THE
WORLD CUP
IN REAL TIME

THE
WORLD CUP
IN REAL TIME

RELIVE THE FINALS
AS IF THEY WERE
HAPPENING TODAY

IAN PASSINGHAM

First published by Pitch Publishing, 2016

Pitch Publishing
A2 Yeoman Gate
Yeoman Way
Durrington
BN13 3QZ
www.pitchpublishing.co.uk

© 2016, Ian Passingham

ISBN 978-1-78531-121-5

Typesetting and origination by Pitch Publishing

Printed by Bell & Bain, Glasgow, Scotland

Contents

Acknowledgements

THANK YOU to everyone who has helped on the road to *66: The World Cup In Real Time*. To Vicky (another reason why 1966 was a special year) for all your encouragement, help and patience. To Ella and Alex for your support. To Vicky, Magnus, Alex, Rob and Shaun for giving up your time to be guinea pigs. And to the staff at the wonderful British Library.

Also, many thanks to Pitch for having faith in this project. I am grateful to everyone at Pitch who worked on the book and particularly to Duncan for his excellent artwork and to Graham for his skill and great patience in fine-tuning the layout and typesetting.

—◇—

Ian Passingham is a journalist with 30 years' experience in local and national newspapers. Having worked as a news reporter, news editor and sports editor with Essex County Newspapers, he joined the *Daily Star* in 1994 as a sports sub-editor. In 2003, he moved to *The Sun* as assistant sports editor and has been a senior *SunSport* production journalist for the last 12 years.

Notes

THE information in this book is drawn mostly from reports published at the time and has been cross-checked against video footage and 1966-related books published since the tournament.

The day-by-day reports in the book are intended to reflect events as they were understood at the time and, therefore, deliberately exclude information which has emerged in the 50 years since the tournament, such as Bobby Moore having been treated for testicular cancer and what Alf Ramsey may (or may not) have told his players or FA officials in private conversations at the time.

The chronology of the story is true to events as they happened. In a few instances, a quote or a trivial story may have been shifted from its original date to give a better balance to the overall narrative. None of these are in any way taken out of context.

The spellings of many participants' names vary in reports published in 1966 and since. The titles attached to some officials also vary. Every effort has been made to report these accurately.

Largely, the spellings of names correspond with those used in Chris Freddi's highly-comprehensive *Complete Book Of The World Cup: 2006 edition,* as the author clearly went to great lengths to clarify them. In the case of the North Korean player, Pak Doo-Ik, Freddi refers to him as Park Doo-Ik, but the use of Pak rather than Park has been so common over the last 50 years that it seemed ridiculous to deviate from the popular version.

The attendances given are the official figures FIFA list today. Surprisingly, the final attendance figure (96,924) is lower than

England's final group game against France (98,270). In fact, according to the same source, the England-France match had the highest attendance of any fixture. Attendances reported at the time differ in some cases from those given now by FIFA, particularly for matches at Wembley. The England-France attendance was actually reported as only 92,500. This and other figures published during the tournament are too conveniently rounded (75,000 for England v Uruguay, for example) to be considered reliable. However, it should be noted that in some instances the FIFA statistics may also be open to question because they possibly include advance ticket sales. Some fans bought packages of tickets for a number of matches and then did not actually attend them all. Other tickets may have been bought by touts and gone unused.

Introduction

'It's only once in a lifetime, you know.'

With these words, Prime Minister Harold Wilson coaxed Alf Ramsey on to the balcony at London's Royal Garden Hotel for English football's reluctant hero to receive the acclaim of the thousands of fans who had gathered below to celebrate.

As Wilson watched the England manager raise the Jules Rimet Trophy on the night of 30 July 1966, little did he know how prophetic his words would be.

Fifty years on and English football is still waiting to host a World Cup again, let alone win one.

To most of us, the story of the 1966 World Cup finals in England has been simplified over those 50 years to something like…

England aren't very good.

Ramsey becomes manager. Ramsey says we will win the World Cup.

The cup is stolen.

The cup is found by a dog.

Ramsey calls Argentina 'animals'.

Russian linesman (who's actually from Azerbaijan) says Geoff Hurst's shot did cross the line.

Kenneth Wolstenholme says, 'Some people are on the pitch. They think it's all over. It is now.' That sums it all up pretty nicely, but there is so much more to the story. And certainly so much more than England's victory.

Home fans welcomed 15 visiting teams and – unlike today, when many overseas stars play in the Premier League and there is widespread TV coverage of football from around the globe –

these foreign players would have seemed exotic and mysterious. In the case of North Korea, they might as well have been men from Mars.

Playing (and, importantly, refereeing) styles were wildly varied around the world and the game in general bore little resemblance to what we see today. There was brutal tackling and little protection for flair players, the game was played with heavy leather footballs and teams got only two points for a win. There were no substitutes, no red and yellow cards and no back-pass rule.

In England, football did not have the mass interest it has today. The FA Cup Final was one of the only matches televised live and English football chiefs were anxious to keep it that way amid concern over falling attendances. Indeed, the level of interest in football was reflected by advance ticket sales for the World Cup, with even the England group matches not coming close to selling out.

Today, our top clubs' stadiums are state-of-the-art all-seater sporting venues after the massive rebuilding programme sparked by the 1989 Hillsborough disaster. Ahead of the World Cup, our ageing grounds were in such a state that it was feared they would be an embarrassment. After a long battle, the FA and Sports Minister Denis Howell convinced the government to pump £500,000 into stadium improvements and work carried on until the last minute at some grounds.

On the field, Ramsey's team were not generally given much chance of success. England had once been regarded worldwide as masters of the game, but by the time Ramsey took charge in 1963, even the most deluded and arrogant among the English football Establishment had long since realised this was a myth.

While English football's standing had been revived to some extent by increasing success in European club competitions, expectations of success for the international team had been dimmed by our dismal failure at four World Cups once the FA had finally deigned to enter, having snubbed the three pre-Second World War editions of the competition.

Opinion was divided over the England manager and his methods. Many fans and pundits predicted failure as Ramsey experimented with personnel and formations right up until the big kick-off.

As a personality, he certainly wasn't universally popular. The bulk of England's support came from the working classes and Ramsey was one of their own. He was very much a players' manager and, privately, he despised the old-school FA 'blazers'. In public, though, his aloof manner and guarded sound-bites, spoken in a carefully cultivated and sometimes almost comical wannabe upper-class accent, meant he came across as one of the Establishment rather than the Dagenham-born son of a straw and hay dealer.

Much has been made of England having home advantage in 1966, but the reality was that disillusionment with the state of the national team was such that Football League chairman Joe Richards felt moved to issue an eve-of-tournament rallying call to fans, saying that the atmosphere at Wembley 'was as cold as any away ground for our players'.

As a major sporting event, the World Cup could not claim to rival the Olympics. It was, though, steadily growing, with the gradual expansion of TV coverage helping to fuel interest, and world governing body FIFA was just beginning to evolve into something like the all-powerful organisation we know today.

Yet this tournament would spark an explosive intercontinental row which threatened to cause a catastrophic split in world football, with 71-year-old FIFA president Sir Stanley Rous, a former international referee and an old-school English administrator, caught up at the centre of it all.

Of the many accounts written about 1966, most have centred almost exclusively on England and have drawn to some degree on recollections of the tournament which, inevitably, are coloured and sometimes distorted by hindsight.

Instead, this book sets out to bring back to life the whole tournament, as if it were being played and reported on today, with all the action, reaction, news and gossip from all 16 competing nations.

So, imagine yourself in the era of Beatlemania, mini-skirts, black and white TV, Wilson's Labour government and the Cold War, and read on.

PRELUDE (PART ONE)

1872–1962…
From Masters To Pupils

1872

ENGLAND and Scotland contest the world's first association football international, a goalless draw at Hamilton Crescent, Partick.

This is the first of 94 full international matches played by England between 1872 and April 1908, in which the only opponents faced are Scotland, Ireland and Wales.

1908

AUSTRIA become the first nation from outside the British Isles to play England in a full international, losing 6-1 and 11-1 in two matches in Vienna.

England are lauded as masters of the game on this first continental tour, which also features a 7-0 thrashing of Hungary in Budapest and a 4-0 victory over Bohemia in Prague.

1923

BELGIUM are the first visiting team from outside the British Isles to play in England and are crushed 6-1 at Highbury.

However, later that year the Belgians hold England 2-2 in Antwerp – becoming the first continental team to avoid defeat against the Three Lions.

1929

AMID frenzied scenes at the Estadio Metropolitano in Madrid, Spain inflict England's first defeat by a continental nation.

England lead 3-2 with only three minutes to play but Jaime Lazcano equalises and delirious Spanish fans pour on to the pitch.

As England's players look on in bewilderment, sword-wielding officers from the civil guard clear the pitch. When play finally resumes, the shell-shocked visitors concede a late winner.

1930–1933

HOSTS Uruguay win the first World Cup in 1930. England don't take part, as the FA had resigned from FIFA in the 1920s in a dispute over the world body's stance on payments to amateur players.

Other major powers also snub the World Cup. One of them, Italy, meet England for the first time in 1933 and, after a 1-1 draw in Rome, Italian captain Umberto Caligaris claims, 'The English played a splendid game and fully deserve to be considered world champions.'

1934

ENGLAND again choose to stay away when Italy host and win the second World Cup. But the new world champions are beaten 3-2 by England at Highbury later that year and the victory is regarded at home as proof that the Three Lions are the world's best.

1938

ITALY retain the World Cup in France as the FA, still not a FIFA member, continues to ignore the tournament.

A shock away defeat to Switzerland's part-timers is one of a number of results which call into question England's standing in world football. It is dismissed as an 'off day' by captain Eddie Hapgood, and FA tour manager Charles Wreford-Brown's stiff-upper-lip reaction is, 'Although beaten, we showed them how to lose.'

A 6-3 win over Germany in Berlin and a 3-0 Wembley victory over the Rest of Europe in a match to mark the FA's 75th anniversary supposedly prove that all is well.

Italy's World Cup-winning coach Vittorio Pozzo, though, derides the state of English football as he takes charge of the Rest of Europe team.

Pozzo claims, 'English football is on the decline. It is no longer what it used to be – the football of artists, the football I saw played before the war.'

1939–1950

THE Second World War means England go six years without an official international.

Before England's first match in 1946, the FA announces it is to appoint its first full-time manager, finally bringing it into line with top continental rivals.

An FA statement explains his duties will include 'tactics, training and style, as well as supervising the players in such matters as diet, smoking, sleep and entertainment'. The team will still be picked by an FA committee, but the statement says the appointment of a manager will 'ensure continuity of style and teamwork, which are essential if British teams are to compete successfully'.

The job goes to Walter Winterbottom, a former Manchester United player with no club management experience. The FA also rejoins FIFA. Under Winterbottom, England lose only four of their next 29 matches and beat world champions Italy 4-0 away in 1948 and 2-0 at home in 1949.

Following the 1948 victory in Turin, FA selection committee chairman Arthur Drewry says, 'To say that the English team was a credit to the country is the sort of understatement of which we English are supposed to be so proud. England could not have sent out a better band of players, who have greatly enhanced the reputation that English football enjoys abroad.'

Winterbottom, though, expresses concern over the development of future players, saying, 'Boys these days are more interested in cinemas, youth clubs and light entertainment than football.'

1950

ENGLAND qualify for the World Cup by winning the Home International Championship and go to Brazil as one of the favourites, despite never having faced a team from outside Europe.

A team featuring world-renowned stars including Billy Wright and Tom Finney, plus future England manager Alf Ramsey, is humiliated 1-0 by the part-timers of the USA in Belo Horizonte and England crash out at the group stage.

FA selection committee chairman Arthur Drewry says, 'I am speechless. It's unbelievable. There is no doubt the tour has taught us that we must reorient altogether our ideas on international football.'

1950–1954

ENGLISH pride is largely restored by a run of only two defeats in 25 matches.

The Three Lions extend their unbeaten home record against opposition from outside the British Isles, but that is shattered by a stunning 6-3 Wembley defeat by Hungary in November 1953.

The skilful and tactically-innovative Magical Magyars, unbeaten in two years, teach England a football lesson. Alf Ramsey is never picked again after being given the run-around.

Hungary captain Ferenc Puskás says, 'England were poorer than we expected. Our team were certainly three goals better. Perhaps England, once the masters, can now learn from the pupils.'

England manager Walter Winterbottom admits, 'We have to decide whether we are going to organise the game to make it a national success or just to get fun out of football. Until clubs demand training by their players and more practice with the ball we cannot hope to compete.'

1954

ENGLAND qualify for the World Cup, but they suffer a record 7-1 defeat by Hungary in Budapest in their final warm-up for the finals in Switzerland.

England captain Billy Wright admits, 'The Hungarians are years ahead of us.'

The FA even faces calls for England to withdraw from the finals, but chairman of selectors Harold Shentall says, 'England would not be so cowardly as to walk out of international football because we are doing badly. We will never improve unless we take the lessons from such games.'

England reach the quarter-finals but are beaten 4-2 by Uruguay and FA secretary Sir Stanley Rous announces a four-year plan to introduce new playing styles to the English game.

Rous says, 'Using basic English principles of football, we will try to introduce pinpoint accuracy in passing, close marking and sharp shooting. The aim is to win the 1958 World Cup.'

1954–1958

WALTER WINTERBOTTOM again steers England to World Cup qualification and a run of only one defeat in 20 matches in the build-up to the 1958 finals in Sweden boosts confidence.

However, the death of key players, including the new young star of English football, Duncan Edwards, in the Munich air disaster in February 1958, is a major setback.

And a 5-0 drubbing by Yugoslavia in Belgrade on the eve of the finals makes a mockery of England's status as one of the tournament favourites. Winterbottom admits, 'It was the worst exhibition by an England team I have ever seen.'

Yugoslav goalkeeper Vladimir Beara says, 'I never expected such an easy game against England. I thought they were one of the best teams in the world...until today.' Another new Manchester United star, Bobby Charlton – a survivor of the Munich tragedy – is made a scapegoat for the Belgrade shambles and does not play a single minute in Sweden as the Three Lions go out at the group stage.

FA chairman of selectors Joe Mears claims, 'I thought we played very well in all the games without a ha'penny of luck.'

Off the field, Englishman Arthur Drewry is elected FIFA president in 1955, a position he will hold until his death six years later.

1959–1960

ENGLAND'S reputation slumps further as they lose all three matches on a 1959 South American tour.

Later that year, World Cup runners-up Sweden win 3-2 at Wembley and their English coach, George Raynor, says, 'England's basic technique was exposed. No matter how fast a ball was played to a Swede, he killed it. It was foot on the ball, pause, play it…the rhythm all football should have, the way England used to play.'

To make matters worse, England lose away to Spain and Hungary in the spring of 1960.

1960–62

A FIFA vote on the hosting of the 1966 World Cup sees England chosen ahead of West Germany.

At a meeting in Rome in August 1960, English delegate Denis Follows argues that the FA is the oldest football organisation in the world and has the necessary experience and facilities.

Spain drop out of the running before the vote, in which England defeat West Germany by 34 to 27.

Englishman Arthur Drewry is the FIFA president at the time of the vote. After his death the following year, FA secretary and former international referee Sir Stanley Rous is elected to replace him.

England suffer only one defeat in each of the 1960/61 and 1961/62 seasons, while qualification for the 1962 World Cup in Chile is achieved in a group featuring Luxembourg and Portugal.

1962

WALTER WINTERBOTTOM'S final tilt at the World Cup ends in more disappointment.

England beat Argentina in the group stage, but eventual champions Brazil down the Three Lions 3-1 in the quarter-finals. Winterbottom admits, 'We would have to lift our game to the highest state of our potential to beat Brazil. We have got to keep working at our football.'

It is announced that Winterbottom is to retire and will step down once his successor is appointed.

The FA is initially reluctant to approach a Football League manager, as it is worried about the potential salary and power the new man might expect. Applications are invited and two unknown university fitness lecturers are among those briefly considered.

Eventually, Alf Ramsey, the manager of Football League champions Ipswich Town, is appointed in October 1962. Although not a universally popular choice, he has all the right credentials.

Ramsey is a former full-back with Southampton, Tottenham Hotspur and England. As a player, his professionalism, dedication to self-improvement, organisational skills and ability to remain calm under pressure earn him the nickname The General.

He can boast 32 England caps, three as captain. His distinguished international career is blighted only by the 1950 World Cup defeat by the USA and the Wembley loss to Hungary in 1953 – his final appearance.

Moving into management in 1955 at unfashionable Ipswich, he moulds a team of unheralded players into a formidable unit, leading the club from the third tier of English football to a surprise League title triumph in 1962. At just 40, age is also on Dagenham-born Ramsey's side. He is actually 42, but it doesn't emerge until 1967 that at the end of the Second World War he knocked two years off his age because he feared clubs would think he was too old to be given a professional playing contract. Ramsey is not the FA's first choice and is only approached after Jimmy Adamson, Bill Nicholson and Stan Cullis all say 'no'. Ramsey is given the job on £4,500 a year and assured he will have total control over selection. He is to take over in December, but will initially work on a part-time basis as he insists on remaining with Ipswich until the club, struggling to reproduce their title-winning form, are safe from relegation.

FA chairman Graham Doggart says, 'I was most impressed by Ramsey's opinions and his broad outlook on the game. I'm convinced he is an excellent choice.'

Ramsey says, 'As England manager I will expect to be judged by the standards applied to a club manager – failure is followed by replacement.

'The World Cup? Well, we have a wonderful chance to win in 1966. We have the potential.

'But I believe that even in the days when England had great players like Stanley Matthews, Tom Finney and Raich Carter, the team would have been better with a rigid plan. Any plan must be adapted to the strengths and weaknesses of the players.'

Winterbottom bows out, saying, 'I'm sure that, with the right support, the World Cup will be ours in 1966.

'The score, in my 17 years, hasn't been a bad one, but the stumbling block has been the World Cup. This is my tragedy and

England football's tragedy. It was something I hoped for all my life… to win the World Cup. Even so, I don't know how the myth has arisen that we can't play football. I wouldn't have taken the job in the first place if that had been so.'

The immediate challenges Ramsey faces are daunting. Public interest has slumped to a point where only 27,500, a record low for an England match at Wembley, watch them beat Wales in Winterbottom's farewell match.

And Ramsey's first match is a tough European Nations Cup clash in France.

The competition, which England have entered after snubbing the inaugural edition in 1960, ranks second only to the World Cup.

With France having held Winterbottom's team 1-1 in the first leg of the preliminary round tie, Ramsey knows he must win in Paris or it will be England's only competitive match in the three-year build-up to the World Cup.

PRELUDE (PART TWO)

World Cup Countdown
27 February 1963–5 July 1966

38 GAMES TO GO
27 February 1963: France 5 England 2
6 April 1963: England 1 Scotland 2
8 May 1963: England 1 Brazil 1

ALF RAMSEY'S reign gets off to the worst possible start as France inflict England's heaviest defeat since 1958 to send them crashing out of the European Nations Cup.

Ramsey says the performance smacks of 'desperation' and complains, 'One does not expect five goals such as the French team got tonight in an international match.'

This is followed by a home defeat by Scotland, in which Leicester City goalkeeper Gordon Banks makes his debut, and a scratchy 1-1 Wembley draw with world champions Brazil.

But Ramsey claims after the Brazil match, 'We have something to base our hopes on. With four, five or six of today's players, I hope it will be possible to find a team good enough to win the World Cup.'

35 GAMES TO GO
29 May 1963: Czechoslovakia 2 England 4
2 June 1963: East Germany 1 England 2
5 June 1963: Switzerland 1 England 8

A CLEAN sweep of wins on a three-match European tour ends the season on a high.

The FA selection committee is disbanded as Alf Ramsey, having left Ipswich Town, takes total control.

He says, 'I dislike the word boss. I dislike the word dictator even more. I am employed by the Football Association to do a job and that is to win the World Cup.'

He makes Bobby Moore, 22, England's youngest captain in place of injured Blackpool right-back Jimmy Armfield and 4-2-4 replaces the long-established 3-2-5 formation with West Ham United half-back Moore employed in central defence as a sweeper.

ALF: WE'LL WIN THE CUP
21 August 1963

ALF RAMSEY boldly promises World Cup victory.

Buoyed by the success of England's end-of-season tour, the usually-reserved manager is in bullish mood at a briefing for sports writers ahead of the new season. He says, 'I believe we will win the World Cup in 1966. We have the ability. We have the determination. We have the strength. We have the personality. We have the character. And we have the players with the temperament.

'We are just starting to build. I shall go on building up a pool of England players, adding here, discarding there, until I find the final pool for the World Cup.'

32 GAMES TO GO
12 October 1963: Wales 0 England 4
23 October 1963: England 2 Rest of the World 1
20 November 1963: England 8 Northern Ireland 3

JIMMY GREAVES and Bobby Charlton mark themselves out as key men as England make it six wins in a row.

Manchester United left-winger Charlton's strike in Wales makes him England's 31-goal record scorer.

Tottenham Hotspur forward Greaves nets in all three games, including four against Northern Ireland.

The Rest of the World – playing at Wembley to celebrate the FA's centenary – are coached by Chilean Fernando Riera and he says, 'Win the World Cup with this team? Of course it is possible for England. And not only in English conditions. I mean anywhere.'

CUP STADIUMS SHAMBLES
7 March 1964

FA CHIEFS warn the government it risks suffering a blow to national prestige unless it helps fund improvements to England's ageing stadiums.

With London, Manchester, Liverpool, Birmingham, Newcastle, Sunderland and Sheffield picked to host matches, FA secretary Denis Follows makes an urgent plea for cash.

He says, 'Without government help, we can certainly stage the World Cup adequately, but we could not hope to do the sort of job for the spectators that was done in Sweden in 1958 and Chile in 1962. The World Cup is a national prestige event.

'This was the original home of football. We want to put on a first-class show and let the world know that England can do things properly.'

Minister for Sport Denis Howell admits, 'No World Cup ground is in a satisfactory state to house the matches.'

29 GAMES TO GO
11 April 1964: Scotland 1 England 0
6 May 1964: England 2 Uruguay 1

JIMMY GREAVES is axed against Scotland and the move backfires as England's winning streak ends.

Greaves insists, 'I'm not worried. I'm not brooding. I'm not crying about it. England know what I can do by now and they either want to use my capabilities or they don't. It's as simple as that. If I'm never picked for England again, then at least I've had a good run.'

He is recalled against Uruguay, when Johnny Byrne scores twice, four days after winning the FA Cup with West Ham United, but the team are booed off after an uninspiring victory. Fulham right-back George Cohen makes his debut.

27 GAMES TO GO
17 May 1964: Portugal 3 England 4
24 May 1964: Republic of Ireland 1 England 3
27 May 1964: USA 0 England 10

JOHNNY BYRNE looks a World Cup cert after a hat-trick against Portugal and another goal in Dublin help England kick off a six-match end-of-season tour in style.

Alf Ramsey's men then fly to New York and crush the USA in a record 10-0 romp.

The win is put into perspective by USA goalkeeper Uwe Schwart – a waiter at England's hotel. He says, 'We've never played together. We've never trained together. We've never even TALKED together.'

24 GAMES TO GO
30 May 1964: Brazil 5 England 1
4 June 1964: England 1 Portugal 1
6 June 1964: England 0 Argentina 1

FA CHIEFS face calls to sack Alf Ramsey after England finish bottom in a four-nation tournament dubbed the Little World Cup.

Hosts Brazil destroy Alf Ramsey's men at the Maracana, but Ramsey claims, 'The margin of the defeat was unfair. We were matching them until they got three goals from nowhere.'

England captain Bobby Moore is left in awe of Brazil superstar Pelé, saying, 'It's incredible. You go into the tackle, you make contact, you think you've got him or the ball – or both – and then you find you haven't got either. He has got through a space a man that big can't get through.'

England's failure in the tournament leaves even Bobby Charlton, a virtual ever-present since 1958, sweating over his future. Ramsey warns, 'He has talent. What he must find is football discipline.'

ALF DOUBLE DRAMA
September 1964

UNDER-FIRE Alf Ramsey vows to tough it out with England after revealing he snubbed an offer to rejoin Ipswich Town.

Ramsey says, 'I consider it a great privilege that Ipswich approached me, but I am now engrossed in my job of building a team for the World Cup.'

There is more drama as Ramsey names his team to face Northern Ireland in the first match of the new season, with Bobby Moore left waiting an unprecedented eight days before being confirmed as captain.

The manager holds talks with Moore, one of seven players who broke a curfew while on England duty at the end of the season, and seeks assurances that he is totally behind him.

Ramsey says, 'I am doing what I think is right. I am building for the World Cup and I must make sure I have the right captain. It might have been handled in a better way to create less publicity, but possibly that has now served a purpose.'

MISTER MISSES MISSUS
October 1964

ENGLAND hopeful Alan Hinton finds out how seriously Alf Ramsey is taking the World Cup build-up – when he has to miss his wedding night.

The Nottingham Forest winger, not picked since Ramsey's first match, is recalled to face Belgium and asks permission to report 24 hours late, the day after his marriage to Joy Roberts.

But Hinton reveals, 'Mr Ramsey said he couldn't bend the rules. But Joy will be at Wembley to see the match and we'll be together again as soon as possible.'

Hinton does play against Belgium and in the next match against Wales, but is never capped again.

21 GAMES TO GO
3 October 1964: Northern Ireland 3 England 4
21 October 1964: England 2 Belgium 2
18 November 1964: England 2 Wales 1
9 December 1964: Holland 1 England 1

BOBBY CHARLTON'S place comes under serious threat as Chelsea youngster Terry Venables gets the chance to become England's key playmaker.

Charlton is switched from the left wing to central midfield against Northern Ireland, but Ramsey replaces him with uncapped 21-year-old Venables for the next match.

Ramsey says, 'Charlton was not a success as the link man against Ireland. Venables is in because we want a man to pass accurately and quickly.'

Venables plays against Belgium and Holland, but he is never capped again as Charlton goes on to excel in the link man role over the next 18 months.

Jimmy Greaves overtakes Charlton as record goalscorer with a hat-trick in Belfast.

VIC SICKENER
7 December 1964

ENGLAND Under-23 captain Vic Mobley's World Cup dream is dashed in the space of four hours.

The 21-year-old Sheffield Wednesday player gets a chance to stake his claim as a potential central defensive partner for Bobby Moore when he is called up to face Holland.

Two days before the game his name is included when the team is announced at noon. But at 4pm devastated Mobley reveals, 'The doctor says I can't play because of a shin injury and has sent me home.'

Unlucky Mobley never wins a senior cap.

17 GAMES TO GO
10 April 1965: England 2 Scotland 2
5 May 1965: England 1 Hungary 0
9 May 1965: Yugoslavia 1 England 1
12 May 1965: West Germany 0 England 1
16 May 1965: Sweden 1 England 2

ALF RAMSEY'S experiments pay dividends with an impressive run to the end of the season.

The five matches include successful debuts for Nobby Stiles, Jack Charlton and Alan Ball, while the manager uses a radical new 4-3-3 formation in the wins over West Germany and Sweden.

The system impresses Germany coach Helmut Schön, who says, 'You defend with seven players and attack with six. Never in the last two years have we had a match which demanded so much speed over 90 minutes.'

By the time England win in Gothenburg, Ramsey appears to have settled on a World Cup back five of goalkeeper Gordon Banks and defenders Charlton, Bobby Moore, George Cohen and Ray Wilson.

In attack, Johnny Byrne's hopes are wrecked by a knee injury he suffers against Scotland and Jimmy Greaves is left fuming when Ramsey drops him against Sweden and says, 'This is my best team on current form.'

BALL FACES THE BOOT
2 June 1965

ENGLAND superkid Alan Ball's World Cup dream looks doomed when he is sent off for throwing the ball at the referee in an Under-23 clash with Austria.

The fiery Blackpool midfielder, outstanding on his introduction to the full side weeks earlier, pleads, 'I go into every game determined that I won't get into trouble. I'm only 20. I want to learn and I know I have got to learn.'

STADIUMS CASH BOOST
27 May 1965

THE government finally agrees to cough up £500,000 towards improvements at World Cup venues. The FA, backed by Minister for Sport Denis Howell, wins a year-long battle for financial help.

Howell says, 'I am convinced the proposals I have been able to set out today will enable England to host the World Cup in an outstanding manner which will reflect credit on the nation.'

With Newcastle having dropped out, Middlesbrough's Ayresome Park will now stage matches. The other venues are London (Wembley and White City), Manchester (Old Trafford), Liverpool (Goodison Park), Birmingham (Villa Park), Sunderland (Roker Park) and Sheffield (Hillsborough).

FA GETS WILLIE OUT
July 1965

FA CHIEFS unveil World Cup Willie – the tournament's first official mascot.

Walter Tuckwell & Associates is employed to handle the 1966 licensing rights and illustrator Reginald Hoye gets the job of designing a mascot.

Hoye, renowned for illustrating children's books by Enid Blyton, comes up with a cartoon lion sporting a Beatles-style haircut and a Union Jack T-shirt emblazoned with the words 'World Cup'.

Willie, who will go on to become a huge success and set a trend for mascots at future tournaments, is to feature on tournament merchandise ranging from T-shirts to key rings.

RED-FACED RAMSEY
August 1965

EMBARRASSED Alf Ramsey admits he wishes he had never said England would win the World Cup.

The manager's bold pledge has been repeatedly thrown back at him over the last two years.

Looking ahead to the season which will end with the World Cup finals, he admits, 'I should have killed that statement. I said it when there were great pressures on me. It has been a great embarrassment.

'One can only try to be in a position to say one has done the best job possible. I hope to be able to say that. I shall be satisfied with nothing less than winning the World Cup.

'We have played a lot of matches and tried lots of players. I think I have nine of the players I want. The months to come are the most important. We shall be better prepared than we have ever been.'

12 GAMES TO GO
2 October 1965: Wales 0 England 0
20 October 1965: England 2 Austria 3
10 November 1965: England 2 Northern Ireland 1
8 December 1965: Spain 0 England 2

ENGLAND make a poor start to World Cup season – until Alf Ramsey hits the jackpot with a stunning away win over European champions Spain.

A dreary draw in Wales is followed by a shock defeat by Austria, who are only the third continental team to win at Wembley.

Ramsey fumes, 'We were beaten by the worst side we have met for a long time. It was ridiculous.' But he insists, 'I regard the lapses as temporary rather than lasting. There is no thought of discarding and starting again. Not at all.'

Ramsey switches back to 4-3-3 against Spain in a team featuring no wingers. He is rewarded with a performance Spain boss José Villalonga describes as 'phenomenal'.

Alan Ball stars against Spain after ending his six-month international exile, but Jimmy Greaves faces a long lay-off with hepatitis.

HOME ALONE
7 December 1965

ENGLAND know they will be the only home nation at the World Cup after Scotland crash out to Italy.

The Scots, the last team still in with a chance of qualifying, lose 3-0 in Naples in a winner-takes-all clash.

Northern Ireland blow their chances by drawing with Albania in their final game to let Switzerland scrape through, the Republic of Ireland are eliminated in a play-off against Spain, while Wales are never in the running after losing three of their first four games in a group won by the Soviet Union.

ALF'S NEW YEAR MESSAGE
1 January 1966

ALF RAMSEY welcomes in World Cup year and promises, 'England will be ready. I won't have to tell my players what it means – they will know.'

With a friendly against Poland and the draw for the finals imminent, Ramsey says, 'The World Cup still seems a long way away. When the draw is made we shall know then what we have to do.

'I shall have a target and, from then on, three teams will be uppermost in my mind. I shall watch them, study them.

'When the draw is made, I shall feel again like a club manager listening to the FA Cup draw. This time there will be three teams to contend with and none of them will be easy.'

8 GAMES TO GO
5 January 1966: England 1 Poland 1

ALF RAMSEY sticks with his 'Wingless Wonders' system at Goodison Park, but it needs Bobby Moore's first England goal to rescue a draw.

Merseyside fans hoping that Liverpool trio Peter Thompson, Gordon Milne and Ian Callaghan will be picked are left disappointed as single-minded Ramsey snaps, 'There are much bigger things at the end of all this than just a good crowd for one match.'

THE WORLD CUP DRAW
6 January 1966

CAPTAIN Bobby Moore welcomes the World Cup finals draw as 'great' after Uruguay, France and Mexico are named as England's opponents in Group One.

Alf Ramsey misses the draw, which is televised live from London's Royal Garden Hotel by the BBC in a 40-minute show, after learning that his father has died.

FIFA officials finalise the rules that morning with a loose seeding arrangement which keeps apart hosts England and champions Brazil and spreads countries from different confederations across the four first-round groups.

Moore says, 'It's a great draw for us. Everyone in the country should be delighted.'

7 GAMES TO GO
23 February 1966: England 1 West Germany 0

ALF RAMSEY slams the Wembley crowd for slow-handclapping England – and even booing when the Germans have an equaliser disallowed.

The England manager says, 'I thought it was very unfair of the crowd to boo and it was most extraordinary that they did so after a visiting team's goal had been disallowed. If that had happened to an England goal somewhere abroad, the crowd would have gone wild with delight.'

With Jimmy Greaves still recovering from hepatitis, the search for forwards continues.

Bobby Smith (Tottenham Hotspur), Johnny Byrne (West Ham United), Fred Pickering (Everton), Frank Wignall (Nottingham Forest), Joe Baker (Arsenal), Derek Temple (Everton), Alan Peacock (Leeds United), Barry Bridges (Chelsea) and Mick Jones (Leeds United) are on a long list who have tried and failed to nail down a place.

Ramsey ignores calls to try Chelsea teenager Peter Osgood and instead gives a debut to West Ham's Geoff Hurst, recently converted from midfield, alongside Roger Hunt.

JULES RIMET TROPHY STOLEN
20 March 1966

FA CHIEFS are left red-faced when the World Cup is stolen from an exhibition at Central Hall, Westminster.

The £30,000 solid gold Jules Rimet Trophy is taken from a display called Sport With Stamps.

Exhibition organising committee chairman Cecil Richardson defends security arrangements as news of the theft is greeted with widespread condemnation from around the world.

Richardson says, 'I think the security was adequate. I don't think it would have made any difference if we had had barbed wire and machine guns.

'This was a very determined attack at the World Cup and I think if a guard had been beside the World Cup we would have had a coshed policeman as well as a missing Cup.'

DOG FINDS TROPHY
27 March 1966

A DOG called Pickles becomes a national hero when the mongrel finds the missing Jules Rimet Trophy a week after it was stolen.

Pickles draws owner David Corbett's attention to a package left by the side of a road near their home in Norwood, South London.

Thames lighterman Corbett opens it and, to his amazement, unwraps the trophy.

Explaining the moment when he realised what he had found, Corbett says, 'I pulled the top off and I could see the top of the statue on the trophy. I looked at the base and I could see "Brazil 1962" and that is what sort of clicked in my mind.'

6 GAMES TO GO
2 April 1966: Scotland 3 England 4

TWO-GOAL Roger Hunt is the star as Alf Ramsey finally records a win over the Auld Enemy. Scotland midfielder Billy Bremner admits, 'This must be the most flattering result of all-time. We should have been murdered.'

MOORE HAMMER BLOW
5 April 1966

BOBBY MOORE admits a dispute with West Ham United could dent his World Cup hopes.

The England captain is put up for sale for £200,000 after rejecting a new contract and Hammers boss Ron Greenwood reveals, 'I've known for eight months that he didn't want to play with us. If the West Ham image doesn't suit him, he's better off where the image does suit him.'

Moore says, 'I don't want any of this business to hinder my chances of leading England in the World Cup.

'It's vital that everything is cleared up before the championship starts in July.'

ALF NAMES 40 HOPEFULS
7 April 1966

ALF RAMSEY leaves the door open for a clutch of rising young stars as he names a 40-man pool from which he expects to select his World Cup 22.

The 11 uncapped players included are: Peter Bonetti (goalkeeper, 24, Chelsea), Gordon West (goalkeeper, 22, Everton), John Kaye (centre-forward, 26, West Bromwich Albion), Peter Osgood (centre-forward, 19, Chelsea), Ian Callaghan (winger, 23, Liverpool), Martin Peters (midfield, 22, West Ham United), John Hollins (midfield, 19, Chelsea), Paul Reaney (full-back, 21, Leeds United), Marvin Hinton (full-back, 26, Chelsea), Chris Lawler (full-back, 22, Liverpool), Tommy Smith (centre-half, 20, Liverpool).

5 GAMES TO GO
4 May 1966: England 2 Yugoslavia 0

MARTIN PETERS makes a late push for a World Cup place as England win their last home match before the finals.

West Ham United midfielder Peters, 22, impresses on debut, while Jimmy Greaves needs just nine minutes to score in his first international since recovering from hepatitis.

SQUAD CUT TO 28
6 May 1966

JOHNNY BYRNE is handed a surprise World Cup lifeline as Alf Ramsey names 28 players who will report for a training camp on 6 June ahead of England's European tour.

Chelsea winger Bobby Tambling and Everton defender Brian Labone are also drafted in.

Fifteen of the original 40-man pool are axed. They are: Joe Baker, Barry Bridges, Fred Pickering, Terry Venables, Tony Waiters, Gordon

West, Chris Lawler, Paul Reaney, Marvin Hinton, John Hollins, Tommy Smith, Peter Osgood, Derek Temple, John Kaye and Gordon Harris.

RAMSEY NAMES FINAL 22
18 June 1966

SIX players suffer heartbreak as Alf Ramsey names the 22 men he wants for the World Cup.

After putting the players through a punishing training camp at Lilleshall, Shropshire, the England manager makes his final call.

Injury rules out Everton defender Brian Labone, while Gordon Milne, Johnny Byrne, Bobby Tambling, Peter Thompson and Keith Newton miss the cut. These five are asked to remain on standby.

The decision is particularly tough on Liverpool midfielder Milne, an almost ever-present in the first 18 months of Ramsey's reign, and on Byrne, whose late push for a place fails.

Martin Peters and Geoff Hurst are picked, while uncapped Ian Callaghan edges out fellow Liverpool winger Thompson.

The party, which is officially submitted to FIFA in early July, is:

1 Gordon Banks (goalkeeper, 28, Leicester City),
2 George Cohen (full-back, 26, Fulham),
3 Ray Wilson (full-back, 31, Everton),
4 Nobby Stiles (midfield, 24, Manchester United),
5 Jack Charlton (centre-half, 31, Leeds United),
6 Bobby Moore (centre-half, 25, West Ham United),
7 Alan Ball (midfield, 21, Blackpool),
8 Jimmy Greaves (inside-forward, 26, Tottenham Hotspur),
9 Bobby Charlton (midfield, 28, Manchester United),
10 Geoff Hurst (centre-forward, 24, West Ham United),
11 John Connelly (winger, 27, Manchester United),
12 Ron Springett (goalkeeper, 30, Sheffield Wednesday),
13 Peter Bonetti (goalkeeper, 24, Chelsea),
14 Jimmy Armfield (full-back, 30, Blackpool),
15 Gerry Byrne (full-back, 27, Liverpool),
16 Martin Peters (midfield, 22, West Ham United),
17 Ron Flowers (centre-half, 31, Wolverhampton Wanderers),
18 Norman Hunter (centre-half/midfield, 22, Leeds United),
19 Terry Paine (winger, 27, Southampton),
20 Ian Callaghan (winger, 24, Liverpool),
21 Roger Hunt (inside-forward, 27, Liverpool),
22 George Eastham (midfield/inside-forward, 29, Arsenal).

4 GAMES TO GO
26 June 1966: Finland 0 England 3
29 June 1966: Norway 1 England 6
3 July 1966: Denmark 0 England 2

JIMMY GREAVES fires a warning to England's World Cup rivals.

The Tottenham Hotspur forward, back on form after recovering from hepatitis, takes his record goals tally to 43 by scoring four in Norway.

He says, 'Sticking the ball in the back of the net is my bread and butter – and I feel business is good right now.'

Alf Ramsey reacts angrily to repeated questions over Manchester United midfielder Nobby Stiles's combative style, insisting, 'Certainly Stiles is a hard player, but there is no more to it than that. I emphasise most strongly that he is not a dirty player. He goes in hard, yes, but only to get the ball.'

Veteran Ron Flowers's bid to oust Jack Charlton in central defence is damaged when his blunder against Norway leads to the only goal England concede on tour.

Winger Ian Callaghan and goalkeeper Peter Bonetti both make their debuts during the tour, but new boy Geoff Hurst's poor performance in Denmark is a blow to his chances of facing Uruguay in the World Cup opener on 11 July.

Off the field, a shadow is cast over the tour after FA chairman Joe Mears dies from a heart attack in Oslo on 1 July.

1 GAME TO GO...

THE WORLD CUP
IN REAL TIME

Tuesday 5 July
Six days to go

GEOFF HURTS
Poland 0 England 1 (Hunt 14)

ROGER HUNT is in Pole position for a World Cup starting place after grabbing the winner in England's final warm-up match today.

And the Liverpool forward's super-show in Chorzow is set to spell heartbreak for Geoff Hurst.

The West Ham United man looked certain to start Monday's tournament opener against Uruguay after playing in four of the five games since his debut in February.

But Alf Ramsey axed him from today's line-up after he had a shocker in Denmark on Sunday.

Alan Ball and Martin Peters both featured in midfield today and, with 4-3-3 now Ramsey's favoured formation, the side included no recognised wingers.

The victory means England finished their four-match European tour with four wins from four, with 11 goals scored and only one conceded.

ENGLAND TEAM: Gordon Banks, George Cohen, Ray Wilson, Jack Charlton, Bobby Moore (capt), Nobby Stiles, Alan Ball, Martin Peters, Bobby Charlton, Jimmy Greaves, Roger Hunt.

ALF DISMISSES MIND GAMES

ALF RAMSEY claims rival managers are playing mind games by tipping England for glory.

The hosts have been backed to win by the likes of West Germany coach Helmut Schön.

But the England manager, who three years ago promised victory, is sticking to his prediction and says his counterparts are guilty of kidology.

Ramsey said, 'It seems extraordinary that managers should tip other teams. It seems I am the only manager who tips their own particular team. I would pay no notice to this. Every manager has one object in mind – to win the World Cup.'

England made it a clean sweep of victories on their four-match European tour by winning in Poland tonight and Ramsey said, 'What we set out to achieve we have achieved on this tour. Match fitness – and this is the most important aspect – plus the good results. By being on tour like this, we have formulated the team spirit you would expect of a top-class club side.

'One of these days someone is going to get a hell of a pasting from this England team.'

Captain Bobby Moore said, 'If we get the breaks, we will want some beating. This is how the whole squad feel.

'The run of the ball and freedom from injuries are important factors, but we honestly believe we have a great chance.'

KID IS 'NEW PELÉ'

SIXTEEN-YEAR-OLD Brazilian Edú is being tipped to rewrite World Cup history when the finals kick off next week.

The Santos forward will be the youngest player at the tournament after the 16 squads were confirmed by FIFA.

He gets his chance after the champions left out Inter Milan forward Amarildo, a key man in their successful title defence in 1962.

Edú, whose full name is Jonas Eduardo Américo, will become the youngest player to appear in a World Cup match if he sees action.

And long-time team physician Dr Hilton Gosling today predicted, 'Edú could be as big a success as Pelé was in the 1958 World Cup.'

England manager Alf Ramsey submitted his squad 24 hours ahead of the official deadline and there were no last-minute changes after Jack Charlton overcame an ankle injury.

Strangely, Hungary are bringing only 18 players, despite naming the maximum 22 permitted by FIFA.

And Argentina manager Juan Carlos Lorenzo showed there is no room for sentiment by leaving out Daniel Onega. He and brother Ermindo featured in their European tour, but only Ermindo is selected.

Meet The 16 Contenders

GROUP ONE

ENGLAND: The hosts have never been beyond the quarter-finals, but home advantage and a solid defence marshalled by captain Bobby Moore gives them a shot. Bobby Charlton is the main creator after his switch to a central role, while record scorer Jimmy Greaves' goals will be vital. Questions remain over Alf Ramsey's best formation and he has struggled to find a settled midfield and attack.

FRANCE: The French gave England a five-goal beating in Alf Ramsey's first match as England manager three years ago, but a repeat of that is highly unlikely. They qualified well with five wins out of six, their only defeat coming away to Yugoslavia. This is their sixth appearance in the finals, but manager Henri Guérin's team are inconsistent and they will do well to make it past the group stage.

MEXICO: The Mexicans have become regulars at the tournament and are making their sixth appearance. However, their win over Czechoslovakia in Chile four years ago was their only victory in 14 finals matches. They easily qualified ahead of Costa Rica and Jamaica in their final three-nation CONCACAF group, but it will be a surprise if another three defeats are not added to their record.

URUGUAY: Two-time world champions and, while few expect them to make it a hat-trick this time, they should be England's biggest threat in Group One. Their mean defence is a tough nut to crack and they have players capable of producing special moments going forward. The nucleus of their side is drawn from Peñarol, winners of South America's equivalent of the European Cup.

GROUP TWO

ARGENTINA: Finalists in the first World Cup in 1930, they could finally be contenders again. Critics question their ability to produce their best football outside of South America. They won the Little World Cup held in Brazil two years ago, beating England, Portugal and the hosts in the process. But they were poor on their recent European tour. Expect a mix of skill and no-nonsense defending.

SPAIN: They aim to become the first country to hold the European and world titles simultaneously after winning the European Nations Cup two years ago, beating the USSR on home soil. One of the most attractive teams in the finals, Spain have some of Europe's most expensive stars. They won a play-off against the Republic of Ireland to qualify after Syria withdrew from a three-team group.

SWITZERLAND: The part-timers are clear outsiders in a tough group. Competing in a sixth finals, they have reached the quarter-finals three times – the last time as hosts in 1954. They edged out Northern Ireland in qualifying and have some talented players, but the professionalism of three of the competition's powerhouses is likely to tell. Expect the Swiss to go home without a point.

WEST GERMANY: Helmut Schön's side have high hopes of winning a second world title after they returned from post-Second World War exile to win in 1954. The experienced striker and captain Uwe Seeler will spearhead their attack and they have added real creativity to their side with the emerging midfield combination of Helmut Haller and the highly-rated youngster Franz Beckenbauer.

GROUP THREE

BULGARIA: The Bulgarians are the outside bet in possibly the toughest group in the competition. They were battered 5-0 away to Belgium in qualifying, but then beat them 2-1 in a play-off in Florence after the two countries finished level on points. Their hopes of progressing will rely heavily on Georgi Asparoukhov, who is one of the most talented centre-forwards in the competition.

BRAZIL: Looking for a third straight world title, they will rely on the heroes of 1958 and 1962. Pelé was the teenage sensation of 1958, but was then injured for most of the next tournament. He arrives here as the world's undisputed number one player. Garrincha, the star of 1962, is one of a number of players who may be past their best. The bookmakers still rate them as favourites.

HUNGARY: This is a new era for Hungarian football after the Magical Magyars dominated international football in the 1950s – albeit without actually winning the World Cup. They may no longer have the genius of Ferenc Puskás, but they still have some exciting talent. Lajos Baróti, who was also in charge in 1958 and 1962, led them to third place in the 1964 European Nations Cup.

PORTUGAL: Making their finals debut, Portugal will be expected to slug it out with Hungary to qualify alongside favourites Brazil. Their attacking players are drawn mainly from the successful Benfica side, notably the exciting strikers Eusébio and José Torres. The Portuguese put paid to 1962 finalists Czechoslovakia in qualifying and could shine here. Defence may be their Achilles heel.

GROUP FOUR

CHILE: They were semi-finalists four years ago, but that was as hosts and it would be a major surprise if they got anywhere close to a repeat. Chile needed a play-off against Ecuador to qualify from a three-team group also featuring Colombia. Their players are mostly part-timers and lack experience outside of South America. It is hard to see them stopping the USSR and Italy progressing.

ITALY: Hopes are high in Italy that their richly-paid superstars can make them, rather than Uruguay or favourites Brazil, the first nation to lift the Jules Rimet Trophy for a third time. That optimism has been fuelled by the emergence of Gianni Rivera, the 22-year-old AC Milan playmaker. Many believe Golden Boy could be the star of the tournament. If he hits top form, this could be Italy's year.

NORTH KOREA: The mystery of the tournament, they took the one place available to Asia, Africa and Oceania virtually by default. An African boycott and South Korea's withdrawal left the way open for them to pip Australia for qualification. Little is known about their players other than that they have a reputation for outstanding fitness. Italy and the USSR could run up big scores against them.

USSR: Alf Ramsey wouldn't agree, but the Soviets are arguably the tournament's most meticulously-prepared team. The Soviets won the first European Nations Cup in 1960 and were finalists again in 1964. Their meeting with Italy is likely to be a shootout for top spot in Group Four. They will be predictable, but could go a long way. Legendary goalkeeper Lev Yashin will want to go out on a high.

Sunday 10 July
One day to go

DOPE TESTING SHOCK

FIFA today revealed shock plans for compulsory drug tests at every World Cup match.

The 16 competing nations and the 31 tournament referees were informed of the scheme at a meeting in London.

Two players from each team will be randomly selected after every match for testing by world football's first anti-doping squad.

The system, involving 25 doctors, sees football follow in the footsteps of cycling, the only other major sport to introduce a random testing programme.

Scientists last year developed a technique for detecting the use of stimulants such as amphetamines and the World Cup experiment will be based on a system trialled in last month's Tour of Britain cycle race, in which two riders were disqualified after positive tests.

FIFA president Sir Stanley Rous said, 'We set this up to make sure that there should be no charges of teams receiving shots in the arm to gain an unfair advantage. We are doing the spot checks as a deterrent.'

FIFA has also given referees the power to nominate any player they suspect of doping.

Arsenal club surgeon Dr Alan Bass, in charge of organising the testing, said, 'We want the referee to be the judge of this because he is the man physically closest to the players. He is best fitted to notice any signs.

'Before each match, the area medical officer will be given the names of the players of each team. They will be put in a hat and two names from each team will be drawn out.'

The urine samples will be sent to a London laboratory, with the results returned within 18 hours.

Any guilty player will be booted out of the tournament – and FIFA could even expel an entire team if an offence is deemed serious enough.

WORLD CUPPA

WORRIED Brazilian officials today asked for confirmation that coffee does not count as a stimulant after FIFA announced dope test plans.

Carlos Nascimento, head of Brazil's World Cup technical commission, said, 'We have no objection whatsoever to the tests, but obviously we want to make quite certain that there is no objection to coffee. Our players do drink an awful lot of it.

'In our opinion, tea is a greater stimulant than coffee and, if we are not allowed to drink coffee, we feel the England team should be banned from drinking tea.'

The anti-doping programme has been condemned by Portuguese FA vice-president António da Silva.

He complained, 'I want the world to know we don't like this slight, this inference that we would stoop to anything so low as doping. It is unthinkable.'

But Soviet Union coach Nikolai Morozov said, 'There is no need for us to worry – we only drink coffee. I think that teams who have never taken dope have a right to feel insulted by the tests, but those who have been guilty of taking it in the past cannot grumble.'

KEEP IT CLEAN

FIFA today pledged to come down hard on the World Cup's hatchet men in a bid to avoid the violence which marred previous tournaments.

In 1954, Hungary's quarter-final win over Brazil was dubbed the Battle of Berne after English referee Arthur Ellis sent off three players and a violent brawl erupted after the match.

And four years ago, there were even worse scenes as hosts Chile beat Italy in the Battle of Santiago.

Two Italians were dismissed by English referee Ken Aston, now in charge of the 1966 match officials, and the game could have been abandoned because of fighting and violent fouls.

Today, the 16 competing nations were lectured by FIFA chiefs at an eve-of-tournament meeting and told that for the first time a special disciplinary committee has been set up to deal with cases during the finals.

FIFA president Sir Stanley Rous, an ex-international referee whose 1938 re-working of the laws of the game are those still used worldwide today, said, 'Tell the players that action will be taken after every match and that the disciplinary committee will be strict.'

Competing nations are taking no chances over the potential for serious injuries to players, with the squads insured for a total of around £20m.

Brazil superstar Pelé has been insured for £250,000, while the England party are covered for a total of £1m. Any England player who suffers a career-ending injury would receive £3,000, while their club would get £45,000.

REF AND READY

ENGLISH referee Ken Dagnall has predicted a trouble-free World Cup – but won't hesitate to come down hard on bad-boys.

Dagnall, a 45-year-old Bolton housing officer, is one of seven home referees among the 31 officials.

He confirmed foul play and indiscipline had been 'high on the agenda' at a briefing on Friday. But he said, 'I very much doubt there will be any trouble. I certainly hope not. I intend to keep a very firm hand on my matches from the start, but I won't hesitate to send a man off if he deserves to go. The only language I speak is Lancashire, but I'm not worried. Football is an international language and a player knows when he has done wrong.'

Ken Aston, a former English referee and now FIFA liaison officer for the tournament match officials, said, 'If a referee has to caution a player, he will politely turn him round and write his number in his notebook.

'If it is necessary to send a man off, he will note his number and clearly point to the touchline and say "Off...allez vous...expulsado" or give the direction in any language he feels will be understood.'

BOOKIES BACK BRAZIL

BRITISH bookmakers have installed world champions Brazil as 2/1 favourites.

Hosts England are rated 4/1 second favourites. The rest of the odds are: Italy 7/1, Argentina 9/1, West Germany 10/1, Russia 11/1, Hungary 22/1, Portugal 22/1, Spain 25/1, France 33/1, Uruguay 40/1, Bulgaria 66/1, Chile 66/1, North Korea 100/1, Switzerland 150/1, Mexico 200/1.

£1K SHOOTOUT

ENGLAND goal king Jimmy Greaves will be shooting it out with the world's top strikers for a £1,000 prize over the next three weeks.

A London casino offered to put up the cash bonus and FIFA chiefs have approved the scheme.

WING AND A PRAYER

LEGENDARY former England winger Sir Stanley Matthews carried the FIFA flag at today's pre-World Cup service at Westminster Abbey.

The service was dedicated to the worldwide fellowship of sport, and FIFA president Sir Stanley Rous and Minister for Sport Denis Howell were among the congregation.

Lessons were read by England squad member Jimmy Armfield, tennis player Virginia Wade, West Indies cricket vice-captain Conrad Hunte and Great Britain athletics captain Menzies Campbell.

The sermon was given by the Venerable Edward Carpenter, Archdeacon of Westminster and a keen Chelsea supporter. He suggested the World Cup could help create a mood 'out of which wider cultural, social and political order might very easily spring'.

EXTRA TIME FOR QUEEN?

THE Queen is keeping fans guessing over whether she will be at the final.

She will attend tomorrow's opening ceremony and England-Uruguay match, but her schedule does not include concrete plans for a return to Wembley on 30 July.

FIFA president Sir Stanley Rous said the issue would be discussed at tomorrow's curtain-raiser.

He said, 'We are hoping the Queen will be at the final, but I think it might depend on whether England get there. In the past it has been the job of the president of FIFA to present the trophy.'

THIS IS ENGLAND

SPORTS MINISTER Denis Howell believes staging the World Cup will showcase the whole of England. Critics have questioned the decision to pump £500,000 of public funds into stadium improvements, but Howell insists it is money well spent.

A year ago, Howell – a former Football League referee and Britain's first Sports Minister – convinced the government to cough up after warning that the ageing grounds needed a facelift if the tournament was to 'reflect credit on the nation'.

Improvements have been carried out at all the venues, with work continuing until the last minute at grounds like Ayresome Park in Middlesbrough.

Howell, MP for Birmingham Small Heath and a proud Brummie, said today, 'It is quite evident that these great international sporting festivals are now matters of major importance in the world. It is extremely important, unlike what some cynics say.

'I keep telling officials in Whitehall that there is a hell of a lot of England north of Watford. This thought should be written in letters of gold in Whitehall.'

Howell will be at matches across the country over the next three weeks and added, 'Some of my colleagues have told me I should be in Parliament discussing the selective employment tax and Vietnam.

'But I feel I can do more for Britain in the field of foreign affairs by being at World Cup matches in London, Manchester, Birmingham, Sheffield, Liverpool, Sunderland and Middlesbrough. I have told other MPs, "In this way I can do more than you for Britain's prestige".'

PETERS KO WOE

MARTIN PETERS was today axed by Alf Ramsey for England's opener against Uruguay.

The West Ham United midfielder's exclusion is the only change to the team which won in Poland last week, with Manchester United winger John Connelly recalled.

Ramsey confirmed his XI at the Three Lions' base in Hendon and insisted he could not be happier with his three-and-a-half-year build-up to the tournament.

The former Ipswich Town boss said, 'If I could start all over again, I don't think I would change anything. I had a lot to learn, not only about the players of other countries, but also the players available here. The first men have been chosen and a way of playing best suited to them has been decided upon. We have done everything we set out to do in the way of preparation. The players know what is demanded of them.

'In three years, we have improved tremendously. It was important we did change our views on the manner in which football is played. I am certain the England team is much stronger now than it was three years ago.'

The team is: Gordon Banks, George Cohen, Ray Wilson, Jack Charlton, Bobby Moore (capt), Nobby Stiles, Alan Ball, John Connelly, Bobby Charlton, Jimmy Greaves, Roger Hunt.

Only four players – Moore, Bobby Charlton, Jimmy Greaves and John Connelly – remain from the team beaten by France in Ramsey's first match back in February 1963.

While Ramsey has a settled defence, he has continued to experiment with tactics and attacking options. Many observers felt Peters and his West Ham team-mate Geoff Hurst would figure.

The inclusion of wideman Connelly means Ramsey has opted not to deploy his Wingless Wonders formation. Connelly will join Greaves and Hunt up front in a 4-3-3.

Asked if he still believed England would win the tournament, Ramsey said, 'I have been saying it for three years and nothing has happened to make me change that view.

'We do have deficiencies and one is the finishing. But I would be more worried if we were not making so many chances.'

The England manager will have a four-strong team of Football League managers watching games in the other groups.

He said, 'I hope to have a good dossier, particularly on teams we are likely to meet in the later stages.'

Uruguay captain Horacio Troche today highlighted Bobby Charlton and Alan Ball as key men, but he vowed, 'We are all in good spirits and we expect to win.'

ENGLAND'S NUMBER 10

PRIME MINISTER Harold Wilson is hoping for a 1966 win double.

He led Labour to victory in the General Election three months ago, putting himself back in 10 Downing Street by increasing the meagre five-seat majority he won in 1964 to a commanding 96.

Now the football-mad PM is backing England for glory. He said, 'After a successful tour of the continent, England are playing together as a team. We will face the best you can put against us with great confidence.'

Wilson opened last week's FIFA Congress and admitted he was relieved the Jules Rimet Trophy had been recovered by Thames lighterman David Corbett and his dog Pickles after being stolen from an exhibition in March.

He told delegates, 'It is something of a relief to all of us to have a Cup to present.

'A few months ago I thought I would come to the meeting to say, "Sorry we have lost the cup." But thanks to the efforts of the British police and a dog, it is now back in a safe place.'

CUP UNDER WRAPS

WORRIED FA chiefs will keep the Jules Rimet Trophy under lock and key until the final.

The theft of the trophy earlier this year was a major embarrassment and the FA will be taking no chances.

FA secretary Denis Follows said, 'It is my duty to look after it. It is in the vaults of a bank and it will not go on show during the tournament if I have my way.'

MEARS TRIBUTE

WORLD CUP organisers have added a tribute to the late FA chairman Joe Mears in the official tournament programme.

Mears, influential behind the scenes in the staging of the tournament, died of a heart attack ten days ago while with the England touring party in Norway.

The programme had already been printed with a welcome message from Mears. A flysheet has now been added informing fans of his death and saying the finals will be a 'tribute to the memory of a fine man'.

In his programme notes, Mears wrote, 'I hope that our visitors will return to their homes having enjoyed a feast of football and the best of English hospitality.'

GREAVES IN THE GROOVE

GOAL machine Jimmy Greaves today warned World Cup defences he is fit and raring to go.

The Tottenham Hotspur striker warmed up for the finals by scoring four goals against Norway.

That helped answer question marks over his fitness after recovering from hepatitis and he said, 'I was very pleased with my personal form on the tour. I feel 100 per cent fit and I hope the goals continue to go in.'

He believes that playing at Wembley will help him boost his national record haul of 43 goals.

Greaves said, 'We are all so ready for the kick-off now. All we need is the breaks and, if we get them, nobody will hold us. This is going to be a defensive World Cup and that is why I am certain that playing at Wembley will be a tremendous factor in England's favour.

'England know Wembley far better than any of the other teams. The ball comes off the pitch fast and the pitch is huge…vast. It is not a pitch for systems, it's a pitch for ability – and ability is going to count in the World Cup. Wembley gives great confidence to a forward. I have played some of my best games there.

'I would rather play against an eight-man defence at Wembley than at any other ground because there is so much room and you have a chance to escape your shadower.'

MOORE IN LIMBO

CAPTAIN Bobby Moore will lead England into the World Cup with his club future in limbo.

The West Ham United defender turned down a new contract and his old deal expired on 1 July.

Hammers manager Ron Greenwood made Moore available for transfer at £200,000 in April, saying he did not want the uncertainty to hinder Moore's World Cup hopes, but no move has materialised.

A player must be contracted to a club to play at the World Cup so Moore has signed a monthly deal. Moore said, 'The most important thing on my mind now is the World Cup. Nothing will be done about my future with West Ham until after that.'

Greenwood – involved in a FIFA tactical study group at the World Cup as well as working as a BBC TV pundit – has also made an eve-of-tournament swoop for England reserve goalkeeper Peter Bonetti.

Bonetti has asked to leave Chelsea and the Hammers have bid £55,000 – a British record for a keeper. Greenwood confirmed, 'Chelsea have received my offer. Now it is up to them.'

Arsenal inside-forward George Eastham also faces an uncertain future. Bertie Mee, temporary manager after Billy Wright left, confirmed Eastham had been transfer-listed.

But Eastham, 29, said, 'I won't be thinking much about my personal future over the next three weeks.'

STARS 'MURDERED'

TRAINER Harold Shepherdson has revealed how the England players were put through 'murder' in the build-up to the finals.

Alf Ramsey ordered right-hand men Shepherdson and Les Cocker to push his 28-man provisional squad to the limit when they reported for duty at Lilleshall ahead of last month's European tour.

And Shepherdson said, 'Honestly, the programme we planned was murder. I felt sorry for the lads. For two weeks they were on their knees, but not one belly-ached.

'Suddenly it happened – they were razor-sharp and, no matter how hard we tried to make them wilt, they just came back for more.'

FLOWERS POWER

ENGLAND veteran Ron Flowers believes a pre-World Cup 'boot camp' has turned the hosts into winners.

Flowers, 32 later this month, made his international debut back in 1955 and played in the 1962 finals, when England failed to get beyond the quarter-finals.

But the Wolverhampton Wanderers centre-half says a punishing training camp at Lilleshall and a winning European tour have primed the squad for success.

He said, 'I cannot see anyone beating England and that includes Brazil. We have developed a tremendous team spirit.

'The past month has been really hard. The pressure was really on when we reported at Lilleshall before the tour. The discipline and training has been maintained from then right through the tour and has been accepted willingly by all the players.'

Flowers, edged out of the starting XI by Jack Charlton, added, 'English players are very much home birds and playing in our own country will greatly influence our chances.

'We are delighted that we will be playing in the right climate with the right food. It should make a vast difference. The chance is there. We must take it.'

PUMP UP THE VOLUME

FOOTBALL LEAGUE president Joe Richards has pleaded with fickle England fans not to give Alf Ramsey's team the 'cold shoulder'.

The Wembley crowd have sometimes turned on the Three Lions and, in February, the home team were booed off despite beating West Germany.

Richards, who retires after the finals, said, 'Let's have none of this infamous Wembley cold shoulder.

'I can only plead with the England fans to roll up for the first match and roar their heads off. For too long Wembley has been as cold as an away ground for our players. Let's see the aloofness changed.

'With the crowd on your side, that is a tremendous psychological advantage. Let's give our lads that advantage.

'We have the best possible man in control in Alf Ramsey. He has chosen a well-balanced squad which has won all its warm-up matches on the continent.

'If we can do that away from home, we are capable of a great run in the competition in our own country.'

49

HEART STOPPER

THE Uruguay squad will have heart tests tomorrow morning to make sure they aren't too stressed out about facing England.

The two-time world champions will delay officially confirming their team until the afternoon and any player who has a quickened heartbeat could be axed.

Team physician Dr Roberto Masliah said, 'This is a precautionary measure to ensure our players are in the best condition. A quickened heartbeat could be a sign of strain or worry. We don't want them to get too worked up. It could affect their performance.'

Uruguay trainer Omar Borrás added, 'If a player's heart is beating too fast on the morning of the match, it means he will be playing the game in his mind before he even gets to Wembley. It could mean it would be unwise for him to play.'

BOY SCOUTS 1 URUGUAY 0

URUGUAY'S final training plans were thrown into chaos today – by a Boy Scouts troop.

They arrived at Harlow Sports Centre in Essex to find a Scouts sports event still in progress. The squad headed back to the Saxon Inn Hotel and worked out in a field there instead.

MAN IN THE MIDDLE

HUNGARIAN referee István Zsolt has the honour of taking charge of tomorrow's opening match.

Zsolt, a 45-year-old stage manager for the Budapest Opera, was the man in the middle at Wembley for West Ham United's European Cup Winners' Cup Final win over Munich 1860 last year.

His linesmen will be Bulgarian Dimitar Roumentchev and Tofik Bakhramov of the Soviet Union.

MEXICAN STAND-OFF

FA CHIEFS today headed off an embarrassing Wembley row with Mexico.

Their squad WILL now be at tomorrow's match between their Group One rivals England and Uruguay after earlier threatening a boycott in a misunderstanding over tickets.

They thought 18 of their 28 tickets were for the terraces and manager Ignacio Trelles complained, 'I will not have my players standing for 90 minutes. They are a World Cup team and are entitled to seats.'

However, it turned out the tickets were marked Grade I and Grade II and that the Mexicans had wrongly assumed Grade II meant standing. An FA spokesman said, 'Both grades provide seats.'

POOR OLD ALF

MEXICO manager Ignacio Trelles says he feels sorry for Alf Ramsey.

Trelles's team will be underdogs when they face England in a Group One clash on Saturday, but he claims all the pressure will be on the hosts.

Trelles – manager since 1957 and a veteran of two previous World Cups – said, 'Playing away is okay – in Sweden in 1958, in Chile in 1962 and now in London. But playing at home? No, that is too much.

'I will want nothing at all to do with the World Cup when it comes to Mexico in 1970. Poor Mr Ramsey. The things he must be feeling now. At home, everyone watches – everyone expects – so much. The Brazilians didn't win in Rio in 1950 and the police had to help them escape. No, I don't want to be like Mr Ramsey.'

Trelles admitted even he cannot predict how his inexperienced side will perform.

He added, 'They can be geniuses one day, the worst team in the world the next. That is the trouble with a team so young. You can never tell what they might do next.'

CHILD'S PLAY

ENGLAND will find facing Group One rivals Mexico like playing against 'children'.

That is the verdict of Switzerland manager Alfredo Foni, whose part-timers drew 1-1 with the Mexicans in a warm-up match in Lausanne last month.

Italian Foni, who won the World Cup as a player in 1938, believes England will easily beat Mexico on Saturday in their second match of the tournament.

Foni – whose team are in Group Two with West Germany, Argentina and Spain – insisted, 'England I believe in, absolutely. Mexico will be no trouble to England.

'Mexico take 20 steps to move one pace forward. They take ten moves to do what Jimmy Greaves would do in two.

'They are infants. I do not mean that nastily, because they have some very good players. But they play like children in international football. They are tactically and technically very young.'

ITALY FLOP FEAR

ITALY manager Edmondo Fabbri fears the worst over their chances and has 'a feeling in his blood' that England will be champions.

The two-time winners are highly fancied, but Fabbri says he has a bad vibe about the Azzurri's prospects.

'I cannot give reasons for my lack of confidence,' he said. 'It is just a feeling in my blood. I can see no other country than England winning.'

Italian football has often been blighted by defensive tactics and violent play, but Fabbri promised, 'We will not kill football. If one of our players is provoked, he will not retaliate. There is a new spirit in the team which makes them realise that fair play is part of the game.

'I know it is the habit of some of our clubs to concentrate on defence, but with the national team we go for goals.

'That is the true spirit of the game and that is how we are going to play. It is wrong to think of Italy as concentrating on defence. In our warm-up games we scored 19 goals to one against. Does that sound like defensive football?'

Chile manager Luis Álamos today backed his men to upset the odds on Wednesday, saying, 'We are pleased to be starting against a team who are strongly fancied to win the competition.

'We think we can spring a surprise and, if we manage that, we must have very good prospects of qualifying for the quarter-finals.'

THE AZZZzzURRI

ITALIAN chiefs have splashed out more than £1,000 on replacing beds and furniture after turning up their noses at their accommodation.

Azzurri officials took one look at the rooms usually used by students at Durham County School of Agriculture and headed to Newcastle to buy 31 beds and easy chairs.

Italy chief press officer Giuseppe Bardigotta said, 'Our players must have every ease and comfort if they are to give of their best. The beds were suitable enough for students, but too small for our players.

'Our new mattresses are very good. Our players like them so much that we are arranging to have the beds transferred wherever we go – Liverpool, London – during the closing stages of the competition.'

KOREANS COM-PLANE

NORTH KOREA hope to be a big noise at their first World Cup – despite being kept awake by aircraft.

The Hornets are staying at the St George Hotel, near Darlington, and are only 300 yards from the runway at the new Teesside Airport.

North Korean spokesman Shin Ha-Taik said, 'The noise from the aeroplanes is tremendous. Although we can tolerate it by day, it is not very pleasant at night when we are trying to rest.'

The squad are training at Middlesbrough's Hutton Road practice ground after complaining that a pitch prepared for them near the hotel was too bumpy.

Korean FA president Kim Ky-Soo said, 'It means we have to travel ten miles into Middlesbrough to do our practice, but it is worth it.'

He added, 'We are handicapped by our lack of experience in England, but we had spies watching the other competing nations and we think we can do well. Our players are dedicated men, who do not drink. They spend their spare time playing chess and cards.'

MEN FROM U.N.C.L.E

THE Soviet Union are ready to vow fans with their football…and hairstyles.

USSR chiefs took the squad to a Durham City salon for a pre-tournament trim and many of the players opted for a new style.

Hairdresser Jack Brown said some chose the Perry Como or Dick van Dyke look, but the most popular was the style sported by Napoleon Solo, the character played by Robert Vaughn in the hit TV show *The Man From U.N.C.L.E.*

Brown said, 'I don't suppose they have even heard of Napoleon Solo, but the style suited some of them very well indeed.'

The Soviets and Italy are both insisting there will be no *Man From U.N.C.L.E*-style espionage while they train on opposite sides of Durham University sports ground.

Italian FA general secretary Dr Franco Bertoldi said, 'When I look out of the window the Russians are there, but I am sure that spying will be ruled out by all sides.'

USSR Vice-Minister for Sport Leonid Nikonov insisted, 'We have nothing to hide. We would not be bothered by the Italians watching us.'

TAKE IT OR LEV IT

GOALKEEPING great Lev Yashin was today warned he won't play in the Soviet Union's opener against North Korea unless he is 100 per cent fit.

Yashin, 38, is regarded as the world's top keeper, but he has been troubled by a knee injury.

USSR Vice-Minister for Sport Leonid Nikonov said, 'Yashin is still our number one goalkeeper. He played in Sweden only a few days ago and brought off some fantastic saves.'

But coach Nikolai Morozov warned, 'Yashin must be perfect to get his place. I will definitely not play him if he is half-fit.'

Yashin vowed, 'I've never worked harder than this time for my third World Cup. I've never been in better form.'

As well as World Cup glory, Yashin has another burning ambition – to go fishing in England.

When the Soviets flew in, Yashin was clutching a fishing rod and joked, 'No football for me. I have come for the fishing. I hope to catch some trout.'

Meanwhile, defender Valentin Afonin says the USSR want to avoid Brazil in the last eight. A year ago, the champions crushed them 3-0 in front of a 103,000 crowd in Moscow, with Pelé scoring twice.

Afonin said, 'I have paid particular attention to the Brazilians' technique. We can learn much from them. Pelé is very fast and you have got to be constantly ready for any kind of trick from him.'

RATTIN IS ALL MOUTH

ARGENTINA captain Antonio Rattin has been given the all-clear to lead their campaign – after emergency dental treatment.

The Boca Juniors midfielder gave the South Americans a scare when he woke up with a bad toothache, but the problem was solved after a hastily-arranged visit to a Birmingham dentist.

The bill will be met by British taxpayers, as the official World Cup handbook states, 'The Ministry of Health has stated that representatives of the nations competing can be regarded as visitors and, as such, are entitled to free treatment under the NHS for emergency conditions.'

NICE JUAN

ARGENTINA manager Juan Carlos Lorenzo has vowed to shake off their image as football bad-boys.

The South Americans were criticised for rough play at the 1962 World Cup and a recent friendly in Italy saw a player from each side sent off. Lorenzo knows his players must keep their discipline, particularly when European referees are in charge.

He said, 'We must be on our best behaviour, on and off the field. The whole football organisation in Argentina has been geared to improve our image in the eyes of the world.

'I have told my players they must behave correctly and accept referees' decisions. They know that European referees will apply the laws as seen in Europe and that this means there will be a certain amount of physical contact.

'As long as they understand this, I think trouble will be avoided. We shall try to avoid physical contact. It is important to be strong physically, but the technical side is just as vital.'

Argentina, who start against Spain on Wednesday, arrived in England two days later than planned because Lorenzo kept them at their camp in Austria for 'punishment' training.

Lorenzo, who was in charge in 1962 but was only recently reappointed, said he was disappointed with the performances in their warm-up matches and had kept the players back for 'extra polishing'.

He won't let up during the tournament, adding, 'My players will obey strict discipline and their routine will be set out each day so they know exactly what is required. Dinner will be at 8pm and I will expect them to be in their rooms by 10pm.

'There will be plenty of work, but enough relaxation. They have televisions in their rooms, so that they can relax. Sightseeing? Maybe Stratford-upon-Avon.'

Lorenzo is sending three players to represent Argentina at the opening ceremony at Wembley. He explained how he chose the trio, saying, 'Roland Irusta, because he is a goalkeeper and we have three goalkeepers. Then Jose Varacka, because he played in the 1958 World Cup and this will be an added honour. And Juan Carlos Sarnari – because he is very handsome!'

SPANISH TUMMY

SPAIN manager José Villalonga has banned his players from drinking English tap water in case it makes them ill.

Villalonga said, 'This is a precautionary measure against stomach upsets, which are so often caused by a change of drinking water.'

The squad will not be subject to a booze ban, though, with Villalonga adding, 'We have one bottle of wine per day between four players, but no spirits.'

GERMANS WRITTEN OFF

WEST GERMANY legend Fritz Walter has written off his nation's hopes of a second world title.

Walter, a national hero after captaining the Germans to victory in 1954, believes home advantage makes England favourites.

He said, 'I do not think the German team will get further than the semi-finals. I take England and Italy for the final.

'Germany have a strong side and are physically tougher and more experienced than the 1954 side, but I cannot see England losing a match on their home ground.'

German coach Helmut Schön claimed, 'We are honestly surprised to find that we are being so strongly tipped as winners. It seems the critics fancy us more than we fancy ourselves.'

IT'S A KNOCKOUT

THE World Cup is giving Switzerland manager Alfredo Foni a headache – in more ways than one.

Foni was knocked out by a shot from Heinz Bäni during training at Abbeydale Park in Sheffield last week and there was concern when he later collapsed again in the dressing room.

The Swiss boss has been given the all-clear, but he admits the challenge facing his side is giving him another headache. His part-timers, whose jobs range from publicans to pastry cooks, have only been together for a week and must tackle the might of West Germany, Spain and Argentina.

Foni admitted, 'We cannot expect to win the group, never mind the cup.'

And captain Heinz Schneiter, a bank clerk, added, 'If we win one point we will be doing well.'

LITTLE BIRD FLYING

BRAZIL star Garrincha says he is ready to repeat his 1962 World Cup heroics.

The 32-year-old winger, nicknamed Little Bird, was the main man as Brazil won a second straight title, but his international career has stuttered since.

Today, though, Garrincha promised he is ready to turn on the style. He said, 'A cartilage operation and a change of clubs meant I missed two years of football. Now I feel very happy and very fit.'

Fellow Brazil superstar Pelé has assured fans he is already looking ahead to the NEXT World Cup.

The Santos ace said, 'I have no thoughts of retiring. Football is my life. I am still only 25, so you can be sure I will be aiming for my fourth successive World Cup competition in Mexico in 1970.'

Brazil have been preparing at Bolton Wanderers' training ground for their opener against Bulgaria and Trotters trainer Bert Sproston believes English players could learn from their methods.

The ex-England full-back said, 'It's a pity some of our clubs couldn't be here to see the Brazilians. They would know then what real training is. These Brazilians are dedicated, even in practice.'

CHEEKY BULGARS

BULGARIA have won a pitch battle with their hosts after complaining about training facilities.

The Eastern Europeans were upset when Chester City refused to let them use their main ground because the pitch had been re-seeded.

The squad were instead directed to a nearby pitch normally used for junior matches.

A Bulgaria spokesman complained, 'We are surprised at being asked to train out in the fields. When the ball went out of play, the players had to chase it a long way.

'I am afraid some of the players have got the impression we are being treated as second-class citizens. They do not visualise the Brazilians training on such a pitch. When a delegation called on Chester in January it was made clear we could use their ground.'

Chester have now had a change of heart and player-manager Peter Hauser said, 'I'm afraid we had to agree. We didn't want any bad feeling.'

The Bulgarians are outsiders in a group featuring Brazil, Portugal and Hungary, but coach Rudolf Vytlačil warned, 'Watch out – we could be the dark horses.

'Taking us lightly would be very dangerous. Bulgarian football is much improved since Chile four years ago. Our tactical plans are better and the players will be fully prepared mentally and physically.

'We have outstanding players. Ivan Kolev, who needs no introduction, and the greatest footballer Bulgaria has ever produced in Georgi Asparoukhov. Yes, I am confident Bulgaria will be in the quarter-finals.'

DREAM MATCH

COUNCIL worker Dave Williams and his mates have already had a World Cup to remember – after playing against Bulgaria.

The Bulgarians wanted a training game, but the FA has put a block on competing nations playing official warm-up matches.

So 20-year-old Manchester Town Hall publicity assistant Williams, an assistant attache to the Bulgarian squad during the finals, rounded up a team of locals to play them. He said, 'I was told my job as an assistant attache was to help the Bulgarians in every way possible!'

Despite a 12-1 thrashing, his brother Graham, a former Manchester United junior, said, 'It was a great experience. We certainly enjoyed it and we hope it was useful for their training.'

WE'VE GOT BALLS

HUNGARY plan to win over English fans by kicking autographed footballs into the crowd before matches.

The Magyars have brought dozens of balls painted in their national colours of red, white and green.

Hungarian FA secretary Gyorgi Hontl said, 'We are a long way from home and we want to get the fans on our side. Having the fans cheering for you can do wonders.'

The Hungarians are staying at the Palace Hotel, Southport, and their dietician is keeping a close eye on what they eat, with beef strictly off-limits on a menu featuring veal, lean pork and chicken.

Hontl said, 'We are taking no chances. The dietician will keep a check on the meals and the players won't necessarily be eating the same food as the hotel residents. We consider beef a second-grade meat. Hungarians eat very little red meat.'

Coach Lajos Baróti is sweating over the fitness of star men Ferenc Bene and Flórián Albert ahead of Wednesday's opener against Portugal.

Both have leg injuries and Baróti said, 'It is like getting ready for the first night of a new play and worrying in case you will be without your leading performers.'

DROP OF PORT

WORLD CUP new boys Portugal are leaving no stone unturned in their bid for glory.

The Portuguese have made themselves at home at the Wilmslow Hotel, Manchester, after arriving with barrels of olive oil, 600 bottles of wine and a huge stock of frozen fish.

Hotel manager Vernon Darby said, 'They are tremendously particular in their preparations. If they play as well as they have prepared, we will certainly be hearing a lot more about Portugal in the next few weeks.'

Portuguese FA vice-president António da Silva has played down their chances, saying, 'We do not expect to win the trophy, but our players will be giving their best and they are under instructions to play in a sporting spirit.

'I think England have as good a chance as anyone of winning, as they are in their home country.'

LAST ORDERS

TIME has been called on a bid for late drinking at a dozen Manchester pubs during the finals.

Wilson's Brewery applied for half-hour extensions on three nights this month, arguing that fans wouldn't be able to get to the pub because they would be watching matches at Old Trafford or on television.

Despite dozens of similar extensions being granted elsewhere in England, the application was rejected at Salford Stipendiary Court.

Stipendiary magistrate Leslie Walsh ruled, 'It seems to me these people try to seize every possible excuse for getting extensions.

'What they are saying, in effect, is that people watching the games are being swindled out of one and a half-hour's drinking and must be given the chance to make it up.'

WEMBLEY OF THE NORTH

EVERTON chairman Edward Holland Hughes says the club are proud that Goodison Park is the Wembley of the North.

The Merseyside ground will host five matches and Hughes says the stadium is in tip-top shape after improvement work costing around £160,000.

And he hopes Goodison's glory will be crowned by a semi-final featuring England.

He said, 'We are delighted with the way the work has gone and we feel it has improved what we have always thought to be the finest league ground in the country.

'We consider ourselves very honoured that Goodison has been rated second only to Wembley in importance as far as the World Cup is concerned.'

While Arsenal's Highbury stadium was ruled out as a London venue because the pitch is too small, the Goodison playing area has been extended by two yards at either end to meet FIFA requirements.

Around 900 seats have been temporarily removed from the Goodison Road Stand to provide high-tech facilities for 700 TV, radio and print journalists.

A 5,000-seat section has been set aside in the Bullens Road Stand for foreign fans, with interpreters and guides on hand to assist them. Hughes promised, 'The arrangements at Goodison will be as good as anywhere.'

STREETS AHEAD

MERSEYSIDERS living near Goodison Park are bringing extra colour to the finals.

Everton's ground will stage matches in Brazil's group, as well as a quarter-final and a semi-final.

Residents of Claudia Street and Leta Street have coughed up 30 shillings per household to deck out their streets with bunting and artificial flowers.

Lord mayor of Liverpool Herbert Allen, invited to a tea party by residents, said, 'This is a fine idea. The World Cup seems to have brought out a wonderful community spirit everywhere.'

NAME GAME

BBC commentators have been working overtime – to make sure they say players' names right.

Many of the overseas players will be almost as unknown to the Beeb's lead commentator Kenneth Wolstenholme and his colleagues as they will be to UK viewers.

A BBC spokesman explained today how Wolstenholme and Co. have been getting to grips with hundreds of pronunciations.

'The boys have had their homework,' said the spokesman. 'We have a pronunciation unit, which has listed all the names alphabetically and phonetically from the appropriate sources.

'The Brazilians, Portuguese and Mexicans pose rather awkward problems, because they often use nicknames. For instance, Edson Arantes do Nascimento becomes Pelé.'

The spokesman admitted the commentators were probably relieved that one particular star didn't make the Brazil squad, adding, 'Olegário Tolóí de Oliveira becomes Dudu…pronounced Doodoo. You will, of course, appreciate the problem.'

Many fixtures will be screened live, with matchday highlights shows on both channels. Unfortunately, coverage will only be available in black and white in the UK, with the highly-anticipated introduction of colour TV expected next year.

While Wolstenholme will be the BBC's number one commentator, David Coleman will double up as presenter and commentator, with Walley Barnes and Frank Bough the other commentators.

Hugh Johns is ITV's lead commentator, with Gerry Loftus, Barry Davies and John Camkin completing the team.

Both channels have signed top names from British football to give viewers expert analysis.

ITV's coverage will be fronted by former *Crackerjack* and *This Is Your Life* star Eamonn Andrews.

He will be supported by a line-up of pundits featuring former England captain Billy Wright, Wales manager Dave Bowen, Liverpool manager Bill Shankly, Celtic manager Jock Stein and Aston Villa forward Phil Woosnam.

Expert views on the BBC will come from Coventry City manager Jimmy Hill, ex-England captain Johnny Haynes, Chelsea manager Tommy Docherty, former Tottenham Hotspur captain Danny Blanchflower and West Ham United manager Ron Greenwood.

BIN AND GONE

UNLUCKY fan Jim Milnes is set to miss matches including the final after claiming his tickets were thrown away by mistake.

The salesman from Huyton, Merseyside, says he had tickets for matches in Liverpool and Manchester, plus the Wembley final – but a relative inadvertently binned them.

Milnes, 53, says he even searched through piles of rubbish at Huyton Tip before writing to organisers asking for replacement tickets.

Today he received a letter from the Wembley box office telling him, 'We are sorry to have to take this line, but we are being inundated with queries of this nature and we are having to refuse all requests to issue duplicate tickets.'

Monday 11 July
Matchday One

England v Uruguay (Group One)
7.30pm, Wembley, London

QUEEN KICKS IT OFF

QUEEN ELIZABETH II called for 'some fine football' as the World Cup got under way tonight with an impressive opening ceremony at Wembley Stadium.

Fifteen minutes before England kicked off against Uruguay, Her Majesty's arrival on to a podium on the pitch was heralded by a fanfare from eight state trumpeters in golden uniforms.

The Queen, flanked by the Duke of Edinburgh and FIFA president Sir Stanley Rous, told the crowd, 'I am very pleased that this country is acting as hosts for the final stages of the World Cup.

'I welcome all our visitors and feel sure that we shall be seeing some fine football. It now gives me great pleasure to declare open the eighth World Football Championships.'

The ceremony was opened at 6pm by the massed bands of guards with a 65-minute music and marching display.

Then 320 boys from schools in Middlesex and London took part in a flag-bearing ceremony to introduce the 16 nations, with the flag of champions Brazil carried in first and England's last.

FIFA chief Rous welcomed fans from around the world in a message in the official tournament programme, writing, 'We hope that whether their team wins or loses, supporters will return home feeling that their visit to England has helped them make friends in sport.'

BLANK OF ENGLAND
England 0 Uruguay 0
Group One, Wembley, London (att: 87,148)

ALF RAMSEY tonight insisted England CAN still win the World Cup, despite this drab display.

The Three Lions failed to break down a stubborn Uruguay defence – the first time in 52 attempts that England have failed to score at Wembley since the end of the Second World War.

Ramsey, whose side had won their previous seven matches, said, 'I was disappointed with the result, but not with the performance. Uruguay were a good side.

'Naturally I was disappointed we did not get a goal. But, with seven or eight opposing players in the 18-yard box, you had to be lucky to get a break.

'With regard to the mass hypnotism after the draw, when everybody thought England were in an easy group, I said at the time that there were 15 other teams and nothing was going to be easy. But I still believe we are able to win the World Cup.'

Before Uruguay left their base in Harlow, Essex, well-wishers presented them with a teddy bear decked out with ribbons in their national colours. But there was nothing soft and cuddly about their play at Wembley.

Coach Ondino Viera defended their cautious approach and predicted they will win the group.

He said, 'My team played controlled football and we got the result we wanted. Having kept England at bay, we should finish top.

'You can see my boys are very happy. I am proud of them. They played with much method and showed plenty of self-discipline.

'While we retain this composure and understanding, we are confident of doing well. England were the powerful ones, the team we feared most. That was before the game…now we fear nobody.'

The Wembley crowd roared England on throughout and showed their frustration by booing the Uruguayans' negative tactics and time-wasting.

England made a bright start, but it was Gordon Banks who had to make the only meaningful save of the first half when he dealt with a shot from Julio César Cortés.

England took until the 65th minute to trouble Uruguay goalkeeper Ladislao Mazurkiewicz with a deflected Bobby Charlton shot and the elusive goal never looked like coming.

ENGLAND: Gordon Banks, George Cohen, Ray Wilson, Nobby Stiles, Jack Charlton, Bobby Moore (capt), Alan Ball, Jimmy Greaves, Bobby Charlton, Roger Hunt, John Connelly.

URUGUAY: Ladislao Mazurkiewicz, Luis Ubiña, Omar Caetano, Milton Viera, Jorge Manicera, Horacio Troche (capt), Julio César Cortés, Néstor Gonçálvez, Héctor Silva, Pedro Rocha, Domingo Pérez.

Group One

	P	W	D	L	F	A	Pts
England	1	0	1	0	0	0	1
Uruguay	1	0	1	0	0	0	1
France	0	0	0	0	0	0	0
Mexico	0	0	0	0	0	0	0

WEE BIT OF HISTORY

BOBBY MOORE and Jack Charlton made history tonight as the first England players to be drug-tested at a World Cup.

The pair, along with Uruguay's Néstor Gonçálvez and Omar Caetano, were selected at random to give urine samples under FIFA's new anti-doping scheme.

FIFA had planned to keep the players' identities secret, but England manager Alf Ramsey was left miffed after the names were leaked.

He said, 'The idea was that the people carrying out the tests should not know who the samples were taken from.'

ROYAL MIX-UP

FOUR England players dropped a royal clanger after the goalless draw with Uruguay tonight.

The two teams and the match officials were meant to stand to attention for the playing of *God Save The Queen* after the game.

The Uruguay team lined up in front of the Queen, but most of the England players had headed for the tunnel when the final whistle blew. They were called back by embarrassed officials, but four – Jack Charlton, Jimmy Greaves, Roger Hunt and John Connelly – were already back in the dressing room when the anthem was played.

The Queen, perhaps unaware of the confusion, looked on, smiling.

HAVING A BALL

REFEREES' chief Ken Aston today demonstrated the ritual officials will go through to choose the balls for every World Cup match.

Aston and match referee István Zsolt put on a pre-match show for reporters at the Kensington Close Hotel ahead of the England-Uruguay game.

First they had to decide which colour ball – white or lime. After Essex school headmaster Aston turned off the lights to recreate the conditions he expected at Wembley, they opted for white.

After pumping up the balls and weighing them, Aston and Zsolt signed them and packed them into a string bag.

The ritual will be repeated before every match and, before setting off for the game, Aston said, 'I'm taking them to Wembley in my car. They will never be out of my sight until we get there.

'Remember that no team can come to the ref and say that the ball is too hard or too soft once it has been signed by us.'

AGAINST ALL ODDS

MEXICO manager Ignacio Trelles has laughed off his side's tag as 200/1 outsiders as they prepare to take on France.

Trelles was in buoyant mood after today's training session at Cheshunt, Herts, ahead of their Wembley opener on Wednesday.

Asked about the bookies writing off his team's hopes, he said, 'What does it matter? We don't think of the odds, only of doing as well as we possibly can.

'England are the best in our group, but I think we will qualify. Everybody starts with the same chances. We are not among the great powers of world football, but we may spring a surprise.

'We are confident about the game against France. It is just a game to us, an important game, but still a game. The World Cup is important and can be called a sporting war, but I still regard football games as football games.'

Trelles's biggest worry is the fitness of his goalkeepers. Number one Ignacio Calderón injured a shoulder in training and deputy Antonio Carbajal – hoping to play at his FIFTH finals – is nursing an injured finger.

Mexican legend Carbajal, 37, announced his retirement at the LAST World Cup, but today he promised this really will be his swansong, admitting, 'I am happy to retire – I am too old.'

ALLEZ LES BLEUS

FRANCE manager Henri Guérin believes his side can reach the last eight – but admits England are favourites to win their group.

The England squad will be at Wembley for Wednesday's France-Mexico match and Guérin thinks they will see enough to worry them ahead of their meeting next week.

Guérin said, 'I am confident we can qualify – most likely as runners-up to England. Our greatest asset could be the high speed of our players. I feel we could do well on the fine Wembley turf.'

Guérin has written off first opponents Mexico, saying, 'They are so weak, so slow. Their forwards have no zest and the defence has no man of steel.'

His players, meanwhile, have reportedly been making a tidy profit by charging schoolboys for autographs at their training ground.

BULGARIAN 'BOMB'

BULGARIA'S star striker Georgi Asparoukhov says they are ready to explode on to the World Cup stage tomorrow against Brazil.

Group Three gets under way when the South Americans kick off their bid for a third straight crown at Goodison Park against a nation yet to record a finals win.

But Asparoukhov, 23, said, 'We're the outsiders, of course, but the ball sometimes plays jokes. And what a bomb will burst in Liverpool if we can win or draw.'

Bulgaria coach Rudolf Vytlačil knows what a tough task his side face after taking charge of the Czechoslovakian team beaten 3-1 by Brazil in the 1962 final.

He is playing his cards close to his chest over who will be detailed to man-mark Pelé, but the job is expected to go to Dobromir Jechev. He has shackled the likes of Bobby Charlton, Italian star Sandro Mazzola and Hungarian great Flórián Albert in the past.

Vytlačil said, 'It is quite evident that Brazil are not as good as they were, but let us be clear about it – they are still one of the best in the world.

'Who marks Pelé? Our best and most intelligent player. This man will be a real gentleman – hard, but fair. Pelé is such a difficult player to plot against, as you never know what role he'll be playing.'

HEAT IS ON PELÉ

SUPERSTAR Pelé admits he is feeling the weight of expectation going into the finals.

The Brazil forward has established himself as the undisputed number one player in the world since inspiring his nation's triumph in 1958.

But he warned ahead of tomorrow's opener against Bulgaria, 'Everyone expects me to be in top form every match, but it is not as easy as that. Opponents perhaps mark me a little harder than other players and I cannot always manage it. I always feel disappointed, though, if I let down the public as well as the team.'

NO-NAG MAGYARS

HUNGARY chiefs have defended their decision to bring only 18 players to the finals.

The other 15 nations have arrived with 22-man squads, but the Magyars have gambled by leaving four players at home on stand-by.

Hungarian FA secretary Gyorgi Hontl explained, 'It is nothing to do with finance. We find that men who do not get a place in the side begin to nag, so we cut down on the nagging by making the party as small as possible. We can fly them over in a few hours.'

Hontl is confident despite Hungary being grouped with champions Brazil, highly-fancied Portugal and improving Bulgaria.

He said, 'I believe West Germany, Italy and England will reach the semi-finals, with Hungary as dark horses. Brazil are a great team, but European conditions are not favourable for South American teams.'

Hungary won extra support in Manchester today when they were the only one of the Group Three nations to send their whole team to a reception hosted by the Lord Mayoress of Manchester, Nellie Beer.

While a handful of Bulgaria and Portugal players attended, Brazil said they didn't want to disrupt their stars' match preparations.

TORRES ON A HIGH

GIANT striker José Torres today fired a warning to Portugal's rivals.

Torres and strike partner Eusébio banged in the goals in training at Cheadle Rovers' ground near Manchester ahead of Wednesday's meeting with Hungary.

And 6ft 4in Torres said, 'I've never felt better. I was beating the goalkeeper so often that it made me so happy. Now I'm looking for lots more goals while we are in England.'

GERMANS ATTACK

HELMUT SCHÖN will send out his West German side against Switzerland tomorrow with the orders, 'Attack, attack, attack!'

Many pundits are predicting the competition will be blighted by defensive tactics but West Germany coach Schön is demanding a positive approach.

He vowed, 'I promise we shall do everything possible to attack. It would be suicidal to go into any match in the competition without a strong defence, but I'm sure the eventual winners will be the country with the best attack. We shall not forget this in any of our matches.

'I feel our present side, in terms of skill and ability, is the best blend we have had for years.'

Schön named his XI after a final training session in Ashbourne, Derbyshire, and the only surprise was the omission of free-scoring winger Lothar Emmerich.

His prolific season with Borussia Dortmund included scoring four times against West Ham United as the German club scored a 5-2 aggregate win in their European Cup Winners' Cup semi-final.

Schön will remind his team how tough it was to beat Switzerland 2-1 in a group game four years ago. He added, 'We shall not underestimate the Swiss. We remember them only too well from Chile.

'Out there, the Swiss were two goals down against us and, when they lost a player through injury, it looked all over. But they got a goal and put up such a fight that we were very hard pushed to hold on.'

PRAM-IER LEAGUE

MADCAP Swiss fan Emile Holliger has made it to Sheffield in time for their first match – after pushing a pram from Zurich.

The window cleaner, 48, made the three-week, 800-mile trek to win a £65 bet. He said, 'If the Swiss win the World Cup, I will push my pram all the way back to Zurich.'

COP SOME KIP

POLICE have been called in to help Argentina's stars get some sleep.

Birmingham cops are carrying out late-night anti-noise patrols around the Argentinians' city centre hotel because the players have been kept awake by noisy motorbikes racing around nearby roads.

An Albany Hotel spokesman said, 'We have complained for some time about the noise from motorcyclists late at night. They use one stretch of road as a racetrack. The Argentinians have been very nice about it, but they are having difficulty in getting to sleep.'

While the South Americans have had disturbed nights, they have had no problems during the day. Each afternoon they take a break from training at the police sports ground two miles away and return to the hotel for a siesta.

SKILL STILL KING

SPAIN manager José Villalonga is confident skill will come out on top against strength in this World Cup.

Spain won the European title two years ago and Villalonga believes his team and the likes of Brazil will be too good for nations who rely on hard work and physical power.

Villalonga, whose side begin their campaign against Argentina on Wednesday, said, 'It does not matter how robust the play is, skill will always win. Both West Germany and England are noted for their hard playing, but skill will come out on top.'

CHILL AGAINST CHILE

ITALY manager Edmondo Fabbri will urge his team to play without fear against Chile on Wednesday.

Fabbri said, 'My only briefing to the team is, "We have to win." I am satisfied that training has gone according to plan. Now they must relax. We have high hopes and faith in this team. I don't intend divulging my tactics. That is like going to war and letting the enemy know your battle plans.'

The Azzurri boss said he was not concerned that group rivals North Korea sent three spies to watch Italy beat Scotland in their final warm-up match.

And he won't even bother scouting the Koreans ahead of their meeting next week.

He said, 'The fact that I permitted them to watch proves, I think, that we are sportsmen. I don't intend to watch the Koreans.'

BAD FOR MY KOREA

SOVIET UNION coach Nikolai Morozov admits even the thought of losing to North Korea would give him sleepless nights.

The Asian side are unknowns on the world stage and pundits are predicting the Soviets could run up a cricket score at Middlesbrough's Ayresome Park tomorrow.

But cigar-puffing Morozov said he had seen enough in the Hornets' 2-0 win over Spartak Moscow two years ago to suggest they won't be a pushover.

He said, 'The only reason I could be afraid of them is that they are practically unknown to us. The only time I have seen them in action was when they beat Spartak a couple of years ago. All we could gather was that they are fit and move very fast. They played it hard. We do not fear the North Koreans, but nor are we saying what the score could be. We don't care how many we win by, we just want the points.'

Asked how he would react to defeat, Morozov replied, 'Please don't ask such questions – I won't be able to sleep at night. It will not be the end of everything if they beat us, but it would be a big blow.'

Morozov will not make his line-up public until tomorrow and said, 'It is not opportune of me to reveal my team until the morning of the game. We must keep our little secrets.'

INTERNATIONAL PIN-UPS

SOVIET UNION chiefs will ensure their players go face-to-face with their opponents even before a ball is kicked.

USSR Vice-Minister for Sport Leonid Nikonov revealed that photos of the opposing team are pinned up on a board before every match and the Soviets are told to study the man they will be up against. Nikonov explained, 'The opposition then become more than just names and numbers. Our players see them as personalities and this is important in the approach to any game.'

POLITICAL FOOTBALL

THE British government has avoided an embarrassing political row by allowing the North Korean flag to fly at Wembley.

Britain has no diplomatic relations with the communist Democratic People's Republic of Korea, but its flag has been raised at the national stadium alongside those of the other competing nations.

Foreign Office officials are understood to be aware of this, but are choosing to turn a blind eye.

The Korean squad are in high spirits and have been amusing staff and guests at the St George Hotel near Darlington with a group sing-along of patriotic songs in the restaurant each morning.

Their breakfast menu has also caused a stir. The players have been tucking into a spread including bread and butter, rice, boiled beef and spaghetti soup, cabbage, cucumber and onions with soy sauce, beef and eggs and apples – all washed down with coffee.

After their final training session ahead of facing the USSR, coach Myung Rye-Hyun said, 'We are very happy and looking forward to a win.

'It should not be forgotten that we have earned the right to meet Russia, Chile and Italy thanks to the sweat of our brow. We have tried to raise our physical and tactical preparations to a very high level. It won't be easy for our opponents, especially in the first quarter of an hour when we play at maximum speed and in the last quarter of an hour when many opponents will be out of breath and we will play at the same pace as at the start of the match.'

TICKET PLEA

FANS have been urged: Don't give your cash to the touts, there are plenty of tickets left.

World Cup organisers cannot block the resale of tickets at inflated prices and one tout today predicted big business during the tournament.

Londoner Bruce Davies, 21, had tickets available for the opening match and said, 'There are plenty more where they came from and I'm in a position to supply any askers at my price.'

However, Football League secretary Alan Hardaker revealed no group match is a sell-out yet. He said, 'There is no need to pay black market prices for tickets. The League have quite a number available for all matches in the preliminary stages.'

Concern over poor ticket sales for the matches in the North-East eased today, as World Cup fever finally appeared to take a grip.

With 168,000 tickets available for the group games at Sunderland and Middlesbrough, only a third have been snapped up in advance sales.

However, there were long queues outside Roker Park today and Sunderland assistant secretary Eddie Marshall said, 'The fans have come forward as the date for the games has drawn nearer. There has been a real rush on tickets today.'

At Ayresome Park, Middlesbrough secretary Harry Green added, 'Ticket sales have picked up considerably in the last few days, but it still looks as though we will have to put them on sale at the turnstiles. There is no time now to deal with postal applications.'

In the North-West, Goodison Park officials have reported excellent advance sales, while around half the available tickets for Old Trafford have been sold so far. Attendances should be healthy in Sheffield and Birmingham. All 24,000 seats at Hillsborough have been snapped up for every game, leaving terrace tickets only, while Villa Park officials have had to open a special box office in Birmingham city centre to cope with a rush of interest.

Tuesday 12 July
Matchday Two

West Germany v Switzerland (Group Two)
7.30pm, Hillsborough, Sheffield

Brazil v Bulgaria (Group Three)
7.30pm, Goodison Park, Liverpool

USSR v North Korea (Group Four)
7.30pm, Ayresome Park, Middlesbrough

SWISS ROLLED OVER
**West Germany 5 (Held 15, Haller 20, pen 77, Beckenbauer 39, 52)
Switzerland 0
Group Two, Hillsborough, Sheffield (att: 36,127)**

HELMUT SCHÖN tonight warned there is more to come from West Germany after this five-star show.

The Germans lived up to their manager's pre-match promise of attacking football as they ruthlessly dismantled the Swiss part-timers in Sheffield.

Schön said, 'I'm not satisfied in every respect, but of course this was the first match and first matches are always difficult – as England found out.'

Switzerland were rocked when Jakob Kuhn and Werner Leimgruber were dropped by manager Alfredo Foni 90 minutes before kick-off for breaking a 10.30pm curfew the night before the game.

And it soon got worse when Sigi Held and Helmut Haller scored fine solo goals and Franz Beckenbauer made it 3-0 by half-time after exchanging passes with captain Uwe Seeler.

Beckenbauer netted again after 52 minutes with a side-footed finish after beating three men. Haller added a penalty when Scottish referee Hugh Phillips blew for an Ely Tacchella foul on Seeler.

Switzerland were upset that Phillips allowed Haller's goal to stand after he tricked goalkeeper Karl Elsener into diving early by pausing as he ran up to take the kick.

The Germans could have scored even more. A Seeler shot was cleared off the line and Wolfgang Overath hit the crossbar, although the battling Swiss did see both Richard Dürr and Robert Hosp hit the woodwork.

WEST GERMANY: Hans Tilkowski, Horst-Dieter Höttges, Karl-Heinz Schnellinger, Franz Beckenbauer, Willy Schulz, Wolfgang Weber, Albert Brülls, Helmut Haller, Uwe Seeler (capt), Wolfgang Overath, Sigi Held.

SWITZERLAND: Karl Elsener, André Grobéty, Heinz Schneiter (capt), Ely Tacchella, Hansrüdi Fuhrer, Heinz Bäni, Richard Dürr, Karl Odermatt, Fritz Künzli, Robert Hosp, Jean-Claude Schindelholz.

Group Two

	P	W	D	L	F	A	Pts
W Germany	1	1	0	0	5	0	2
Argentina	0	0	0	0	0	0	0
Spain	0	0	0	0	0	0	0
Switzerland	1	0	0	1	0	5	0

FREE KICK KINGS
Brazil 2 (Pelé 15, Garrincha 63) Bulgaria 0
Group Three, Goodison Park, Liverpool (att: 47,308)

TWO brilliant free kicks gave Brazil a winning start to their bid for a third straight world title.

Star men Pelé and Garrincha both scored as the South Americans overcame a brave, but sometimes brutal, Bulgaria.

Pelé, closely marked throughout by Dobromir Jechev, was on the end of some tough challenges.

But Brazil were ready to mix it too – with the foul count 20 by Bulgaria and 21 by the champions.

Indeed, Pelé was fortunate not to face more severe punishment from West German referee Kurt Tschenscher for one vicious lunge on Jechev.

The opener came when Pelé swerved in a free kick, given when he was chopped down by Dimitar Yakimov after escaping the attentions of Jechev for once.

Not to be outdone, Garrincha doubled the lead in the second half with another great dead-ball strike. Little Bird was fouled just outside the box and, with Bulgaria expecting another Pelé special, it was Garrincha who crashed the free kick high into the net.

Brazil did have one big scare when, leading 1-0, goalkeeper Gylmar spilled a through pass, but Georgi Asparoukhov could only steer the ball into the side netting.

Ominously for Brazil's rivals, long-time team physician Dr Hilton Gosling claimed the champions had plenty more in reserve. He said, 'We were only 80 per cent effective in this game.'

Bulgaria coach Rudolf Vytlačil was unrepentant about the rough treatment dished out to Pelé, saying, 'I think every team will take care of Pelé in the same manner.'

BRAZIL: Gylmar, Djalma Santos, Paulo Henrique, Denílson, Hideraldo Luiz Bellini (capt), Altair, Garrincha, Antônio Lima, Alcindo, Pelé, Jairzinho.

BULGARIA: Georgi Naidenov, Aleksandar Shalamanov, Dimitar Penev, Ivan Vutzov, Boris Gaganelov (capt), Stoyan Kitov, Dobromir Jechev, Dinko Dermendjiev, Georgi Asparoukhov, Dimitar Yakimov, Ivan Kolev.

Group Three

	P	W	D	L	F	A	Pts
Brazil	1	1	0	0	2	0	2
Hungary	0	0	0	0	0	0	0
Portugal	0	0	0	0	0	0	0
Bulgaria	1	0	0	1	0	2	0

HORNETS STUNG
USSR 3 (Malafeyev 31, 88, Banishevsky 33) North Korea 0
Group Four, Ayresome Park, Middlesbrough (att: 23,006)

NORTH KOREA coach Myung Rye-Hyun accused the Soviet Union of putting the boot in – then promised his side will come back stronger against Chile.

Although the Asian mystery men were comfortably beaten on their World Cup debut tonight, they won the hearts of the Middlesbrough crowd.

The Ayresome Park fans were on the Hornets' side from the opening minutes when Soviet hardman Murtaz Khurtsilava put in some crunching challenges. He became the pantomime villain after leaving Kang Ryong-Woon in a heap with a foul which earned him a lecture from Spanish referee Juan Gardeazábal.

And coach Myung Rye-Hyun complained, 'We expected Russia to put up a better performance. We are sorry that they had to commit so many fouls. Their tackling was very hard and they are a tough team.

'The crowd were wonderful. All the team said it was like playing at home. The supporters were on our side right from the start and I am glad we are playing all our games at Ayresome Park.

'We learned a lot of lessons from Russia and they were the team we feared more than any other. I am convinced we can benefit from those lessons in the game with Chile.'

Shin Yung-Kyoo headed an early Anatoly Banishevsky effort off the line, but the USSR struck twice in the space of three minutes just after the half-hour mark.

First, goalkeeper Lee Chan-Myung dived at the feet of Banishevsky, but could only deflect the ball into the path of Eduard Malafeyev. Then Banishevsky headed in a Iosef Sabo cross.

Korean winger Pak Doo-Ik did force two excellent saves from Anzor Kavazashvili, playing after Lev Yashin failed to convince USSR chiefs he was fully fit, but the Soviets made it 3-0 near the end when Sabo set up Malafeyev for his second.

USSR: Anzor Kavazashvili, Vladimir Ponomaryev, Leonid Ostrovsky, Georgy Sichinava, Murtaz Khurtsilava, Albert Shesternev (capt), Igor Chislenko, Iosif Sabo, Anatoly Banishevsky, Eduard Malafeyev, Galimzian Khusainov.

NORTH KOREA: Lee Chan-Myung, Park Lee-Sup, Shin Yung-Kyoo, Kang Bong-Chil, Lim Zoong-Sun, Im Seung-Hwi, Park Seung-Jin (capt), Han Bong-Jin, Pak Doo-Ik, Kang Ryong-Woon, Kim Seung-Il.

Group Four

	P	W	D	L	F	A	Pts
USSR	1	1	0	0	3	0	2
Chile	0	0	0	0	0	0	0
Italy	0	0	0	0	0	0	0
N Korea	1	0	0	1	0	3	0

0-0 TO 007

ALF RAMSEY was happy to have a spy in the camp today – when his players met James Bond.

The England manager gave his squad a break with a visit to Pinewood Studios, where actor Sean Connery is filming the fifth *007* movie, *You Only Live Twice*. The players, invited by the Rank Organisation, met other big-name entertainers including movie star Yul Brynner and pop singers Lulu and Cliff Richard.

Scotsman Connery told the squad not to worry about the result of their opener, saying, 'You were great against Uruguay last night. I thought you were really unlucky not to score at least three goals.'

Comic actor Norman Wisdom had the squad in stitches when he gave Jimmy Greaves an impromptu training session in how to jump and head an imaginary ball.

Reflecting on yesterday's match, Greaves said, 'Alf warned us all along that Uruguay would be tough to beat. They didn't want to make a game of it, but I'm convinced that once we get through to the quarter-finals the opposition will have to come at us.'

KICK IN THE GAULS

ENGLAND'S chances have been savaged in the French press after the bore draw with Uruguay.

The Three Lions face France next week and newspapers across the Channel are predicting disaster for the hosts.

France Soir reported, 'This was the most humiliating result for England at Wembley since the 6-3 defeat by Hungary in 1953. It is difficult to see why they are second favourites.'

And sports paper *L'Equipe* sneered, 'England lacked class. Uruguay lacked ambition. France cannot lose to this England team and they will beat Uruguay.'

NO DOPES

ANTI-DOPING chiefs have confirmed the World Cup's first random drug tests came back all clear.

Bobby Moore, Jack Charlton and two Uruguay players were chosen after the opening match to give urine samples.

Professor Mihailo Andrejevic, FIFA anti-doping committee chairman, said today, 'It was as we expected, but these checks must be done.'

TICKETY BOO

MORE than 12,000 fans who bought tickets for England's opening match didn't bother showing up.

The number of tickets sold was 87,148, but it is thought only around 75,000 fans actually passed through the turnstiles.

A Wembley spokesman said today, 'Thousands of people who bought tickets in block form for this and other matches in order to obtain a ticket for the final presumably didn't trouble to use their ticket for this match.'

In Middlesbrough, 23,006 fans watched tonight's USSR-North Korea match after a late rush for tickets left hundreds of fans queuing outside until just before kick-off.

Ayresome Park was the last venue chosen by organisers, with St James' Park, Newcastle, having originally been included.

The ground was only just ready in time for tonight's game after around £100,000 worth of improvement work.

But Middlesbrough mayor Jack Boothby said, 'Some people have said it was an accident that Middlesbrough was chosen as a ground for these games. I think it was an Act of God. The people of Middlesbrough now feel that they are part of the country.'

BATTLE STATIONS

SWISS referee Gottfried Dienst has warned Italy and Chile he won't allow a repeat of the infamous Battle of Santiago.

The two countries meet tomorrow in a rematch of their 1962 clash, which saw police go on to the pitch to restore order.

Italy had two players sent off as English referee Ken Aston struggled to keep control in a match which shamed world football.

FIFA today appointed experienced ref Dienst, a veteran of 86 internationals and eight European Cup matches.

Dienst said, 'I don't think it will be necessary to speak to the teams before the game. I have two good eyes in my head and I can see what is going on. I shall make sure there is no trouble.'

Today, both managers promised there would be no repeat of four years ago. Chile manager Luis Álamos said, 'Chile did not start it in 1962 and Chile will not start anything again. My players will not retaliate, even if provoked.'

Opposite number Edmondo Fabbri vowed, 'There will be no repeat of the rough-house in Santiago. We have come to play football and that is what we shall do. I have a new team with a new spirit.'

CAUGHT NAPPING

LOCAL World Cup organisers in Sunderland today issued an urgent appeal for householders to put up foreign visitors.

A late influx of fans into the area for the opening Roker Park match tomorrow has caught the Sunderland World Cup committee on the hop, with accommodation running low.

A committee spokesman said, 'We prepared a rough estimate of what we would need in the way of accommodation from the number of advance bookings for the match between Italy and Chile.

'Now, however, hundreds of supporters have come to the town with the hope of paying at the gate, which means our list of people prepared to offer beds is totally inadequate.'

GIVE IT A REST

HUNGARY coach Lajos Baróti is upset that his team will have to play twice in 48 hours this week while the likes of England get more rest.

The way the fixtures have been arranged means one nation in each group gets just one full day to recover between their opening fixtures.

Baróti complained, 'It is not right that a team like England should have four full days' rest between their first two matches while others, like us, receive only one full day. This must be looked into in future World Cups.'

Baróti's men kick off against Portugal at Old Trafford tomorrow and he fears they could be blown away by strikers José Torres and Eusébio, two of five Benfica players included. Benfica have reached four European Cup finals since 1961, winning two, and Eusébio was European Footballer of the Year last year.

Benfica suffered a 5-1 European Cup battering in Lisbon from a George Best-inspired Manchester United in March, but Baróti believes Torres and Eusébio are peaking for the World Cup.

'They are just finding their form again, unfortunately for us,' warned Baróti. 'They are vivid, rapid, ingenious. Torres excels in the air, but the best is still Eusébio, not only from the strength of his shots, but by their placing and suddenness.'

REINS ON SPAIN

SPAIN manager José Villalonga says his side will rein in their attacking style – so they aren't made to look like 'mugs'.

The European champions, who start their campaign against Argentina at Villa Park tomorrow, boast one of the most feared forward lines in world football.

But Villalonga will warn his side not to go gung-ho against an Argentina team who defend in numbers and hit opponents on the counter-attack.

He said, 'Our natural game is to attack and this is what we must hope to do, but we shall also be defensive. We shall not be mugs.

'Why should we go all-out on the attack and lose and look like mugs when others just defend for success? The real truth is the result. We will be happy with a one-goal win.'

Spain's 1964 Euro triumph answered critics who claimed a lack of unity among the nation's rival factions would stop them matching their clubs' successes on the big stage.

And Villalonga predicted, 'This competition is our chance to show the world that we now have a Spanish spirit and that we now have a truly Spanish team.

'In the past, our international side has been a collection of individuals. Now we want to show that our national side is as good a team as any of our club sides.'

REF MAKES A SPLASH

WEST GERMAN referee Rudolf Kreitlein is making waves in Sunderland – with daily dips in the North Sea.

The tailor from Stuttgart, who takes charge of Italy's clash with the Soviet Union on Saturday, is keeping up his fitness with a daily routine which involves jogging from his hotel to the beach and taking a swim in the sea.

Kreitlein said, 'The water is a lot colder than in Germany at this time of year, but I must keep in trim.'

Wednesday 13 July
Matchday Three

France v Mexico (Group One)
7.30pm, Wembley, London

Argentina v Spain (Group Two)
7.30pm, Villa Park, Birmingham

Portugal v Hungary (Group Three)
7.30pm, Old Trafford, Manchester

Italy v Chile (Group Four)
7.30pm, Roker Park, Sunderland

DON'T WRITE US OFF
France 1 (Hausser 62) Mexico 1 (Borja 48)
Group One, Wembley, London (att: 69,237)

MEXICO manager Ignacio Trelles tonight fired a warning to England after the supposed World Cup whipping boys defied the odds against France.

The Mexicans – written off as 200/1 outsiders to lift the trophy after just one victory in their previous 14 finals matches – could easily have doubled that win tally at Wembley.

And a delighted Trelles said, 'I was pleased with the team and I thought we were the better side. I am sure the public was satisfied. Our next games will be harder, but I think we will give England a good match.'

France manager Henri Guérin was furious that his players failed to deliver against a side he had dismissed as 'weak and slow'.

Guérin complained, 'I was disappointed. We chose a style of play that did not work. It was a tragic mistake. I will make changes for the next game.

'My team was both nervous and physically slow. It was not a good game and the technique was generally disappointing.'

The warning signs were there for France even before they fell behind. Mexico were denied a penalty when Gabriel De Michele handled inside the box – only for Israeli referee Menachem Ashkenazi to award Mexico a free kick just outside the area.

Debutant Enrique Borja beat the ground in frustration after heading wide and the Mexican fans were left disappointed when Javier Fragoso had the ball in the net, but was flagged for offside.

There were wild celebrations on and off the pitch, however, when Borja broke the deadlock just after the interval. His shot was blocked by goalkeeper Marcel Aubour, but Borja buried the rebound.

Goalkeeper Ignacio Calderón, who played after passing a fitness test on his injured shoulder, sprinted the length of the pitch to hug the goalscorer. Gérard Hausser spared France's blushes when he fired in the equaliser from the edge of the box.

As with England-Uruguay, thousands of fans who bought tickets as part of multi-match packages stayed away.

More than 69,000 tickets were sold, but the actual attendance was probably closer to 55,000.

FRANCE: Marcel Aubour, Robert Budzinski, Jean Djorkaeff, Marcel Artelesa (capt), Bernard Bosquier, Gabriel De Michele, Joseph Bonnel, Roby Herbin, Néstor Combin, Philippe Gondet, Gérard Hausser.

MEXICO: Ignacio Calderón, Arturo Chaires, Gustavo Peña (capt), Gabriel Núñez, Guillermo Hernández, Isidoro Diaz, Salvador Reyes, Magdaleno Mercado, Enrique Borja, Javier Fragoso, Aarón Padilla.

Group One

	P	W	D	L	F	A	Pts
France	1	0	1	0	1	1	1
Mexico	1	0	1	0	1	1	1
England	1	0	1	0	0	0	1
Uruguay	1	0	1	0	0	0	1

EL OF A KICKING
Argentina 2 (Artime 65, 79) Spain 1 (Pirri 71)
Group Two, Villa Park, Birmingham (att: 42,738)

SPAIN manager José Villalonga hit out at Argentina's tough tackling after two-goal Luis Artime condemned them to an opening defeat.

Villalonga slammed Bulgarian referee Dimitar Rumenchev for failing to protect his exciting forwards, with star man Luis Suárez the main target.

But he admitted the counter-attacking Argentines deserved their win and that he now fears going home as a laughing stock if Spain go out.

Villalonga moaned, 'Argentina were a much better side. They did not let us settle down and they have great ability to keep possession. They deserved to win.

'Our lack of speed was a disappointment. I thought speed would be our strong point, but our bid was not helped by the assault tactics on Luis Suárez.

'The treatment handed out to Suárez shocked me. He took some terrible knocks. He was kicked out of the game. The referee should have been stricter on some of the tackling.

'He was tackled unfairly quite a few times when he didn't have the ball. He was physically thrown out of the game. He has a thigh injury and is doubtful for the later matches.

'If we don't qualify, it will be regarded as a national disaster and the fans will laugh at us when we go home.'

Argentina's hero was centre-forward Artime, nicknamed The Handsome One. He hooked in the opener from a superb Jorge Solari pass, only for Spain to level with a scrambled effort from Pirri.

But Artime lashed in a late winner from the edge of the box after being released by Ermindo Onega.

Manager Juan Carlos Lorenzo said, 'We could win this group if we carry on playing this well.'

ARGENTINA: Antonio Roma, Roberto Perfumo, Silvio Marzolini, Roberto Ferreiro, Rafael Albrecht, Antonio Rattin (capt), Jorge Solari, Alberto González, Luis Artime, Ermindo Onega, Oscar Mas.

SPAIN: José Ángel Iribar, Manuel Sanchís, Eladio, Pirri, Gallego, Ignacio Zoco, Luis Del Sol, Luis Suárez, José Armando Ufarte, Joaquín Peiró, Francisco Gento (capt).

Group Two

	P	W	D	L	F	A	Pts
Argentina	1	1	0	0	2	1	2
W Germany	1	1	0	0	5	0	2
Spain	1	0	0	1	1	2	0
Switzerland	1	0	0	1	0	5	0

MAGYARS GO MISSING
Portugal 3 (Augusto 2, 67, Torres 90)
Hungary 1 (Bene 60)
Group Three, Old Trafford, Manchester (att: 29,886)

HUNGARY face an uphill battle to make it to the last eight after gifting Portugal victory in Manchester tonight.

The Magyars, for so long the powerhouse of European football, handed the Portuguese an early lead and then threw away the match after battling back into it.

Coach Lajos Baróti had admitted he was worried Benfica duo José Torres and Eusébio could wreak havoc. That fear seemed to have been transmitted to his players when they were so distracted by the aerial threat of Torres that they allowed José Augusto an easy header from a corner inside two minutes.

The Hungarians had several chances to equalise. Flórián Albert headed against the crossbar and Kálmán Mészöly blazed over with goalkeeper Joaquim Carvalho on the ground and the goal gaping.

When they did level, it was down to luck more than good play, as keeper Carvalho dropped the ball under pressure from Albert and Ferenc Bene pounced.

Portugal went back in front when goalkeeper Antal Szentmihályi allowed a harmless-looking cross to bounce off his body and Augusto tapped in his second. Hungary's misery was complete when Torres headed in a Eusébio cross.

Eusébio suffered a nasty cut above his eye after a clash with the Hungarian keeper, but Portugal physician Dr João da Silva said, 'The cut needed stitching, but it's not too deep and I'm sure he'll be fit to play against Bulgaria.'

Hungary meet champions Brazil next, but coach Baróti believes they can shock Pelé and Co. He said, 'We almost shackled Eusébio, so why should we not be able to keep a tight rein on Pelé?'

PORTUGAL: Joaquim Carvalho, João Morais, Alexandre Baptista, Vicente, Hilário, Jaime Graça, Mário Coluna (capt), José Augusto, José Torres, Eusébio, António Simões.

HUNGARY: Antal Szentmihályi, Sándor Mátrai, Benõ Káposzta, Kálmán Mészöly, Ferenc Sipos (capt), Kálmán Sóvári, Ferenc Bene, István Nagy, Flórián Albert, Gyula Rákosi, János Farkas.

Group Three

	P	W	D	L	F	A	Pts
Portugal	1	1	0	0	3	1	2
Brazil	1	1	0	0	2	0	2
Hungary	1	0	0	1	1	3	0
Bulgaria	1	0	0	1	0	2	0

ANGELS OF THE NORTH
Italy 2 (Mazzola 8, Barison 88) Chile 0
Group Four, Roker Park, Sunderland (att: 27,199)

ITALY let their football do the talking tonight as the Battle of Santiago rematch passed off peacefully.

Violent scenes during the Azzurri's 2-0 defeat by hosts Chile four years ago brought disgrace on football.

But both teams were on their best behaviour at rain-lashed Roker Park, Sunderland, as two-time world champions Italy delighted thousands of flag-waving Azzurri fans who had made the trip to the North-East.

Italy manager Edmondo Fabbri believes there is plenty more to come now his side have got the opening-night nerves out of their system. He said, 'We concentrated on defence until we scored the first goal. Our players felt emotional because this was the first match, but I think it will be different for the next one.'

Italy's hero was Roma winger Paolo Barison. He had a hand in the opener when his fierce shot was parried into the path of Sandro Mazzola and then had two efforts cleared off the line before wrapping up the win with a thunderous long-range strike.

Chile rarely threatened and their hopes were effectively dashed when, ten minutes before half-time, forward Armando Tobar was carried off after a collision with Giacomo Bulgarelli and the South Americans had to play the rest of the match with ten men.

ITALY: Enrico Albertosi, Tarcisio Burgnich, Giacinto Facchetti, Giovanni Lodetti, Roberto Rosato, Sandro Salvadore (capt), Marino Perani, Giacomo Bulgarelli, Sandro Mazzola, Gianni Rivera, Paolo Barison.

CHILE: Juan Olivares, Luis Eyzaguirre, Hugo Villanueva, Humberto Cruz, Elías Figueroa, Rubén Marcos, Pedro Araya, Ignacio Prieto, Armando Tobar, Alberto Fouilloux, Leonel Sánchez (capt).

Group Four

	P	W	D	L	F	A	Pts
USSR	1	1	0	0	3	0	2
Italy	1	1	0	0	2	0	2
Chile	1	0	0	1	0	2	0
N Korea	1	0	0	1	0	3	0

HI-TECH RAMSEY

ALF RAMSEY is using the latest TV technology to boost England's chances.

The England manager has arranged for broadcaster ITV to give his squad a special screening of the goalless draw with Uruguay.

The footage will be piped into their Hendon headquarters tomorrow via a closed-circuit line as Ramsey examines what went wrong at Wembley.

He said, 'It could help us gain a point or two.'

The players will watch Friday's France-Uruguay match on TV, but Ramsey will attend the match to get a touchline view of the French, England's final group opponents.

Ramsey today put his players through drills on breaking down blanket defences and was relieved when Bobby Charlton and Alan Ball, who picked up ankle and foot injuries respectively against Uruguay, were able to take part in the session.

MOORE THAN SATISFIED

CAPTAIN Bobby Moore has played down worries over England's slow start to the tournament.

Monday's goalless draw with Uruguay has raised fresh questions over the hosts' hopes, but West Ham United defender Moore today reassured England fans.

Moore said, 'We were all very pleased with Monday's performance. Naturally we were all a little bit disappointed with the fact we didn't win, but we all feel that Uruguay will be one of the most difficult teams in the tournament to beat, so we are all quite happy.'

His central defensive partner, Jack Charlton, believes all England need is an early goal to open up the game when opponents set out to frustrate them. The Leeds United man said, 'They are all very good players in defence and are hard to beat. What you need is an early break. If you get an early break, they have to come for you.'

IT'S A CAT FIGHT

ENGLAND reserve goalkeeper Peter Bonetti admits he is in the dark about his future after reports over a possible transfer to West Ham United.

The Chelsea stopper, nicknamed The Cat, was the subject of a £55,000 eve-of-tournament bid by the Hammers – an offer the Blues have turned down.

Bonetti said, 'The only thing I knew about West Ham's bid was what I read in the newspapers. If I do move, I would like to stay in London.'

With Alex Stepney having arrived from Millwall for £50,000 in May, it is expected Bonetti will start the new season as Chelsea's second-choice keeper unless West Ham up their bid to £60,000.

FRENCH STINKER

BRENT TOWN HALL was left reeking of Pernod tonight after 900 French fans enjoyed a pre-match party ahead of their draw with Mexico.

The supporters were winners of a huge World Cup ticket competition run by French newspapers and the firm which produces the aniseed-based spirit.

Fans knocked back free measures of Pernod before heading for Wembley armed with 30,000 carnations which they handed out to women along the way.

SWISS WAGS FLY IN

THE wives of two axed Swiss stars are flying to England after reports the players had been out womanising.

Jakob Kuhn and Werner Leimgruber were dropped for the part-timers' 5-0 defeat by West Germany for failing to be back at their Sheffield hotel at 10.30pm the night before yesterday's match.

Kuhn, a printing engraver, and plumber Leimgruber arrived 58 minutes late, along with reserve goalkeeper Leo Eichmann.

It has emerged that the trio were driven back to the Hallam Tower Hotel by two local women.

While Swiss officials accepted this was 'all quite innocent', the players were upset to hear of reports in their homeland that they had been out womanising.

This morning, Kuhn and Leimgruber demanded to be flown home, with Leimgruber saying, 'We never want to play again after this humiliation.'

But after the pair held talks with Swiss officials, selector Willy Wyttenbach claimed, 'Everything has been smoothed over. Both players will be in our team to play Spain in Sheffield on Friday.'

Edgar Obertüfer, assistant general secretary of the Swiss FA, said, 'The players asked to go home because they were upset that stories of them being out with girls would upset their wives.

'We didn't want them to go, so we arranged to fly their wives over here to sort out the problem.

'After hearing from another English witness what happened, we are satisfied it was all quite innocent. The two ladies brought the players back in their car after they asked for a lift. The players had been given a lift into the city and forgot the time.

'They have been disciplined for being out late and now we want to forget the incident.'

SCHÖN SHOW-OFFS

WEST GERMANY coach Helmut Schön today knocked his side down a peg after their demolition of Switzerland.

The Germans romped to a 5-0 win at Hillsborough last night, but Schön was upset his players were showboating in the final stages.

He said, 'Everything was fine for 60 minutes, but there was too much over-elaboration for the rest of the match. I will not have big-heads in my team. For the first hour, I have rarely seen an international side play better.

'But then some players began to play for themselves instead of the team. They began to take risks and indulged in personal tricks to show off to the crowd. The players were told about their mistakes – in the dressing room after the match, in the coach travelling to the hotel and again this morning.

'I have told them a repeat of this sort of performance against the stronger teams in our group, Argentina and Spain, could be disastrous.'

Schön – applauded by pressmen over Germany's performance when he arrived to speak at their headquarters in Ashbourne, Derbyshire – added, 'It was satisfying, but we do not intend to get big-headed about it. We must keep our feet on the ground.'

The manager did, however, single out Bologna ace Helmut Haller and rising Bayern Munich star Franz Beckenbauer for special praise over the way they bossed the midfield.

He added, 'They are like the hinges of a door, opening and closing an attack at will. They are the sort of men needed by any team hoping to win the competition.'

HANS OFF THAT CAKE!

HELMUT SCHÖN is taking West Germany's preparations so seriously he banned the team from eating goalkeeper Hans Tilkowski's birthday cake.

Tilkowski was 31 yesterday – the same day he made his first appearance at a World Cup.

The Borussia Dortmund keeper was presented with a cake at the Peveril of the Peak Hotel in Ashbourne and said, 'It was a wonderful double celebration.

'I travelled to Sweden and Chile with the previous World Cup squads, but I never played. This is one of the proudest moments of my life.'

But coach Schön barred the squad from eating the cake, saying, 'This sort of food is not on our diet, so we cannot let the players have any.'

PAUSE FOR THOUGHT

WORLD CUP referees' chief Ken Aston has defended the decision to allow Helmut Haller's controversial penalty kick against Switzerland.

The part-timers, already trailing 4-0, were upset when Haller tricked goalkeeper Karl Elsener into diving early by pausing as he ran up to take the spot-kick.

The Swiss felt Scottish referee Hugh Phillips should have disallowed it for ungentlemanly conduct.

But Aston, a former World Cup referee and now FIFA liaison officer for the 1966 officials, said, 'You cannot lay down hard and fast rules in cases like this.

'The referee could decide that the goalkeeper was upset by the attitude of the penalty-taker and award a free kick for ungentlemanly conduct or, if the kicker had failed to score, that the goalkeeper had moved and order the kick to be retaken.

'But if this slow motion move is ungentlemanly conduct, then what would be the ruling if the penalty-taker ran up slowly and then suddenly raced the last few yards?'

NOT INTER-ESTED

BIG-SPENDING Inter Milan are set for double disappointment in their bid to land two of the World Cup's top stars.

Foreign imports are banned in the Italian League to encourage the development of homegrown players, but the embargo could be lifted next summer if Italy have a successful World Cup.

Inter are already eyeing Brazilian superstar Pelé and Bulgarian hotshot Georgi Asparoukhov.

Manager Helenio Herrera was at Goodison Park on Tuesday to watch them in action and Inter aim to tempt both with lucrative deals.

However, it is understood Pelé wants to stay with Santos in Brazil to be near friends and family.

And Inter are also likely to fail with their bid for Levski Sofia goal machine Asparoukhov.

The 23-year-old is a student at Sofia Institute of Sport and earns only £35 a month for playing, but the communist authorities in Bulgaria would almost certainly block a move abroad.

SCORE BLIMEY!

FANS watching World Cup matches at Hillsborough are getting a glimpse of the future – a hi-tech electronic scoreboard.

Sheffield Wednesday chiefs have taken the scoreboard on loan as an experiment during the tournament and supporters got a first look at it during the West Germany-Switzerland game.

As well as match facts and public service announcements, the scoreboard flashed up advertisements in English and German.

Hillsborough has already undergone £200,000 of improvement work for the tournament, but the club are considering forking out around £40,000 to keep the scoreboard.

Owls general manager Eric Taylor said, 'We only have it on loan from a firm in Bolton for the World Cup games, but we hope to make it a permanent fixture at Hillsborough.

'A board like this makes our conventional scoreboards look 90 years old. Supporters deserve a modern information service. We plan to be the first English club to give it to them.'

Roy Brown, joint managing director of scoreboard supplier Hird-Brown, said, 'It costs a lot of money, but it's a lot of scoreboard.'

Thursday 14 July
Rest Day One

ALF ON THE ATTACK

ALF RAMSEY today snapped back at England's doubters by promising they will 'definitely' be world champions.

The Three Lions manager – who boldly predicted three years ago that England would win the World Cup – has been stung by criticism of the goalless draw with Uruguay.

Today, riled when a press man quoted him as having said he 'thinks' the hosts will win, Ramsey said, 'I did not say I THINK anything. England will definitely win the World Cup.'

Despite his confidence, Ramsey is promising his team won't be fooled into taking outsiders Mexico lightly at Wembley on Saturday.

The hosts are expected to qualify comfortably for the quarter-finals after Mexico and France both looked beatable in their 1-1 draw yesterday.

But Ramsey, who was at Wembley to watch England's group rivals, said, 'For me, the game was extremely interesting and I learnt from watching it, but it would be dangerous to come to any conclusions because of it. I know that France can play far better than this and I must admit that Mexico produced better football than I expected.

'I have not made up my mind yet as to when I will name the team. We shall have another training session tomorrow and I will select the side when I am ready. Alan Ball is the only casualty. Alan's ankle is still quite sore, but it is nothing serious.'

Ramsey spent the day drilling his players on the art of breaking down massed defences after England's failure to open their goalscoring account against Uruguay.

He gave the squad a tactical talk at their Hendon headquarters before the players tried out Ramsey's ideas in a training session at

Highbury. Ramsey added, 'Our work today has, I believe, helped us in overcoming these very tight defensive systems.

'We went over the match against Uruguay again and then watched a film of it. The object of discussing the game before seeing the film was to make sure the players knew what to look out for.'

NO ARM DONE

FORMER England captain Jimmy Armfield reckons France's draw with Mexico was the best result the hosts could have hoped for.

The Blackpool full-back, one of the most experienced men in Alf Ramsey's squad, admitted he was relieved that neither the French nor Mexicans had seized the initiative in Group One.

He said, 'It's back to square one really. The draw is the best result for us because it puts us all on level pegging again.

'If either side had won and moved into the leading position in the group, it would have been more difficult for us. Also, in Uruguay, I think we have already met the best side in our group.'

GREAVES: NO FEAR

JIMMY GREAVES believes England's chances of World Cup glory are as good as ever.

The Tottenham Hotspur forward is in confident mood despite the disappointing draw with Uruguay and says he has seen nothing to scare the hosts after watching the opening round of group matches.

Greaves said, 'The more the games have gone on, the more I have rated England's chances.

'I mean, I saw Brazil play Bulgaria and, to me, Bulgaria were unlucky to be beat. It was by two magnificent free kicks, but there were no opportunities created by Brazil.

'I think our chances are still as high as they ever were.'

SUM-THING IS UP

TWO draws in England's group have left World Cup bosses at the centre of a mathematical debate.

Goal average – where the number of goals scored is divided by goals conceded – is being used to separate teams who are equal on points in the group stages.

Two draws in Group One, 0-0 between England and Uruguay and 1-1 in the France-Mexico game, have sparked a debate over which result is better.

Zero is not divisible by zero, but FIFA secretary general Helmut Kaiser today claimed, 'In my opinion, 0-0 is better than 1-1, but at this stage it doesn't really matter.'

However, if the rest of the games in Group One were to finish goalless, it WOULD matter.

Kaiser added, 'It is a matter for the appropriate committee and if a decision is necessary, then we will make it.'

Professor Ambrose Rogers, a renowned mathematician at London University, said, 'A most amusing situation. Mathematicians have agreed that you cannot make sense of nought-over-nought. You can regard it as either smaller or greater than one-over-one according to personal prejudices.'

BULLISH MEXICAN

MEXICAN forward Enrique Borja is ready to lock horns with Jack Charlton on Saturday – after turning his back on a career as a bullfighter.

The 20-year-old university student scored on his debut in the 1-1 draw against France yesterday.

But rather than playing football, he could just as easily have followed his father into bullfighting.

Borja revealed, 'My father was a top bullfighter in Mexico and is now a leading manager of toreros. I wanted to be a bullfighter and I fought them in the training ring.

'But I decided the horns were very dangerous! Football is less dangerous, so I switched.

'Jackie Charlton is big and strong like a bull and I respect him as the best of England's players. But I would still prefer to face him than a bull. He has no horns!'

Borja's debut performance against France caught the eye of England manager Alf Ramsey.

Ramsey said, 'Borja is only lightly built, yet his running off the ball was intelligent and he never gave the French defenders a moment's peace.'

SECOND BEST

URUGUAY trainer Omar Borrás is billing tomorrow's White City Stadium clash with France as a straight shootout to join England in the quarter-finals.

The Three Lions were held by Uruguay in their opener, but Borrás believes the hosts will crush Mexico and France to claim top spot.

He said, 'The winners of tomorrow's match will qualify and we think it will be us. We shall be second to England. England will take three goals from both France and Mexico.'

Borrás again defended Uruguay's negative tactics against England, saying, 'We came here hoping to win the World Cup, but we have to be realistic.

'Certainly we could have arranged offensive plans against England, but then what would we have had left but defeat?

'England are too strong for us to attack at Wembley and not many teams in the world would have decided to adopt offensive plans in this match. They dare not.

'We did try to win and we had a few good chances, but England were so strong they drove us back.'

PELÉ KO FEAR

BRAZIL could be without Pelé against Hungary tomorrow after he was forced to sit out today's training session in Bolton.

Pelé has been named in an unchanged team from their opening win over Bulgaria – but officials stressed the line-up was 'depending on medical revision'.

Team physician Dr Hilton Gosling rates Pelé's chances at only 50-50 because of a knee injury.

Dr Gosling said, 'If we were playing the World Cup Final tomorrow, then Pelé could play. But we have several more games, we hope, and although tomorrow's match is an important one, it is not the vital one.'

Pelé managed only one full match at the last World Cup before being ruled out by injury and Brazil are worried history could repeat itself if they risk him against Hungary.

If Pelé is ruled out, his Santos team-mate and possible successor as the star of Brazilian football, 16-year-old Edú, could become the World Cup's youngest player.

HUNGARY FOR AN UPSET

HUNGARY coach Lajos Baróti believes his side can shock Brazil tomorrow in a 'World Cup of surprises'.

The Magyars are already on the brink of elimination after losing to Portugal, but Baróti is confident they can keep their hopes alive with an upset against the champions.

He said, 'If we do not get at least a point from Brazil we are finished in the competition.

'We were unlucky against Portugal. The team played well and fought well, but failed to take their chances. In this World Cup there will be a lot of surprises. Tomorrow's match could be one of them.'

THAT'S SCHÖN 'EM

WEST GERMANY coach Helmut Schön today revealed he barred his players from watching the Argentina-Spain match – because he doesn't want them interfering in tactics.

The squad had asked to go to the Villa Park clash between the two teams they have yet to face in Group Two, but Schön went without them.

He made it clear who is in charge when he said, 'I am the one who checks on our future opponents and dictates tactics. It is better that there should be one view – mine – rather than 22 others.'

FRANZ FANS

ARGENTINA admit they fear the threat of new West German sensation Franz Beckenbauer.

The 20-year-old announced himself to the world with two goals in the 5-0 thrashing of Switzerland.

And Argentina trainer Rodolfo Torrecillas, preparing the team to face the Germans on Saturday, said, 'Men we fear are the link men Franz Beckenbauer and Helmut Haller. Beckenbauer is truly a world-class player.

'From what we have seen of the World Cup matches, Germany are the best side in the competition. They are strong and very fast and will give us a hard fight. But now we have beaten Spain, we are sure we will qualify.'

West Germany coach Helmut Schön today predicted a huge future for Beckenbauer, saying, 'This boy can be the toast of Europe before he is 21 – and that is in November.

'The best is yet to come and it could well be that the fierce competition of the World Cup will draw it out of him.'

'GANGSTER' RAP

SPAIN star Luis Suárez faces a race against time to be fit for tomorrow's crucial clash with Switzerland after a 'gangster' hit on him by Argentina.

The £180,000 Inter Milan forward was the victim of some tough tackling in the 2-1 defeat yesterday and may not recover in time from a leg injury.

Suárez complained, 'The tackling was too hard. One tackle, in fact, was like that of a gangster.'

Spain manager José Villalonga has also been rocked by the news that key defender Eladio is out of the tournament after damaging knee ligaments in the first match.

REBELS WITH A CAUSE

SWITZERLAND have made sweeping changes for tomorrow's match with Spain – including a recall for rebel duo Werner Leimgruber and Jakob Kuhn.

The pair were axed for the defeat by West Germany for breaking a curfew and then threatened to boycott the rest of the tournament.

But manager Alfredo Foni today included them in a team featuring seven new faces, with one of them, René Brodmann, taking over from Heinz Schneiter as captain.

Foni said of the two players at the centre of the curfew row, 'They have been punished and that is the end of it.'

The players' wives, Alice Kuhn and Terese Leimgruber, flew in today, but made no comment as they arrived at the Hallam Tower Hotel in Sheffield.

The head of Switzerland's World Cup delegation, Ernst Thommen, said, 'The wives will be allowed to see their husbands, but not for long. Tonight all the players are going out for a walk together and then they will have an early night. From now on, the players must all go out together, always.'

Only goalkeeper Karl Elsener, defender Hansrüdi Fuhrer, midfielder Heinz Bäni and forward Robert Hosp retain their places in the team to face Spain.

BLUNDERLAND

SUNDERLAND officials were almost dropped in the alphabet soup when they staged Italy's win over Chile.

The letter 'I' was missed out in one Roker Park stand when the row markings were painted in a stadium facelift.

The blunder came to light when local pensioner William Smith dropped in the day before the match to see where his seat was and couldn't find it.

The 78-year-old said, 'When I went to the ticket office and pointed out the error, I was given tickets for row B instead.'

With hundreds of other tickets sold for row I, a painter was hurriedly found to re-letter the rows.

OH BOY!

THIRTEEN Italian orphan boys were the happiest fans at their nation's opening victory over Chile.

The lads are enjoying a six-week holiday in Sunderland and an anonymous Good Samaritan dropped 13 match tickets through the letterbox of a local Roman Catholic presbytery where they are staying.

FLAG SWAG

CHEEKY thieves have stolen the Soviet Union flag from their training camp at Durham University sports ground.

The giant flag went missing last night while the USSR party were in Sunderland watching the match between group rivals Italy and Chile.

Sports ground chief Alec Henderson said, 'I think it is a very poor show to steal a flag at a time like this.'

HORNETS BUZZING

NORTH KOREA coach Myung Rye-Hyun today predicted his side will cause a sensation by qualifying for the quarter-finals.

The Hornets were overpowered by the Soviet Union in their opening match, but their coach is confident they will beat Chile tomorrow and go on to qualify alongside the USSR.

He said, 'I watched Italy and Chile play and I was not greatly impressed. We are not hard tacklers, I know, but we can move the ball around and we have the ability to beat both Chile and Italy.

'This way we would qualify for the quarter-finals along with Russia and that is the way I think it will end.

'We profited a good deal from our 3-0 defeat by Russia. We learned lessons and we have now had the opportunity of seeing our other opponents as well.'

OUT-STAN-DING

FIFA president Sir Stanley Rous says the World Cup is a success so far – despite concerns over attendances and ultra-defensive football.

Although organisers say well over 300,000 fans watched the opening eight matches, no game sold out and only a late rush at the turnstiles boosted the crowd figures at Middlesbrough and Sunderland to a respectable level.

On the pitch, the first round of games produced only 21 goals at an average of 2.6 a game. Chile four years ago averaged 2.8 for the tournament – the lowest ever. But Rous, heading for the North-East to take in the next two matches in Group Four, said, 'I think it is going very well and I hope it will go on just as successfully. I have known other World Cups that have not started so well.

'The general conduct of the players has been first-class and I am well satisfied with the standard of sportsmanship and referee control.

'All the teams I have spoken to are very happy and local people have taken the teams to their hearts – especially if they are underdogs, which is rather typical of the British.

'The attendances in the North-East seem to indicate that there was above average interest for a Tuesday or Wednesday night. There were empty seats, but on a filthy, wet night I am not surprised.'

BBC WON

BBC CHIEFS are delighted after viewing figures for Monday's Wembley curtain-raiser revealed they bashed rivals ITV.

More than 13m watched the opening ceremony on the BBC, with the figure swelling to around 19m for the England-Uruguay game.

ITV only attracted around 5m for the match, while figures for Britain's top-rated show, *Coronation Street*, slumped to 6.5m as viewers deserted the soap opera to watch BBC coverage of the Queen getting the World Cup under way. *Corrie* has come close to 9m on occasions.

RING OF STEAL

POLICE chiefs are deploying a special squad of officers to clamp down on pickpockets who have targeted World Cup fans.

In the capital, around £250 has already been reported stolen from wallets and handbags since the start of the tournament, with foreign visitors passing through London Airport the main victims.

Met Police detective inspector William Mitchison said, 'The pickpockets are obviously professionals who have been attracted by the increased number of visitors. Appropriate action has been taken to bring these thefts to an abrupt stop.'

ROUGH ON REFS

FIFA chiefs were today branded 'mean' over their treatment of match officials.

In contrast to the pampered players, the referees are being put up in bed and breakfast with a daily allowance of around £4.

Cyril Jackson, spokesman for the 15,000-strong English Referees' Association, claimed, 'They are hand-picked as the best referees in world football and should be treated royally while they are in England, but this is not happening. It is all very mean. With all the profit being made from the World Cup, you would have thought FIFA would look after them better.'

However, League Referees and Linesmen's Association secretary George Readle said, 'We know our financial rewards are poor compared with the players, but I have had no complaint from any of the referees. They regard it as an honour to be selected.'

Former linesman Readle admitted, meanwhile, that the match officials' job was becoming harder because of an increase in gamesmanship. He added, 'Life is tougher these days because the players get up to more tricks.'

Friday 15 July
Matchday Four

Uruguay v France (Group One)
7.30pm, White City, London

Spain v Switzerland (Group Two)
7.30pm, Hillsborough, Sheffield

Hungary v Brazil (Group Three)
7.30pm, Goodison Park, Liverpool

Chile v North Korea (Group Four)
7.30pm, Ayresome Park, Middlesbrough

URUGUAY GO TOP
Uruguay 2 (Rocha 27, Cortés 32)
France 1 (De Bourgoing pen 15)
Group One, White City, London (att: 45,662)

URUGUAY coach Ondino Viera insists Group One is still wide open despite his side fighting back from a goal down to claim top spot.

The Uruguayans, watched at the White City Stadium by England manager Alf Ramsey, now look hot favourites to progress, with only outsiders Mexico left to face.

But Viera said, 'I reckon the group is wide open. I have great respect for all Uruguay's opponents and the last match against Mexico could still be quite difficult.'

The South Americans threw off the defensive shackles and put one foot in the quarter-finals thanks to goals from Pedro Rocha and Julio César Cortés.

But they had to do it the hard way after France went ahead when captain Horacio Troche brought down Yves Herbet and Héctor De Bourgoing converted the penalty.

Uruguay missed several chances to level before Rocha eventually equalised with a thumping shot. Five minutes later Cortés caught out goalkeeper Marcel Aubour with a shot from a tight angle.

Uruguay's positive approach brought 23 attempts on goal – but it also allowed France to have 13.

Viera added, 'I don't think my team was more vulnerable because of playing a more open game than against England. And France's penalty came from an offence that was committed a yard outside the area.'

Defeat leaves France on the brink of elimination. Manager Henri Guérin admitted, 'We have to beat England to have any chance at all of qualifying.'

URUGUAY: Ladislao Mazurkiewicz, Luis Ubiña, Omar Caetano, Milton Viera, Jorge Manicera, Horacio Troche (capt), Julio César Cortés, Néstor Gonçálvez, José Sasia, Pedro Rocha, Domingo Pérez.

FRANCE: Marcel Aubour, Robert Budzinski, Jean Djorkaeff, Marcel Artelesa (capt), Bernard Bosquier, Yves Herbet, Joseph Bonnel, Héctor De Bourgoing, Jacky Simon, Philippe Gondet, Gérard Hausser.

Group One

	P	W	D	L	F	A	Pts
Uruguay	2	1	1	0	2	1	3
Mexico	1	0	1	0	1	1	1
France	2	0	1	1	2	3	1
England	1	0	1	0	0	0	1

SPAIN BOUNCE BACK
Spain 2 (Sanchís 57, Amancio 75)
Switzerland 1 (Quentin 28)
Group Two, Hillsborough, Sheffield (att: 32,028)

SPAIN needed a half-time rocket from manager José Villalonga to get their campaign back on track tonight.

The European champions, rocked by defeat against Argentina, looked to be heading out when René Pierre Quentin gave the Swiss part-timers a shock 1-0 lead.

But Villalonga tore into his flops and they turned it around after the break, with Real Madrid trio Manuel Sanchís, Francisco Gento and Amancio at the heart of their revival.

Villalonga said, 'I was afraid the Swiss were going to win, so I gave my team a talk at half-time.

'I made them attack more through the middle and we managed to get away with it. But we must remould our play in time for the next match.'

Switzerland recalled Jakob Kuhn and Werner Leimgruber, axed for the opening defeat by West Germany for breaking a pre-match curfew, and Kuhn helped create Quentin's goal.

But the Spanish fightback was on when Sanchís, playing in only his fourth international, scored a sensational equaliser. He skipped past a series of challenges and beat goalkeeper Karl Elsener.

The winner came when captain Gento crossed for Amancio to score with a spectacular diving header which knocked him out cold and left him needing five minutes' treatment before returning.

The Swiss thought they had salvaged a point when Quentin turned the ball into the net, but Soviet referee Tofik Bakhramov controversially ruled that goalkeeper José Ángel Iribar had been fouled in the build-up. The decision sparked a chorus of boos from the Sheffield crowd.

SPAIN: José Ángel Iribar, Manuel Sanchís, Severino Reija, Pirri, Gallego, Ignacio Zoco, Luis Del Sol, Luis Suárez, Amancio, Joaquín Peiró, Francisco Gento (capt).

SWITZERLAND: Karl Elsener, Hansrüdi Fuhrer, René Brodmann (capt), Werner Leimgruber, Kurt Armbruster, Xavier Stierli, Heinz Bäni, Jakob Kuhn, Vittore Gottardi, Robert Hosp, René Pierre Quentin.

Group Two

	P	W	D	L	F	A	Pts
Argentina	1	1	0	0	2	1	2
Spain	2	1	0	1	3	3	2
W Germany	1	1	0	0	5	0	2
Switzerland	2	0	0	2	1	7	0

BRAZIL STUNNED
Hungary 3 (Bene 2, Farkas 64, Mészöly pen 73)
Brazil 1 (Tostão 14)
Group Three, Goodison Park, Liverpool (att: 51,387)

HUNGARY coach Lajos Baróti predicted the start of a new golden era for the Magical Magyars after they inflicted Brazil's first World Cup finals defeat since 1954.

The defending champions were floored by a brilliant performance to rival those of the Ferenc Puskás-inspired team which thrilled the world in the 1950s.

Now Brazil, forced to play without their injured talisman Pelé, face a make-or-break showdown with Portugal.

Brazil's last World Cup loss came in the quarter-finals 12 years ago against the original Magical Magyars in the infamous Battle of Berne.

And delighted coach Baróti said, 'This was the best game Hungary has played since the 1954 World Cup. Everyone at Goodison could see how brilliant they were. I realised at half-time that this was not the Brazilian team of old and I was quite convinced they could be beaten.

'Undoubtedly it might have been a different picture with Pelé in the Brazilian team, but even had he been there, I think we would have achieved a draw at least. I feel this Hungary side can equal that of the Puskás era.'

Hungary, desperate for victory after losing to Portugal, got the perfect start when Ferenc Bene scored a superb solo goal after two minutes.

Brazil chose to replace Pelé with 19-year-old Tostão, rather than making 16-year-old Edú the World Cup's youngest player. And Tostão marked his debut by crashing in the equaliser after 14 minutes.

But Hungary weren't to be denied and János Farkas put them back in front after 64 minutes with a powerful right-foot finish following a great run by Bene.

The game was up for the champions when Bene's run into the box was halted by Paulo Henrique's foul and Kálmán Mészöly scored from the spot.

Hungary closed it out, despite Mészöly having to play the later stages with his arm in a sling after suffering a suspected broken collarbone.

Brazil coach and chief selector Vicente Feola said, 'We played badly and they played beautifully. Their win was completely justified and I extend my congratulations to such great players.'

HUNGARY: József Gelei, Sándor Mátrai, Benõ Káposzta, Kálmán Mészöly, Ferenc Sipos (capt), Gusztáv Szepesi, Ferenc Bene, Imre Mathesz, Flórián Albert, Gyula Rákosi, János Farkas.

BRAZIL: Gylmar, Djalma Santos, Paulo Henrique, Antônio Lima, Hideraldo Luiz Bellini (capt), Altair, Garrincha, Gérson, Alcindo, Tostão, Jairzinho.

Group Three

	P	W	D	L	F	A	Pts
Portugal	1	1	0	0	3	1	2
Hungary	2	1	0	1	4	4	2
Brazil	2	1	0	1	3	3	2
Bulgaria	1	0	0	1	0	2	0

TEAR WE GO
Chile 1 (Marcos pen 26)
North Korea 1 (Park Seung-Jin 88)
Group Four, Ayresome Park, Middlesbrough (att: 13,792)

NORTH KOREA'S players left the pitch tonight crying tears of joy after securing their country's first World Cup point.

Only 13,792 fans watched this game between two of the tournament's supposedly weaker nations.

But those who did show up loved every minute of an error-strewn, yet exciting encounter and hailed the Koreans at the end as if they had won the World Cup.

Rubén Marcos, booked for dissent early in the game, put Chile ahead from the penalty spot after Pedro Araya was tripped as he burst on to a pass from captain Leonel Sánchez.

Marcos headed a Sánchez free kick just past the post and Honorino Landa somehow shot wide with the goal gaping.

The Hornets, buoyed by those let-offs, twice came close when captain Park Seung-Jin and winger Pak Doo-Ik both saw shots fly narrowly off target.

Korea kept plugging away and were rewarded two minutes from the end when Park Seung-Jin netted a shot from the edge of the box.

CHILE: Juan Olivares, Alberto Valentini, Hugo Villanueva, Humberto Cruz, Elías Figueroa, Rubén Marcos, Pedro Araya, Ignacio Prieto, Honorino Landa, Alberto Fouilloux, Leonel Sánchez (capt).

NORTH KOREA: Lee Chan-Myung, Park Lee-Sup, Shin Yung-Kyoo, Lim Zoong-Sun, Oh Yoon-Kyung, Im Seung-Hwi, Park Seung-Jin (capt), Han Bong-Jin, Pak Doo-Ik, Lee Dong-Woon, Kim Seung-Il.

Group Four

	P	W	D	L	F	A	Pts
USSR	1	1	0	0	3	0	2
Italy	1	1	0	0	2	0	2
Chile	2	0	1	1	1	3	1
N Korea	2	0	1	1	1	4	1

PETERS, PAINE GET NOD

ALF RAMSEY has called up Martin Peters and Terry Paine for tomorrow's clash with Mexico.

They are the only two changes to the team held by Uruguay as the England manager looks for goals to kick-start the Three Lions' campaign.

West Ham United midfielder Peters, unfortunate to miss out on Monday after featuring in England's final warm-up in Poland, replaces Alan Ball, who has a bruised foot.

Southampton winger Paine gets his chance as part of a front three in a 4-3-3 formation after Manchester United's John Connelly failed to unlock Uruguay's defence.

Paine, a regular in Ramsey's first two and a half years, has only featured twice since last October.

After Connelly's disappointing display, Paine will try to convince Ramsey that England need at least one winger and that he is the man.

Bobby Charlton has overcome a minor injury and was fit enough to show off his batting skills today when the squad relaxed with a knockabout game of cricket.

PICK 'N' MEX

VETERAN Mexico goalkeeper Antonio Carbajal is standing by to make World Cup history against England tomorrow – but hopes he won't be needed.

The 37-year-old will become the first man to appear in a FIFTH successive finals if first-choice Ignacio Calderón fails a fitness test on the shoulder injury which almost kept him out of the opening match.

Carbajal said, 'Wembley is a wonderful place. I would love to play there before I retire.

'It would be a great honour, particularly against England in the World Cup, but we must wait and see what happens to my friend Ignacio.

'He is a very, very good goalkeeper. He is better than me, better even than the great Lev Yashin of Russia. He is the best goalkeeper in the world. If he plays against England they will find him a very hard man to beat.'

Manager Ignacio Trelles still believes England will win Group One, despite their stalemate with Uruguay.

Trelles knows his side need at least a draw at Wembley, but he admitted, 'We know it will be very tough. We are not optimistic of victory, but we shall do our best.

'We are certainly not fooled by England's display against Uruguay. I personally still think England will win this group.

'But I was extremely pleased with our performance against France and I hope we can reproduce this form against England.'

BOBBY WHO?

NORMA CHARLTON today lifted the lid on the personal sacrifices the England squad are making in their bid for glory.

Bobby Charlton's wife is travelling from Manchester to London for tomorrow's clash with Mexico, but the players' partners will only be allowed a brief chat with their other halves.

She said, 'It will be worth coming all this way just to say "hello" to them for a few moments. Otherwise we might forget what they look like!

'Bobby rings me every day, but I have only seen him for a weekend and one and a half days since the end of May. But when you marry a footballer, you expect it.

'I've been keeping the garden in shape and tidying up the garage. I mean, you've still got to do your work, World Cup or not, haven't you?'

VILLA PARK SPARKS

ARGENTINA have warned they are ready to put the boot in tomorrow to stop West Germany.

Yugoslav referee Konstantin Zečević could have a busy day at Villa Park as the Argentines look to contain a team who crushed Switzerland 5-0.

Argentina manager Juan Carlos Lorenzo said, 'We are thinking of bringing in some heavier players to face the Germans. It will be a hard game. They are very physical.

'I saw them beat Switzerland and I know what to expect. It will now be up to the referee to see things don't get out of hand. I'm quite happy to leave it to him.'

YOU CAN'T KID ME

WEST GERMANY coach Helmut Schön says group rivals Argentina fooled the world with their poor pre-finals form.

The South Americans looked like long-shots when they struggled on a European tour which included defeats in Italy and Austria.

But they beat European champions Spain in their World Cup opener and Schön warned ahead of their meeting tomorrow, 'It seems clear that the Argentinians are a much better side than their earlier showings would indicate.

'Their performance against Spain didn't surprise me, but most certainly they deceived many people by their performances before coming to England.

'We're looking at the match in a realistic light – the result could well decide the group winners.'

Villa Park officials are hoping for a sell-out crowd of 50,000-plus, with tickets selling fast and around 7,000 Germans supporters expected to be there.

BULGAR BATTLERS

RUDOLF VYTLAČIL insists he can still sign off as Bulgaria coach by taking them into the knockout stages.

After losing to champions Brazil, the Bulgarians must take at least a point from Portugal tomorrow.

Vytlačil, who takes over at Rapid Vienna in his native Austria after the finals, led Czechoslovakia to the final in 1962 and feels this Bulgaria side have similar potential.

He said, 'We certainly haven't given up hope of reaching the quarter-finals. Another two years with this Bulgarian team and they would be better than my Czech team.'

Experienced winger Ivan Kolev – dubbed the Stanley Matthews of the Balkans – has been dropped for the Portugal game along with playmaker Stoyan Kitov. Kolev, 37, is a football legend in Bulgaria, but Vytlačil said, 'He's quite old now and we shall need greater pace and punch against Portugal.'

GEORGI BEST

PORTUGAL coach Otto Glória fears ace hitman Georgi Asparoukhov could wreck their dream start to the World Cup.

The Portuguese beat Hungary in their first-ever finals match, but Glória knows victory over Bulgaria tomorrow could be vital, with champions Brazil still to come.

Hungary paid for missing several chances against Portugal and Glória fears Asparoukhov will not be so charitable.

He said, 'We let the Hungarians come into the game too much and if their finishing had been better we would have been in trouble.

'We have tightened up our tactics, because we know Asparoukhov's reputation for snatching goals.'

RUSSIAN ROULETTE

SOVIET UNION legend Lev Yashin admits a long-term knee injury threatens to end his career.

Goalkeeper Yashin, 38, missed the opener against North Korea, but he hopes to be fit to face Italy in Sunderland tomorrow in a game expected to decide who tops Group Four.

He said, 'The injury has pursued me for a long time. I hope to stay in the sport. Specialist treatment will be necessary when I return to Moscow if I am to continue playing.

'It's very disappointing, because it's every footballer's wish to play in every game. Whether I turn out in this competition depends on the coach.'

GOLDEN BOY AXE

ITALY'S new superstar Gianni Rivera is set to be axed for tomorrow's showdown with the Soviet Union.

The 22-year-old AC Milan playmaker – tipped as one of the stars of the tournament – was out of sorts in Italy's win over Chile.

And the indications from Italy's Durham training camp are that manager Edmondo Fabbri will sideline the man dubbed Golden Boy.

Fabbri dropped a huge hint when he said, 'Rivera was not impressive and I was not satisfied with the way the team played.

'I have 22 players to choose from and a man cannot keep his place purely on reputation. I shall consider changes.'

Rivera's fate could hinge on whether Giacomo Bulgarelli, the Bologna star who pulled the strings against Chile, recovers from a knee injury. Bulgarelli and Chilean Armando Tobar both suffered leg injuries in the same tackle. Tobar has been ruled out of the tournament.

Fabbri said, 'It's impossible to say how long it will be before Bulgarelli is fit. We're just hoping we can get him ready for tomorrow's game. His knee has improved slightly, but he's still very doubtful.'

The Italians and Soviets are based virtually next door to each other in Durham. The USSR have been happy for crowds to watch training sessions at the university sports centre, but Italy have done their best to keep onlookers away from their Durham County School of Agriculture workouts.

Fabbri claimed he wasn't playing mind games with the Soviets by delaying the naming of his side, saying, 'I'm not trying to be mysterious – I want to make sure all my players are fit.'

However, he then admitted, 'When we played Russia in Moscow two years ago, they gave out one team and fielded another. I am saying nothing until just before the game.'

PASS MASTERS

SUNDERLAND manager Ian McColl says English football must take its head out of the sand to keep pace with the rest of the world.

The former Scotland boss believes domestic clubs should ditch long-ball football for the skilful play he has seen from Italy and the Soviet Union at the World Cup.

McColl has been impressed by the two favourites in the Sunderland and Middlesbrough-based Group Four.

He said, 'All of these players have a great number of attributes and I'd like to think we'll see the day when Football League players have the same ball control and poise.

'Many people in the North-East, accustomed to more direct and forceful football in our own First Division, wouldn't like to see this type of play on a regular basis.

'But I admire a great deal about their play and I'm quite certain that, if we had the same skills and control, our game would improve out of all recognition.'

Saturday 16 July
Matchday Five

England v Mexico (Group One)
7.30pm, Wembley, London

Argentina v West Germany (Group Two)
3pm, Villa Park, Birmingham

Portugal v Bulgaria (Group Three)
3pm, Old Trafford, Manchester

USSR v Italy (Group Four)
3pm, Roker Park, Sunderland

BATTLE OF BRUM
Argentina 0 West Germany 0
Sent off: Rafael Albrecht (Argentina, 65)
Group Two, Villa Park, Birmingham (att: 46,587)

RAFAEL ALBRECHT today pleaded for leniency over the tournament's first sending-off – claiming he was punished for the WRONG FOUL.

The Argentina defender got his marching orders for clattering into Wolfgang Weber during a brutal stalemate in Birmingham this afternoon.

And the match threatened to spiral out of control as the South Americans' manager, Juan Carlos Lorenzo, ran on to the pitch and confronted the match officials.

In a bizarre defence of his part in the controversy, Albrecht said of the clash with Weber, 'We were both going fast and I went in hard to stop him. We collided. Then, when I came round, I thought the referee wanted me to go off for more treatment.

'I couldn't believe I was being sent off for the foul. Indeed, I thought my rugby tackle earlier in the game might have got me sent off.

'I was worried about that foul, but not about this one, and the other players told me it looked much worse than it really was. My boots were on the ground when we collided.'

Asked if he thought he would get no more than a one-match ban from the FIFA disciplinary committee, Albrecht added, 'I hope so. I would never forgive myself if my actions should affect Argentina's chances. I hope they will be lenient.'

Manager Lorenzo defended his arm-waving reaction to the clash, saying, 'I don't feel I did anything wrong. It was an instantaneous reaction as soon as I saw both players on the ground. I thought there had been fractures.

'It was most important I should go on to the pitch. First, to find out whether Albrecht had been sent off. Secondly, to alter the tactics for the rest of the match.

'I stayed talking to the referee, because I could not discover what was going on. At home, we think it is important that a coach should go on to the field to find out these sort of things.'

The flashpoint came after 66 minutes when Albrecht appeared to lead with his knee, catching Weber in the groin in a high-speed collision which left both players writhing on the ground.

That led to an angry melee, as players from both sides squared up to each other and Lorenzo ran on to confront Yugoslav referee Konstantin Zečević.

When Zečević finally restored order, he gave Albrecht his marching orders and the player was led away, still limping, by two Argentine medical staff.

ARGENTINA: Antonio Roma, Roberto Perfumo, Silvio Marzolini, Roberto Ferreiro, Rafael Albrecht, Antonio Rattin (capt), Jorge Solari, Alberto González, Luis Artime, Ermindo Onega, Oscar Mas.

WEST GERMANY: Hans Tilkowski, Horst-Dieter Höttges, Karl-Heinz Schnellinger, Franz Beckenbauer, Willy Schulz, Wolfgang Weber, Albert Brülls, Helmut Haller, Uwe Seeler (capt), Wolfgang Overath, Sigi Held.

Group Two

	P	W	D	L	F	A	Pts
Argentina	2	1	1	0	2	1	3
W Germany	2	1	1	0	5	0	3
Spain	2	1	0	1	3	3	2
Switzerland	2	0	0	2	1	7	0

PORTU-GOALS
Portugal 3 (Vutzov og 17, Eusébio 38, Torres 81) Bulgaria 0
Group Three, Old Trafford, Manchester (att: 25,438)

PORTUGAL dumped Bulgaria out of the World Cup today – and plan to send champions Brazil packing too.

The Portuguese players have been told they will each pocket £125 for reaching the last eight, plus another £125 for beating Brazil.

And tonight they were already drawing up plans to snuff out the threat of Brazil superstar Pelé on Tuesday.

Bulgaria found Benfica duo José Torres and Eusébio too hot to handle at Old Trafford.

Torres, known for his aerial prowess, showed his ability on the ground with a cross which defender Ivan Vutzov headed past his own goalkeeper.

Eusébio made it two before the break with a powerful cross-shot – his first goal of the tournament – and Torres then accepted a simple chance from a poor backpass by captain Boris Gaganelov.

Now Portugal will look to make it three wins out of three against Brazil and Belenenses midfielder Vicente is being lined up to take care of Pelé.

The pair have clashed six times before and on the five occasions Vicente marked Pelé, he only scored twice.

Vicente said, 'The first time I faced him, I was playing for Belenenses against Santos and I knew nothing of Pelé. He was 16 then and he scored four goals.

'But since then, I have proved it is not impossible to stop him. I mark him very closely or else he becomes a catastrophe. I run everywhere he goes.

'You can only think of Pelé the whole match. The team must not expect you to do anything else.

'There is only one ball and if you have it, he can't have it as well. So you must be quick to get to the ball before Pelé does.

'I know I can't get there first every time and Pelé must get the ball sometimes.

'Once he has it, it is fatal to look at his body or his feet. If you do, he will dribble past you immediately. You must always look at the ball, just the ball.

'Pelé is not the cleanest player of all-time, but if you play him well and cleanly he will say to you "Well played" every time you take the ball from him. And, at the end, he will shake hands and say "Thanks for the game".'

PORTUGAL: José Pereira, Alberto Festa, Vicente, Hilário, Germano, Jaime Graça, Mário Coluna (capt), José Augusto, José Torres, Eusébio, António Simões.

BULGARIA: Georgi Naidenov, Aleksandar Shalamanov, Dimitar Penev, Ivan Vutzov, Boris Gaganelov (capt), Dobromir Jechev, Dinko Dermendjiev, Petar Zhekov, Georgi Asparoukhov, Dimitar Yakimov, Aleksandar Kostov.

Group Three

	P	W	D	L	F	A	Pts
Portugal	2	2	0	0	6	1	4
Hungary	2	1	0	1	4	4	2
Brazil	2	1	0	1	3	3	2
Bulgaria	2	0	0	2	0	5	0

BLUE BOTTLERS
USSR 1 (Chislenko 57) Italy 0
Group Four, Roker Park, Sunderland (att: 27,793)

ITALY manager Edmondo Fabbri admitted his players bottled it in today's clash of the big guns.

Fabbri's side looked resigned to defeat once they fell behind in a match billed as the battle for top spot in Group Four.

And asked if Italy showed a lack of heart when it came to the crunch, he said, 'I had that impression – particularly after the goal.'

With Giacomo Bulgarelli passed fit after hurting his knee against Chile, Fabbri dropped Gianni 'Golden Boy' Rivera, explaining, 'I decided it was not the type of game that would suit him.'

But the move backfired as his attack rarely troubled USSR goalkeeper Lev Yashin, back after a knee problem kept him out against North Korea.

Sandro Mazzola blew a chance to give Italy the lead when played in one-on-one with Yashin and the Azzurri were made to pay when Igor Chislenko cut inside and hammered home the winner.

The closest Italy came to salvaging a draw was when Ezio Pascutti, one of three changes to the side which beat Chile, saw his header from a Bulgarelli cross blocked.

USSR: Lev Yashin, Vladimir Ponomaryev, Vasily Danilov, Iosif Sabo, Murtaz Khurtsilava, Albert Shesternev (capt), Igor Chislenko, Valery Voronin, Anatoly Banishevsky, Eduard Malafeyev, Galimzian Khusainov.

ITALY: Enrico Albertosi, Tarcisio Burgnich, Giacinto Facchetti, Giovanni Lodetti, Roberto Rosato, Sandro Salvadore (capt), Gianfranco Leoncini, Luigi Meroni, Giacomo Bulgarelli, Sandro Mazzola, Ezio Pascutti.

Group Four

	P	W	D	L	F	A	Pts
USSR	2	2	0	0	4	0	4
Italy	2	1	0	1	2	1	2
Chile	2	0	1	1	1	3	1
N Korea	2	0	1	1	1	4	1

ENGLAND STUMBLE ON
England 2 (B. Charlton 37, Hunt 75) Mexico 0
Group One, Wembley, London (att: 92,570)

ALF RAMSEY tonight watched England labour to their first World Cup win and told fans: I said it wouldn't be easy.

Having seen the USSR and Portugal record impressive wins earlier in the day, the Wembley crowd turned up hoping to see the hosts put on a show to worry the tournament's big hitters.

But Ramsey has repeatedly warned that getting out of Group One would be tough.

And, after goals from Bobby Charlton and Roger Hunt broke Mexico's resistance, the England manager said, 'When the draw was made, people were saying England had an easy group. The games we have played so far show how wrong that was.

'We have had to work tremendously hard to get anything. We have been forced to change our approach and I think that was evident against Mexico.

'We made far more chances than against Uruguay, but the same defensive structure presented the same problems. It is not easy to overcome. I am satisfied my players gave everything they had. The players were over-anxious before the match. The tension had been building up after the disappointing result on Monday.

'England have never been able in these matches to settle down and play the football that they are capable of. In our two matches, our opponents have not set out to beat us, but to stop us scoring.

'I am concerned about the finishing, but the ball did not run for us in front of goal against the Mexicans. We might have scored many more. There was never any doubt we would win.'

Southampton winger Terry Paine, who replaced John Connelly, fared no better and, worryingly for Ramsey, Jimmy Greaves has yet to open his account.

Even Mexico manager Ignacio Trelles commented, 'Greaves is in such poor form.'

The biggest positive for Ramsey was the brilliant performance of Bobby Charlton, now fully justifying the England manager's decision to switch him from the left wing to a central playmaker's role.

England's frustration was growing, particularly after Hunt had a header disallowed when Peters was harshly deemed guilty of a push.

But after 37 minutes, Charlton rewarded the home fans' patience with one of the great England goals.

Receiving the ball from Hunt, he ran at the retreating defence, made space with a clever body swerve and crashed a shot into the top corner.

Mexican goalkeeper Ignacio Calderón, who recovered from injury in time to deny Antonio Carbajal the chance to appear in a record fifth World Cup, had no chance with that one.

But he was rarely troubled in the second half and the second England goal didn't come until 15 minutes from time.

Charlton released Greaves and, when his shot came back off Calderón, Hunt slotted in the rebound.

ENGLAND: Gordon Banks, George Cohen, Ray Wilson, Nobby Stiles, Jack Charlton, Bobby Moore (capt), Terry Paine, Jimmy Greaves, Bobby Charlton, Roger Hunt, Martin Peters.

MEXICO: Ignacio Calderón, Arturo Chaires, Gustavo Peña (capt), Jesús Del Muro, Gabriel Núñez, Guillermo Hernández, Isidoro Diaz, Salvador Reyes, Ignacio Jáuregui, Enrique Borja, Aarón Padilla.

Group One

	P	W	D	L	F	A	Pts
Uruguay	2	1	1	0	2	1	3
England	2	1	1	0	2	0	3
France	2	0	1	1	2	3	1
Mexico	2	0	1	1	1	3	1

TESTING TIMES

BOBBY MOORE and Jack Charlton were tonight drug-tested for the second match running.

The England duo made history after the opener against Uruguay as the first England players to be picked for random testing under the new World Cup anti-doping scheme.

And incredibly, captain Moore and central defensive partner Big Jack both saw their names pulled out of the hat again after the win over Mexico.

FIFA has confirmed that all tests taken in previous matches have come back negative.

TERRY VISION

ENGLAND reject Terry Venables is turning his World Cup snub to good use by going on a personal scouting mission.

Tottenham Hotspur splashed out £80,000 earlier this year to land the highly-rated midfielder from Chelsea, but Alf Ramsey left him out of his finals squad after capping him twice 18 months ago.

Rather than staying away from the tournament, the 23-year-old is using the time off to boost his football knowledge.

He watched group games in London and Liverpool before switching to the Midlands. Having seen Argentina-West Germany, he plans to take in more action from Group Two.

He said, 'I feel the Argentine, Germany and Spain are three teams of such contrasting techniques that they are all worth careful study. If I learn just one thing which makes me a better player, it will be worthwhile.'

SWISS CHEESED OFF

SWITZERLAND are blaming Scottish linesman Hugh Phillips for their early exit.

The Swiss are out after Spain beat them 2-1, but they claim René Pierre Quentin had an equaliser wrongly ruled out because Phillips flagged for a foul.

Swiss selector Willy Wyttenbach complained, 'We were not satisfied with the judgment of the linesman when he waved his flag and the referee disallowed what we were sure was a good second goal.'

Manager Alfredo Foni moaned, 'It was a bad decision which robbed us of a chance of qualifying.'

BACK IN ARM'S WAY

IRON man Kálmán Mészöly is set to feature in Hungary's crucial match with Bulgaria – despite finishing the win over Brazil with his arm in a sling.

The Vasas SC defender, 25 today, feared he had broken his collarbone in yesterday's thriller against the world champions.

But the injury is not as serious as initially thought and the tough defender has already declared himself fit for Wednesday's final Group Three match. Coach Lajos Baróti said, 'He has 74 caps and I think that if he is alive he will play this one too.'

The Hungarians won't know exactly what they have to do until after Brazil and Portugal play on Tuesday.

But Baróti says that, even if Hungary go out, they have already restored the Magical Magyars' reputation by beating the world champions.

'I think Brazil will beat Portugal,' he added. 'And Bulgaria will probably play better against us than against anyone. But even if we fail, we shall go home proud of our performance against Brazil.'

THE LION KING

THE man who created World Cup Willie has explained how he came up with the idea for the hugely successful tournament mascot.

The FA awarded Walter Tuckwell & Associates the job of handling merchandising for the tournament and it was illustrator Reginald Hoye who hit upon the idea of a lion sporting a Beatles-style haircut and a Union Jack T-shirt.

Hoye, renowned for his work illustrating children's books by Enid Blyton, met FA chiefs to discuss designs for a tournament emblem, but the conversation turned to the possibility of a first World Cup mascot.

Hoye explained, 'We at last got round to the idea of a mascot. Somebody suggested a little man in a bowler hat, but that was too regional.

'Then came the suggestion of a man in a cloth cap, but that had a class ring about it.

'I suddenly remembered these old prints of boxers standing with their muscles flexed – you know, you see them a lot in pubs.

'Then, because my son is called Leo, I decided to turn this character into a lion with a Union Jack.

'I don't think the result is pompous. It is just to show that we're not as clapped out in Britain as some people think we are.'

Hoye received a fee for his work, but the FA holds the licensing rights for the many products on sale during the tournament.

Willie features in merchandise ranging from hats, tracksuits and rosettes to plastic figurines, snow globes and drinking glasses. Hoye added, 'Willie is corn, but he is good corn.'

Sunday 17 July
Rest Day Two

FRENCH RESISTANCE

FRANCE manager Henri Guérin has told his players they can beat England in their own backyard.

A draw at Wembley on Wednesday will send England through and eliminate the French, but a three-goal win for Guérin's men would see them qualify and send the hosts tumbling out.

Guérin has been busy at their Welwyn Garden City base building up his men to pull off an upset after their disappointing performances against Mexico and Uruguay.

He said, 'We know only too well the position. All is not lost yet. We can do much, much better. We all know this and now we must prove it. England can be beaten and must be beaten.'

Alf Ramsey will not underestimate France, having lost 5-2 to them in his first match three years ago.

The England manager said, 'Their performances before the World Cup against Yugoslavia and Italy were impressive.

'We must not under-rate them and we must be prepared for a hard game.

'The French would have to murder us to have a chance of qualifying, but they will be playing as much for their honour as anything else.'

Ramsey has been boosted by the news that Jack Charlton and Terry Paine, who both suffered concussion in the Mexico win, have been given the all-clear.

PELÉ S.O.S

PELÉ is ready to save Brazil's World Cup after proving his fitness for their make-or-break date with Portugal.

The Samba superstar missed the shock defeat by Hungary with a knee injury, but he came through a full training session held in heavy rain in Bolton today. And asked how he felt as he jogged off the training pitch, Pelé smiled and said, 'Fine.'

Brazil know that to guarantee their passage into the last eight, they must win by at least three clear goals. Anything less will leave them relying on the result of the Bulgaria-Hungary match.

The Brazilians went into lockdown at the Lymm Hotel, Cheshire, today. Police stood guard outside and a notice by the front door read, 'The entrance of the press and of any member of the public has been expressly forbidden on any pretext by the technical committee of the Brazilian delegation.'

Team physician Dr Hilton Gosling, who has been working overtime to get Pelé ready, did break the media blackout, though, to call on Brazil to show why they are world champions.

Dr Gosling said, 'We are fighting for our football lives. We have got to prove we are true champions. We stand or fall on Tuesday and the players know the chips are down.

'We must rely on ourselves, not look for others to fail. We must play this match with our heads and our hearts. I don't like it when our players think it is easy. Now they know it isn't easy. They know they HAVE to play well.

'This is the ideal situation. It is a good test for them to show if they are world champions. The players know that we need to beat Portugal by three goals – 3-0, 4-1 or anything higher will be good enough for us. We know we must play on the attack.

'It is no use relying on Bulgaria to beat Hungary. The onus is on us to do the job for ourselves. But Portugal are 80 per cent qualified by virtue of their two victories and they can dictate tactics. A draw would suit them fine.'

ARGENTINA IN THE DOCK

WORLD CUP chiefs look sure to come down hard on Argentina tomorrow when they discuss the Battle of Villa Park.

Defender Rafael Albrecht became the first player to be sent off in the tournament after appearing to knee West Germany's Wolfgang Weber in the groin during an ill-tempered goalless draw.

FIFA is anxious to avoid any repeat of the unsavoury on-field scenes which marred the 1962 finals.

Disciplinary chiefs will discuss the Villa Park match in London tomorrow when they receive Yugoslav referee Konstantin Zečević's report. FIFA secretary general Helmut Kaiser warned, 'Several members of the FIFA committee saw the match on television and, although the normal penalty for a sending-off is one match, this tackle was considered to be rather blatant.'

Argentina manager Juan Carlos Lorenzo could also be in hot water after running on to the pitch and confronting the match officials.

Another case on the agenda will be that of French forward Jacky Simon, who allegedly spat at Czech referee Karol Galba as they lost to Uruguay on Friday.

FIFA president Sir Stanley Rous said, 'All managers were warned of our intentions before the series started. If we think any incidents have brought the game into disrepute, then they will be dealt with.'

OH MY WORD!

POST OFFICE staff took nearly SIX HOURS to cable an Argentine journalist's mammoth report on the Battle of Villa Park to his magazine editors in Buenos Aires.

Osvaldo Ardizzone wrote a staggering 20,246 words – the equivalent of one quarter of a typical novel – on the Argentina-West Germany match.

At a cost of £1 a minute to cable, it set back bosses at *El Grafico* a whopping £340.

After the 20ft-long cable had been sent, Ardizzone insisted he had no regrets, saying, 'After all, this is football…and the World Cup as well.'

RUNNING SCARED

ITALY manager Edmondo Fabbri says his players are facing a crisis of confidence ahead of their crunch clash with North Korea.

Fabbri, whose mood has swung between pessimism and optimism in the opening week of the tournament, today admitted the lame defeat by the Soviet Union has left morale at a new low.

'The players have lost some faith in themselves,' he said. 'They are afraid of losing when they take to the field. We are unlucky in having to meet the Koreans after the other two teams in our group have played them.

'The Koreans were poor against Russia in their first match, better against Chile when they held them to a draw and they will be better still when we play them.'

KOREANS TUNE UP

NORTH KOREA'S squad won more fans in Middlesbrough – by singing in front of 400 guests at a mayoral reception.

The Hornets gave an impromptu performance of a song called *Warm Friendship* at an event hosted by mayor Jack Boothby at Middlesbrough Town Hall.

Official interpreter Kim Moore explained, 'It is really a Korean pop song. The team did not know they were going to sing.

'But they are always singing, so they thought they would show their thanks for the friendliness they have received in a way that everyone would understand.'

Government officials, meanwhile, have confirmed the Koreans will be invited to a ministerial reception for losing teams if, as expected, they lose to Italy and go out at the group stage.

Britain does not officially recognise the Democratic People's Republic of Korea, but that will not stop the squad being asked to attend the Lancaster House reception for the eight first-round losers.

CHOCS AWAY

WEST GERMANY bosses have given 700 bars of chocolate to a children's home in Derby because the players aren't allowed to eat them.

The sweet treats were sent to the squad by a German firm, but press officer Dr Wilfried Gerhardt said, 'The players like a bit of chocolate, but unfortunately it is not on their diet and it doesn't help their training.'

A group of German players took the chocolates to St Christopher's Orphanage, where captain Uwe Seeler handed them over to the children.

An orphanage spokesman said, 'We cannot thank the team enough. They went to endless trouble to arrange this presentation. The children were rather overawed, but delighted.'

GALS AND GOALS

PORTUGAL'S stars had mixed views today on the merits of women's football after they were guests of honour at a match.

The squad saw an England team beat an All-Star XI 3-2 in Salford and Eusébio said, 'It was a good match. I enjoyed it.'

But team-mate Germano was less than impressed, claiming, 'I didn't like it at all. I don't think women should be allowed to play football.'

FORWARD THINKERS

FIFA president Sir Stanley Rous is tipping a panel of experts to unlock the key to more World Cup goals.

The world governing body has set up a study group, including West Ham United manager Ron Greenwood, to compile a report on tactics at the finals.

Answering criticism over defensive tactics and a lack of goals in the finals so far, Rous today promised FIFA was determined to come up with answers.

He said, 'The only criticism seems to be that the play is more defensive than was hoped for.

'But tactics and systems have changed in recent years and it is hoped that the study group we have had at work will perhaps suggest ways in which defences may be penetrated by forwards.'

Monday 18 July
Rest Day Three

BEHAVE OR GO HOME

WORLD CUP bosses have warned Argentina they will be kicked out of the tournament if they step out of line again.

FIFA's disciplinary committee met in London today and banned defender Rafael Albrecht for tomorrow's final Group Two game with Switzerland following his sending-off against West Germany.

And manager Juan Carlos Lorenzo and his squad have been cautioned over their future conduct.

FIFA president Sir Stanley Rous said, 'If we thought any team was setting out deliberately to break the rules, that team could be asked to leave the country.'

Albrecht accepted his suspension, saying, 'It's a lesson for myself and the whole team. I'm very happy with the decision, although I didn't expect to be punished more.'

But Lorenzo reacted angrily to the sanctions and claimed Argentina are victims of a pro-European conspiracy.

He said, 'It is some of the European press that have caused all this trouble. We are not a rough team and I cannot understand why we should be regarded as such. When Italy played West Germany in the 1962 World Cup, it was like the Battle of Waterloo! All right, we had 21 fouls given against us when we played Germany, but sometimes a side can have 21 corners. It's just how a game goes.

'I shall pass on the committee's decision to my players, but I shall not give them any instructions on how to conduct themselves.

'They have already been told how to play and they must see for themselves how the game goes.

'Argentina have a long tradition of good football and artistry. I cannot understand why people are calling us a rough side.

'We will not change our approach when we meet Switzerland.'

He defended Albrecht, adding, 'In Argentina, he has the reputation of being our number one clean player. He has never been censured or sent off before.'

However, West Germany coach Helmut Schön claimed Albrecht had 'got off rather lightly'.

NAMED AND SHAMED

FIFA today issued a roll of shame of players officially warned over their future conduct.

The governing body named nine stars – including sent-off Argentinian Rafael Albrecht – who have been reported by match officials. The other eight are Eusébio (Portugal), Franz Beckenbauer (West Germany), Denílson (Brazil), Jacky Simon (France), Ivan Kolev (Bulgaria), Dinko Dermendjiev (Bulgaria), Murtaz Khurtsilava (USSR) and Iosif Sabo (USSR).

ENGLAND STUMPED

ENGLAND'S stars today relaxed by watching cricket at Lord's – and probably wished they hadn't bothered.

Alf Ramsey's men witnessed a dreary day's play as Middlesex and Essex scored just 200 runs between them in 97 overs on day two of their County Championship match.

ALF BACKS JIMMY

ALF RAMSEY looks set to stand by out-of-sorts striker Jimmy Greaves.

England's record scorer hasn't looked like adding to his 43-goal tally and Ramsey is under pressure to axe him against France.

Ramsey today backed the Tottenham Hotspur man, but admitted he wants to see more goal threat. He said, 'Jimmy has worked very hard in both matches, but he has been coming back too deep at times and this, or course, is not his best function.'

JACK DREAM DOUBLE

JACK CHARLTON has revealed he is hoping for a magical double on 30 July – a World Cup Final win and to become a father again.

Charlton's wife, Pat, is due to give birth to their third child at around the time the tournament ends.

And the Leeds United defender said, 'A World Cup winner's medal and a son on the same day. Could a man ask for more?'

MEXICANS FULL OF BEANS

MEXICO manager Ignacio Trelles will tell his players to throw off their defensive shackles against Uruguay.

Only a handsome win would give the Mexicans a chance of a quarter-final place, but Trelles insists they will go for it. He said, 'We are obliged to do this. We have some doubts about the tactics we have been using so far.'

WORLD CHUMPS

PORTUGAL coach Otto Glória today had a pop at Brazil as the world champions face up to the threat of an early exit.

Brazil need to beat Glória's side by three goals tomorrow to scrape into the knockout stages.

But Glória, born in Brazil to Portuguese parents, has warned his team will be going all-out for a third straight win and believes the champions blundered with their squad selection.

He said, 'This is the worst Brazilian team I have seen and it is the one with the least heart.

'Where are their good players? There are 2m registered players in Brazil and I believe that some of those who have stayed at home should be here. Politics have come into the selection.

'I would like Brazil AND Portugal to qualify, but we shall be on the attack from the start. We want to go through as winners of this group.'

CHEWING THE FAT

BRAZIL boss Vicente Feola today admitted he has 'many doubts' ahead of their do-or-die clash with Portugal.

Coach and chief selector Feola, a national hero when he led the nation to a first world crown in 1958, faces the biggest test of his illustrious career.

The portly Feola, dubbed The Fat One by fans, insists he is under no extra pressure, because expectations at home are so high that he is ALWAYS under pressure.

He has been busy discussing the make-up of the team to face Portugal with his fellow selectors and a major shake-up appears likely.

Injuries will play a part, with Pelé a doubt and Zito and Alcindo definitely out. But there could also be tactical changes, with veteran stars Garrincha, 32, and Djalma Santos, 37, among those who could be axed.

Feola admitted, 'We have many doubts. We shall play a normal game because it is essential we score goals, but it is equally important that we don't give any goals away.

'This means we cannot, under any circumstances, name a team tilted heavily towards attack.'

The thought of returning home early to face the anger of their fans should spur on Brazil.

Carlos Nascimento, head of Brazil's World Cup technical commission, said, 'We have 80m critics – the 80m people of Brazil.'

PELÉ'S ROUGH RIDE

EUSÉBIO has told Pelé that getting a kicking is all part of the game.

Pelé missed Brazil's defeat by Hungary after he was injured against Bulgaria and is still not certain of facing Eusébio's Portugal tomorrow.

Brazil fear the Portuguese could put the boot in on Pelé, but Eusébio said, 'If a man is a good player he has to expect this. Without doubt, Pelé is the best player in the world.

'He is the complete player and he has to be stopped. Sometimes it gets a little rough. I try to forget or ignore the mean things that happen to me.'

EX-ASP-ERATING

BULGARIA coach Rudolf Vytlačil has pointed the finger at star striker Georgi Asparoukhov over their early exit.

The Bulgarians are out with a game to spare after back-to-back defeats by Brazil and Portugal.

Levski Sofia forward Asparoukhov, the teetotal poster boy of Bulgarian football, came into the competition with a reputation as one of Europe's best goalscorers.

But he has failed to fire for the goalless Bulgarians and Vytlačil has slammed his performances. He said, 'He was not effective. He is a most elegant player, but he did not show enough fight.'

SPAIN FACE PAIN

EUROPEAN champions Spain have been told their fancy football will lead to an early exit.

The Spanish need a win against West Germany on Wednesday, but Swiss midfielder Heinz Bäni has faced – and lost to – both teams and has no doubts who will come out on top.

'The Spanish play was too complicated against us,' said Bäni. 'I don't think they have any chance against the Germans.'

Spain may drop their £600,000 Italian-based stars Luis Suárez, Luis Del Sol and Joaquín Peiró in a bid to keep alive their campaign. Captain Francisco Gento's place is also under threat.

Switzerland's part-timers, meanwhile, will sign off against Argentina tomorrow with a sentimental gesture.

Goalkeeper Leo Eichmann, a publican with only one previous cap, will play in place of first-choice Karl Elsener.

Switzerland selector Willy Wyttenbach said, 'Both goalkeepers are of similar class. Elsener has now played twice in the competition, so it is only right that Eichmann should get a chance.'

KOREA MOVE

CONFIDENT North Korea are already making preparations for the quarter-finals.

The outsiders in the North-East group pulled off a surprise by holding Chile and are now eyeing second place by beating mighty Italy.

Officials are so confident of qualifying that they have started looking for a Merseyside hotel ahead of a potential quarter-final in Liverpool.

North Korea coach Myung Rye-Hyun said, 'The Italians are worried after their defeat by Russia. We are confident after our game against Chile – we should have beaten the Chileans.'

Italy manager Edmondo Fabbri has urged his under-performing stars to show their true colours after losing to the USSR.

He said, 'I have told my team they must attack, attack, attack. We must make sure of a good victory to boost our confidence.'

HOT CHILE

CHILE manager Luis Álamos is backing North Korea to shock Italy – and throw his side a lifeline.

An Italian victory tomorrow would eliminate the disappointing Chileans even before their final group game against the USSR.

But Álamos said, 'If my boys find that a win against Russia can keep us in the competition, then they will really sparkle, well beyond their form so far.

'We depend on North Korea beating Italy or, at the worst, playing a draw. Our great hope must be that Korea will beat Italy by one goal and, on Italy's form, this could happen. Then a one-goal margin for us against Russia would put us into the last eight.

'If Italy draw, we would need three goals against Russia to survive and that is a big task.'

Tuesday 19 July
Matchday Six

Mexico v Uruguay (Group One)
4.30pm, Wembley, London

Switzerland v Argentina (Group Two)
7.30pm, Hillsborough, Sheffield

Brazil v Portugal (Group Three)
7.30pm, Goodison Park, Liverpool

North Korea v Italy (Group Four)
7.30pm, Ayresome Park, Middlesbrough

URUGUAY HIT THE BOOS
Mexico 0 Uruguay 0
Group One, Wembley, London (att: 61,112)

URUGUAY booked their place in the last eight – amid a chorus of boos.

The frustrated Wembley crowd made their feelings known as the South Americans shut up shop to ensure they got the point they needed.

Despite the 4.30pm kick-off – this was the only weekday fixture not scheduled as a night game – the match attracted a healthy attendance.

The fans saw Mexico have 28 goal attempts to Uruguay's 19 and the Mexicans also forced twice as many corners, with ten.

They went all-out for the two-goal win they needed, but couldn't find the killer touch.

Mexican FA president Guillermo Cañedo said, 'I am depressed with this result. My team had enough chances to have won.'

Veteran goalkeeper Antonio Carbajal, 37, was in tears as he said farewell after playing in a record FIFTH World Cup and keeping his country's first clean sheet in a finals match.

Ernesto Cisneros saw a shot come back off the post after 11 minutes and Uruguay goalkeeper Ladislao Mazurkiewicz produced a string of saves to preserve their record of not conceding a goal in open play.

Mexico kept plugging away in torrential rain, but Carbajal had to react smartly to keep out Pedro Rocha's header and stop Uruguay pinching it.

The result means England will qualify from Group One if they draw with France and a win will see them top the pool. France need a three-goal win to leapfrog the hosts.

MEXICO: Antonio Carbajal, Arturo Chaires, Gustavo Peña (capt), Gabriel Núñez, Guillermo Hernandez, Isidoro Diaz, Magdaleno Mercado, Salvador Reyes, Ernesto Cisneros, Enrique Borja, Aarón Padilla.

URUGUAY: Ladislao Mazurkiewicz, Luis Ubiña, Omar Caetano, Milton Viera, Jorge Manicera, Horacio Troche (capt), Julio César Cortés, Néstor Gonçálvez, José Sasia, Pedro Rocha, Domingo Pérez.

Group One

	P	W	D	L	F	A	Pts
Uruguay	3	1	2	0	2	1	4
England	2	1	1	0	2	0	3
Mexico	3	0	2	1	1	3	2
France	2	0	1	1	2	3	1

WE JUAN FAIR AND SQUARE
Switzerland 0 Argentina 2 (Artime 53, Onega 81)
Group Two, Hillsborough, Sheffield (att: 32,127)

ARGENTINA were on their best behaviour as they eased into the last eight and a possible showdown with England.

The South Americans – threatened by FIFA with expulsion from the tournament – were booed mercilessly by the Hillsborough crowd.

They kept their cool, though, and were too good for the part-timers of Switzerland. But Argentina manager Juan Carlos Lorenzo fired an ominous warning that they would use strong-arm tactics in the knockout stages if required.

Lorenzo said, 'The Swiss were sporting enough to allow us more time to play the type of football people expect from Argentina.

'We had no need to play it hard. We played hard against the Germans because they have a reputation for hard play.'

Plucky Switzerland kept Argentina goalkeeper Antonio Roma and his defence busy, with Jakob Kuhn, René Pierre Quentin and captain René Brodmann all going close.

Argentina, though, always looked the more likely winners and got the breakthrough early in the second half when Luis Artime punished some slack defending for his third goal of the tournament.

Any doubts were settled when Ermindo Onega exchanged passes with Alberto González and lobbed goalkeeper Leo Eichmann.

ARGENTINA: Antonio Roma, Roberto Perfumo, Silvio Marzolini, Roberto Ferreiro, Oscar Calics, Antonio Rattin (capt), Jorge Solari, Alberto González, Luis Artime, Ermindo Onega, Oscar Mas.

SWITZERLAND: Leo Eichmann, Hansrüdi Fuhrer, René Brodmann (capt), Kurt Armbruster, Xavier Stierli, Heinz Bäni, Jakob Kuhn, Vittore Gottardi, Fritz Künzli, Robert Hosp, René Pierre Quentin.

Group Two

	P	W	D	L	F	A	Pts
Argentina	3	2	1	0	4	1	5
W Germany	2	1	1	0	5	0	3
Spain	2	1	0	1	3	3	2
Switzerland	3	0	0	3	1	9	0

CHAMPS GET THE BOOT
Brazil 1 (Rildo 73) Portugal 3 (Simões 15, Eusébio 27, 85)
Group Three, Goodison Park, Liverpool (att: 58,479)

PORTUGAL tonight defended their treatment of Pelé after kicking him and champions Brazil to the brink of elimination.

Only a mathematical miracle can save Brazil after the Portuguese beat them with a mixture of brutality and brilliance.

Brazil were already reeling from two early goals when a shocking double hack by João Morais reduced Pelé to a passenger for the last hour. The world's greatest player had already been the victim of three nasty fouls before the clash with Morais, but Portugal selector Manuel Afonso insisted his players weren't to blame.

He said, 'Pelé was troubled by a previous injury and by some mischance he injured himself again.'

Garrincha and Djalma Santos were among those axed as the Brazil selectors made NINE changes to the team beaten by Hungary, but the shake-up couldn't stop them falling behind after 15 minutes.

A poor punch by Manga, replacing the unconvincing Gylmar in goal, was headed straight back into the net by António Simões.

Just 12 minutes later, José Torres nodded the ball across goal for Eusébio to head past the hapless Manga.

Brazil's fading hopes were effectively extinguished by Pelé's injury. Morais hacked him down from behind and, when the Brazilian leapt to his feet and tried to play on, Morais cut him down again with a knee-high challenge.

English referee George McCabe awarded a free kick and ruffled Pelé's hair in sympathy as he writhed in agony. But the official decided the offence was worthy of nothing more than a ticking-off.

Pelé courageously returned after being carried off for treatment, but he was hobbling for the rest of the match, even when he emerged after half-time with heavy strapping around his right knee.

Without his dribbling and running power, Pelé was never a real threat. He did, however, provide the pass which started the move from which Rildo halved the deficit with 17 minutes left.

But Brazil needed to win by three goals and the game was up when Eusébio slammed in a spectacular half-volley. Brazil now need Bulgaria to beat Hungary 2-0 and, even then, would have to draw lots with the Magyars for second place in Group Three.

Brazil coach Vicente Feola and his shell-shocked stars left Goodison Park without commenting. But one member of the Brazil delegation, Gunnar Goransson, admitted, 'We are very disappointed. Everybody expected us to reach the semi-finals at least. We haven't done so because other countries have improved.'

Portugal selector Afonso said, 'We came here very quietly and we are now in the quarter-finals. We have great hopes. We'll just continue fighting and playing good football.'

PORTUGAL: José Pereira, João Morais, Alexandre Baptista, Vicente, Hilário, Jaime Graça, Mário Coluna (capt), José Augusto, José Torres, Eusébio, António Simões.

BRAZIL: Manga, José Maria Fidélis, Hércules Brito, Denílson, Orlando (capt), Rildo, Jairzinho, Antônio Lima, Walter da Silva, Pelé, Paraná.

Group Three

	P	W	D	L	F	A	Pts
Portugal	3	3	0	0	9	2	6
Hungary	2	1	0	1	4	4	2
Brazil	3	1	0	2	4	6	2
Bulgaria	2	0	0	2	0	5	0

ITALIAN SOB
North Korea 1 (Pak Doo-Ik 42) Italy 0
Group Four, Ayresome Park, Middlesbrough (att: 17,829)

ITALY manager Edmondo Fabbri admitted they got what they deserved tonight after one of the biggest upsets in World Cup history.

A goal from North Korean winger Pak Doo-Ik knocked out the two-time world champions in a giantkilling to rank alongside England's 1950 defeat by the USA.

And the Italian boss conceded they had been guilty of underestimating the supposed no-hopers, who will go through to face Portugal unless Chile beat the USSR tomorrow.

Fabbri said, 'We are bitterly disappointed. It has been an enormous shock. But the team cannot be accused of not trying. The Koreans were better than we thought.'

North Korea coach Myung Rye-Hyun hailed the Ayresome Park crowd, who again backed the underdogs.

He said, 'The players have lived up to the honour of the fatherland. We have improved with each game in England through the encouragement and support of the Middlesbrough fans.

'It is very difficult to predict the winners of our quarter-final against Portugal, but we will do our best. It will be a marvellous game.'

Luck wasn't with Italy, who had to play for 55 minutes with ten men after the influential Giacomo Bulgarelli was injured.

Italy saw Marino Perani thwarted three times by goalkeeper Lee Chan-Myung in the first half.

And after Korea went ahead, Gianni 'Golden Boy' Rivera – recalled after being dropped for the defeat against the Soviet Union – saw the keeper brilliantly deny him.

But the Koreans, roared on by the majority of what was a disappointingly low crowd of 17,829 at Ayresome Park, fully deserved their victory.

At 1-0, the crowd even taunted the Italians with chants of 'We want two' and the Koreans nearly obliged when Im Seung-Hwi narrowly failed to get on the end of a Han Bong-Jin cross.

NORTH KOREA: Lee Chan-Myung, Shin Yung-Kyoo, Lim Zoong-Sun, Ha Jung-Won, Oh Yoon-Kyung, Im Seung-Hwi, Park Seung-Jin (capt), Han Bong-Jin, Pak Doo-Ik, Kim Bong-Hwan, Jang Sung-Kook.

ITALY: Enrico Albertosi, Spartaco Landini, Giacinto Facchetti, Romano Fogli, Aristide Guarneri, Francesco Janich, Marino Perani, Giacomo Bulgarelli (capt), Sandro Mazzola, Gianni Rivera, Paolo Barison.

Group Four

	P	W	D	L	F	A	Pts
USSR	2	2	0	0	4	0	4
N Korea	3	1	1	1	2	4	3
Italy	3	1	0	2	2	2	2
Chile	2	0	1	1	1	3	1

BOOKIES TIP PORTUGAL

BOOKIES tonight installed Portugal as the new favourites after one of the most dramatic days in World Cup history. Champions Brazil, still 9/2 favourites before their second defeat, are now 100/1.

Portugal have been cut to 6/4, although surprise package North Korea are still big outsiders at 66/1. England are second favourites at 4/1, followed by Hungary (5/1) and Argentina and West Germany (6/1).

PAIN FOR PAINE

IAN CALLAGHAN has been handed the chance to get England's attack firing in tomorrow's make-or-break meeting with France.

The Liverpool winger comes in for Terry Paine in the only change from the side which laboured to overcome Mexico on Saturday.

Callaghan is the third winger tried by Alf Ramsey in as many matches as he sticks with a 4-3-3 formation. Martin Peters keeps his place after replacing Alan Ball against the Mexicans.

Ramsey stands by out-of-form Jimmy Greaves and has ignored calls for him to ditch defensive midfielder Nobby Stiles in favour of Norman Hunter of Leeds United.

ROCKET LAUNCH

MISFIRING striker Philippe Gondet gets the chance to shoot down England after an impassioned plea to France manager Henri Guérin.

The man dubbed Rocket Shot seemed certain to be axed as the French look for the three-goal win needed to qualify.

In a public appeal to his manager, Gondet said, 'This game matters more to me than anything else. Please let me play and I shall do all I can to help France to victory.'

And when Guérin named his XI, the 24-year-old was handed a reprieve. Fellow forward Héctor De Bourgoing, though, has been left out, despite scoring from the penalty spot against Mexico.

Jacky Simon also plays after being cleared of spitting at an official in the defeat against Uruguay.

Guérin will employ an attacking 4-2-4 formation and said, 'Against England it will be necessary. We have to win to stay in the tournament and we shall try to do so.'

He admitted, however, that holding England at Wembley would at least salvage some pride, adding, 'A draw would give us some little reward to face the French people with.'

LET'S STAY LONGA

SPAIN manager José Villalonga has told the misfiring European champions: It's now or never.

The Spanish must beat impressive West Germany at Villa Park tomorrow to keep alive their hopes.

Defeat by Argentina was followed by an unconvincing win over Switzerland and Villalonga admits Spain will be a laughing stock at home if they go out.

Today he issued a rallying call to his flops, saying, 'We need power as well as quality in our play if we are to win.

'I was most disappointed we didn't play faster and better in our first two matches. We must have more force, much more.'

Villalonga seems sure to drop his big-money Italian-based stars, adding, 'I must remould the side to have any chance of us reaching the quarter-finals.'

The Spaniards' choice of preparation the night before the match has raised eyebrows, however.

They were at a smoke-filled hall until midnight watching a boxing show, while the Germans relaxed with a quiet film screening at their Derbyshire retreat.

REF JUSTICE

WEST GERMANY claim Franz Beckenbauer is the victim of a FIFA mix-up after he was warned over his future conduct.

The rising star of German football was on a list of players named and shamed by FIFA yesterday after being reported by referees.

The governing body said the Bayern Munich midfielder was booked during the ill-tempered clash with Argentina, but the Germans insist he is innocent.

Coach Helmut Schön said, 'He was never anywhere near any of the incidents during the Argentina match.

'I have spoken to Beckenbauer in an attempt to clear up this mystery. He insists that the referee never came near him, either to speak to him or to look at the number on his back and certainly not to write his name in his book.

'The only explanation we can think of is that the referee might have confused him with Wolfgang Overath. But how could he mistake Beckenbauer's number four for Overath's number 12?'

The Germans will NOT appeal – even though another booking could mean a suspension.

CHILE CAUGHT COLD

CHILE manager Luis Álamos today admitted his team are World Cup lightweights.

The Chileans must beat the USSR tomorrow to avoid an early exit after losing to Italy and drawing with North Korea.

Boss Álamos said, 'We have been hit by injuries, but that is not the only explanation for our poor form.

'We would have had a better chance in the same group as Mexico and Uruguay. The Russians and Italians have too much physical force for our lightweight team.

'I'm very disappointed with our standard of play. I shall bring in men who are more used to physical contact.'

He has made sweeping changes, dropping two of his top stars, full-back Luis Eyzaguirre and forward Alberto Fouilloux.

NO EASTERN BLOCK

BULGARIA have rubbished Brazilian whispers they will roll over to let Hungary reach the last eight.

Brazil know only a 2-0 Bulgaria win tomorrow will do – and even then they would have to draw lots with Hungary for second place in Group Three.

Bulgaria are already out, but coach Rudolf Vytlačil has hit back at talk that an Eastern European pact could come into play at Old Trafford. He vowed, 'We shall beat them.'

Star striker Georgi Asparoukhov aims to finally show what he can do after Vytlačil branded him 'ineffective'.

The 23-year-old said, 'Either I do something or nothing in a match. This time I will do my best to make it *something*.'

Hungary coach Lajos Baróti warned his side, 'Bulgaria are better than they have shown so far and it's very unlikely an international side will play three bad games in a row.

'I'm convinced they will attack tomorrow, because their defensive players have failed them so far and they will feel they now have to rely on their forwards.'

He promised the attack-minded Hungarians won't play for a draw, adding, 'We'll play our usual game.'

Wednesday 20 July
Matchday Seven

France v England (Group One)
7.30pm, Wembley, London

West Germany v Spain (Group Two)
7.30pm, Villa Park, Birmingham

Bulgaria v Hungary (Group Three)
7.30pm, Old Trafford, Manchester

Chile v USSR (Group Four)
7.30pm, Roker Park, Sunderland

STILL IN THE HUNT
France 0 England 2 (Hunt 38, 75)
Group One, Wembley, London (att: 98,270)

ALF RAMSEY watched England edge into the last eight and declared: We fear no one.

Two goals from birthday boy Roger Hunt, 28 today, set up a quarter-final date with Argentina at Wembley on Saturday.

The only worries for the England manager are that Jimmy Greaves could miss the game with a gashed leg and that Nobby Stiles faces more scrutiny after he was lucky not to be sent off.

Ramsey said, 'I see no reason why we should be afraid of anybody now.

'It will be a good quarter-final against Argentina. I have reports on them and quite obviously they have an excellent defence. This will be difficult to overcome, but I have no fears about the game.'

Ramsey admitted the weight of expectation had stopped England playing with freedom so far.

He said, 'I am completely stunned by the amount of pressure we have been under. It is not a fear. I don't think we are afraid of anything. I most certainly am not afraid of anything.

'It is just the occasion. Everyone wanting to do well. Wanting to please not only themselves, but their family, their friends, the spectators, the public. They have been subjected to a tremendous amount of pressure. We have all felt this, even myself. I had no idea that the tension and the pressures would be so severe.

'Looking around at the players before matches, at training sessions, in discussions and what have you, I think that these players haven't been allowed to play with any freedom at all because of the emotional effects brought about by the tremendous pressures they have been subjected to.'

He added, 'I did not think our performance was up to the standard of the two that went before. We were too casual and, after scoring the first goal, that seemed to sweep through the whole team.'

England, cheered on by a near-full house at Wembley, started like a whirlwind, but repeatedly fell into France's offside trap.

An easy win looked on the cards as England created several early chances and France were reduced to ten fit men when Roby Herbin was injured.

Goalkeeper Marcel Aubour grabbed the ball at the feet of Hunt after he was set up by Martin Peters and a 30-yarder from Ian Callaghan forced another good save.

Greaves – who hurt his shin in a first-half collision – netted with an acrobatic shot after half an hour, but was flagged offside.

But the breakthrough came after 38 minutes when Hunt finished from close range after Jack Charlton's downward header came back off the post. England were strangely cautious in the second half and, after Bobby Charlton had an effort disallowed, the fans had to wait until 15 minutes from time for the killer second.

Callaghan, the third winger tried by Ramsey in as many games, crossed and the keeper fumbled Hunt's header into the net.

Manchester United midfielder Stiles had a wretched night. Having been left limping when he was knocked over in a freak collision with Peruvian referee Arturo Yamasaki, Stiles was later booked for a foul and was then lucky not to be sent off after a dreadful late tackle on Jacky Simon.

Victory means England are unbeaten in 13 matches, including 11 wins, and they are the only team not to have conceded a goal so far in the tournament.

ENGLAND: Gordon Banks, George Cohen, Ray Wilson, Nobby Stiles, Jack Charlton, Bobby Moore (capt), Ian Callaghan, Jimmy Greaves, Bobby Charlton, Roger Hunt, Martin Peters.

FRANCE: Marcel Aubour, Robert Budzinski, Jean Djorkaeff, Marcel Artelesa (capt), Bernard Bosquier, Yves Herbet, Joseph Bonnel, Roby Herbin, Jacky Simon, Philippe Gondet, Gérard Hausser.

Group One

	P	W	D	L	F	A	Pts
England	3	2	1	0	4	0	5
Uruguay	3	1	2	0	2	1	4
Mexico	3	0	2	1	1	3	2
France	3	0	1	2	2	5	1

SPAIN BOSS QUITS
West Germany 2 (Emmerich 38, Seeler 84) Spain 1 (Fusté 22)
Group Two, Villa Park, Birmingham (att: 42,187)

TEARFUL José Villalonga tonight quit football after seeing Spain crash out.

The Spain manager announced his retirement immediately after the European champions' hopes were killed off by West Germany in Birmingham.

Former Real Madrid chief Villalonga said, 'I quit. I'm retiring from football. Tonight I'm finished with the game. Spain's defeat has been too much for me.

'We did our very best and perhaps we didn't deserve to lose this game. But the defeat by Argentina…that was another matter.'

Villalonga, who replaced some of his big-name players with new faces against the Germans, said, 'My old stars had the skill, but not the fight.

'The new boys were so good tonight, but West Germany were too strong for us because we had injuries. Amancio was limping for three-quarters of the game and Manuel Sanchís was also injured. The handicap was too much.'

He thought Spain's fortunes were looking up when Brazilian referee Armando Marques allowed José María Fusté's opener to stand, ignoring German protests he had handled in the build-up.

Villalonga insisted, 'It was a good goal and at that stage I thought we could win.'

Their hopes were rocked by possibly the goal of the tournament so far from Borussia Dortmund winger Lothar Emmerich, given his chance after being overlooked for the opening two games.

It seemed the best Emmerich could manage was a cross after he chased what looked like a lost cause to stop the ball going out for a goal kick. But the man who broke the German League scoring record with 31 goals last season somehow unleashed a scorching half-volley on the turn and the ball rocketed into the roof of the net.

Any doubts about the Germans' place in the last eight were dispelled when captain Uwe Seeler converted a Sigi Held cross.

The victory confirmed West Germany as Group Two winners and sets up a meeting with unbeaten Uruguay, who have yet to concede a goal in open play.

Coach Helmut Schön said, 'It will be a difficult match, but I think we can break down their famed defence.'

WEST GERMANY: Hans Tilkowski, Horst-Dieter Höttges, Karl-Heinz Schnellinger, Franz Beckenbauer, Willy Schulz, Wolfgang Weber, Werner Krämer, Lothar Emmerich, Uwe Seeler (capt), Wolfgang Overath, Sigi Held.

SPAIN: José Ángel Iribar, Manuel Sanchís, Severino Reija, Jesús Glaría, Gallego, Ignacio Zoco (capt), Adelardo, José Maria Fusté, Amancio, Marcelino, Carlos Lapetra.

Group Two

	P	W	D	L	F	A	Pts
W Germany	3	2	1	0	7	1	5
Argentina	3	2	1	0	4	1	5
Spain	3	1	0	2	4	5	2
Switzerland	3	0	0	3	1	9	0

MAGYARS IN, BRAZIL OUT
Bulgaria 1 (Asparoukhov 15)
Hungary 3 (Davidov og 43, Mészöly 45, Bene 54)
Group Three, Old Trafford, Manchester (att: 24,129)

HUNGARY booked a date with the Soviet Union after a comical own goal killed Brazil's chances of an unlikely lifeline.

The champions needed Bulgaria to win 2-0 to set up the drawing of lots for a place in the last eight.

That appeared possible when Georgi Asparoukhov scored Bulgaria's first goal of the competition.

But Brazil's dream died two minutes before the interval when Ivan Davidov – making his debut – inexplicably diverted a harmless Gyula Rákosi cross into his own net.

Hungary took the lead just before half-time with Kálmán Mészöly's half-volley from 20 yards.

Ferenc Bene headed the third nine minutes into the second half to continue his goal-a-game record in the competition.

Bulgaria coach Rudolf Vytlačil admitted, 'We are not yet ready for the World Cup finals. In every match we have played, we have shown our weaknesses and inexperience.'

HUNGARY: József Gelei, Sándor Mátrai, Benõ Káposzta, Kálmán Mészöly, Ferenc Sipos (capt), Gusztáv Szepesi, Ferenc Bene, Imre Mathesz, Flórián Albert, Gyula Rákosi, János Farkas.

BULGARIA: Simeon Simeonov, Dimitar Largov, Dimitar Penev, Ivan Vutzov, Boris Gaganelov (capt), Dobromir Jechev, Ivan Davidov, Ivan Kolev, Georgi Asparoukhov, Dimitar Yakimov, Nikola Kotkov.

Group Three

	P	W	D	L	F	A	Pts
Portugal	3	3	0	0	9	2	6
Hungary	3	2	0	1	7	5	4
Brazil	3	1	0	2	4	6	2
Bulgaria	3	0	0	3	1	8	0

CHILE HEARTBREAK
Chile 1 (Marcos 32) USSR 2 (Porkujan 28, 85)
Group Four, Roker Park, Sunderland (att: 16,027)

NORTH KOREA breathed a sigh of relief tonight after Chile almost wrecked their World Cup party.

The USSR made NINE changes as they rested players ahead of the quarter-finals and Korea were left sweating as Chile threatened to snatch a place in the last eight.

Playing in heavy rain in front of a crowd of only 16,027, the South Americans bravely tried to keep their dreams alive right up until the moment debutant Valery Porkujan lobbed a late winner.

The result means Korea will play new World Cup favourites Portugal in the last eight, with Group Four winners, the Soviet Union, facing Hungary.

Porkujan scored the opener from close range when a Valery Voronin shot was deflected into his path.

Yet it was Chile who did much of the pressing and they equalised four minutes later when midfielder Rubén Marcos – pushed up front after suffering a groin injury early on – scrambled the ball past the unconvincing goalkeeper Anzor Kavazashvili.

The keeper – standing in for Lev Yashin for the second time in three games – repeatedly struggled to hold on to the slippery ball.

He did, though, make a number of important saves, including one superb stop from Chile captain Leonel Sánchez as the South Americans had the best of the chances. But Porkujan's late goal won it to push his case for a place in the Soviets' quarter-final XI.

Chile FA official Mauricio Vinar admitted they would have to adapt their game to succeed in future World Cups.

He said, 'It is very sad that Chile is out of the competition. We have learned that strength and speed are important. The Chilean and Latin game is based on attractive and artistic football.'

USSR: Anzor Kavazashvili, Viktor Getmanov, Aleksei Kerneyev, Leonid Ostrovsky, Albert Shesternev (capt), Valentin Afonin, Slava Metreveli, Valery Voronin, Viktor Serebrianikov, Eduard Markarov, Valery Porkujan.

CHILE: Juan Olivares, Alberto Valentini, Hugo Villanueva, Humberto Cruz, Elías Figueroa, Rubén Marcos, Pedro Araya, Ignacio Prieto, Honorino Landa, Guillermo Yavar, Leonel Sánchez (capt).

Group Four

	P	W	D	L	F	A	Pts
USSR	3	3	0	0	6	1	6
N Korea	3	1	1	1	2	4	3
Italy	3	1	0	2	2	2	2
Chile	3	0	1	2	2	5	1

ITALIAN INQUEST

FURIOUS Italian MPs today demanded action from the country's President over the nation's World Cup shame.

Questions were tabled in Parliament in the wake of Italy's stunning defeat by North Korea and their early exit.

President Giuseppe Saragat sent a telegram to the team congratulating them on having 'suffered with sportsmanship'.

But a group of Christian Democrats, majority party in the coalition government, want action from President Saragat to ensure 'a more dignified and more moral regulation of Italy's most popular sport'.

And a statement from Socialist MPs slammed Italy's elimination as a 'scarcely edifying outcome'.

Before the squad left Durham to catch a train to London at the start of their journey home, manager Edmondo Fabbri said, 'Last night's result was a great shock.

'I haven't spoken to the players yet, because they are too upset. What is the use of talking to them? They are like a family without parents.'

Fabbri, handed an eight-year contract after the last World Cup, faced a grilling from angry Italian reporters, with some demanding he should resign.

He added, 'You have been disappointed and hurt, but for me it is worst of all. No one can understand how bad this feeling is.

'In the state I'm in at the moment, I'm not prepared to give opinions on individual players or the match itself.

'The result has shaken me. Italy were improving with each match. I cannot blame the players for what happened. I am in charge of the team, so I must shoulder the responsibility.

'After four years of hard work, I'm not going to criticise. You can criticise, but I will not. I'll ask the Italian Football Federation to examine all my work over four years. They will decide what to do.'

KOREA CHANGE

FA CHIEFS have stepped in to find giantkillers North Korea somewhere to stay.

The Hornets hadn't booked accommodation beyond the first round and were struggling to find a new base on Merseyside after reaching the quarter-finals.

Italy had reserved rooms at a Jesuit retreat at Rainhill, near Liverpool, on the assumption they would get through, so the FA contacted the retreat to ask if the Koreans could stay instead.

The Korean squad's reward today for their shock win over Italy was to be sent on a five-mile training run before breakfast.

And, unlike opponents Portugal, they won't be paid a bonus for their success.

Korean FA chairman Kim Eung-Sir said, 'In our country we don't have bonuses. Our players are amateurs who have other jobs. When they are preparing and playing with the national team, their employers continue to pay them.

'There is nothing extra. They play for the honour.

'When we go home, perhaps the government will make them Merited Sportsmen according to our system of honours.'

PELÉ AGONY

BRAZIL'S team doctor has revealed how Pelé was willing to risk a career-threatening injury in a bid to save the world champions.

Pelé – reduced to a hobbling passenger after barely half an hour by brutal tackling in the defeat by Portugal – pleaded with Dr Hilton Gosling to give him a pain-killing injection at half-time.

But the doctor said 'no' because he feared the superstar could cause even worse damage to his injured knee.

Gosling said, 'I refused. Without the pain to warn him, he may have seriously ruptured the ligaments. He is a human being first, then a professional footballer.

'Whether we won or lost a World Cup match came last in my order of priorities.'

The Brazilians will head home with NINE of their 22-man squad carrying injuries.

Gosling added, 'The team has received more injuries in the eight days they have been in England than in the previous eight years. Even if we had qualified, we wouldn't have been able to field a good side, as we have so many men injured.

'We can't understand why Portugal became so violent. When they were already two goals ahead, there was no reason at all for those savage tackles on Pelé.

'There was more violence than enthusiasm in Portugal's play. Pelé was unfairly and unnecessarily tackled from behind and has severely strained ligaments.

'It is all the fault of the new style of football, which is tougher and faster. We will have to create new players who are stronger, but less technically perfect.

'I dread to think what the future holds. It looks as though we're drifting towards the American Football idea, where all the players will have to be padded up for protection and go out in suits of armour like something from the 17th century.'

BRAZIL BOSSES QUIT

BRAZIL'S World Cup big-wigs will all resign when they arrive back in Rio de Janeiro.

As the champions awaited confirmation of their elimination, the seven-strong Brazil delegation held a crisis meeting at their Cheshire hotel in the wake of their shock defeat by Portugal.

It was agreed that they should all hand in their resignations to Confederation of Sport president João Havelange.

Team physician Dr Hilton Gosling – a key man alongside coach Vicente Feola in the nation's past successes – admitted the Brazilian public would not accept excuses.

'They won't ask us what went wrong – they will tell us,' he said.

In Brazil, rioting followed the defeat by Portugal. Fighting broke out in Sao Paulo, with Brazilians clashing with people of Portuguese origin in the central Cathedral Square where thousands gathered to listen to radio commentary relayed by loudspeakers.

Police arrived in force to break up the disturbances.

Angry fans in Rio broke into a Portuguese shop and trashed it after the owner let off fireworks to celebrate the result.

An effigy of coach and chief selector Feola was strung up in Rio with a banner demanding 'We want Feola, who robbed us of the attack' in a reference to the changes made against Portugal.

SAMBA SLUMBER

PORTUGAL coach Otto Glória today claimed champions Brazil have paid the price for complacency.

The Samba Stars, favourites for a third successive world title, were out-fought and out-played by Hungary and Portugal.

Brazilian-born Glória said, 'Instead of Brazil accepting the fact that other nations might have something new to show them, they fell into a rut.

'This should be a warning to any nation at a time when it is enjoying success.'

WEDDED BLISS

NEWLYWEDS Michael and Tina Taylor had unexpected guests at their wedding reception – the Portugal squad.

The couple from Bramhall, Greater Manchester, were stunned when the players joined in the celebrations at the city's Wilmslow Hotel, where the squad are staying.

Eusébio even posed for pictures with the happy couple when the wedding snaps were taken.

ROUS-ING STUFF

FIFA president Sir Stanley Rous has thanked teams for being on their best behaviour in the final round of group matches.

World Cup chiefs laid down the law after a number of unsavoury incidents in earlier games – notably Argentina's explosive clash with West Germany.

Now Rous has written to all competing delegations, saying, 'I am writing to tell you how much my colleagues and I, of the organising committee, appreciate the support and co-operation you have given to our request that matches should be kept free from unpleasant incidents.

'Managers and players in almost every match have responded splendidly. I would ask you to thank them.'

BOO-BOYS BLASTED

ARGENTINA manager Juan Carlos Lorenzo has slammed the boo-boys who jeered them as they reached the last eight for the first time since 1930.

The South Americans beat Switzerland 2-0 yesterday to set up a quarter-final against hosts England.

But Lorenzo was upset that the Hillsborough crowd turned on them in the wake of their controversial clash with West Germany.

He fumed, 'We are surprised that people in England do not appreciate our play. We have had more shots than our opponents in each match – despite all the talk of our concentration on defence.

'Our vigour against West Germany was produced only because the situation demanded it. We shall meet each situation as it comes along.

'We are building up so well. We dropped only one point and we didn't play near our peak.'

THE QUARTER-FINAL LINE-UP
England v Argentina (Saturday, 3pm, Wembley)
West Germany v Uruguay (Saturday, 3pm, Hillsborough)
Portugal v North Korea (Saturday, 3pm, Goodison Park)
USSR v Hungary (Saturday, 3pm, Roker Park)

Thursday 21 July
Rest Day Four

ALF IN STILES FURY

ALF RAMSEY today accused World Cup bosses of 'gross intimidation' after they issued a public warning to England midfield terrier Nobby Stiles.

The Manchester United player was booked against France and was then lucky not to be sent off after a shocking late tackle on Jacky Simon.

FIFA's disciplinary committee today issued a statement warning Stiles he faces serious punishment if he steps out of line again and Ramsey now faces huge pressure to drop him for Saturday's match with Argentina.

The statement read, 'The committee decided to inform the Football Association that if Stiles is reported to the committee again, either by a referee or official observer, serious action will be taken.'

The England manager responded, 'I regard this as gross intimidation of a player. Are all the other players who have been cautioned also under observation from the stands?'

FIFA president Sir Stanley Rous hit back, 'It is standard practice to have an observer at all international matches. It is in the regulations. His job is to report on the referee and we did not think the referee in the England-France match had done his job.'

Ramsey knows Stiles may now not be able to play his natural game. If he decides it is too big a risk to play him, 22-year-old Norman Hunter would be the obvious replacement.

Asked how he would tackle the issue, Ramsey answered frostily, 'I will do what I have to do.'

Ramsey today warned his players they will have to stay 100 per cent focussed against the dangerous Argentinians, even if they get ahead.

'There must be no slackening, no relaxing,' he said. 'We must keep on top all the time. It is natural to relax when in front, but in football anything can happen and when a team comes from behind they want some stopping.'

The England boss plans behind-closed-doors sessions to work on out-witting the sort of massed defence they are again likely to face.

He added, 'We want at least one training session in private so that we can concentrate on the points in question. We are taking too much time in building up our moves.'

JIMMY STITCHED UP

JIMMY GREAVES faces a race against time to be fit for England's quarter-final.

The 43-goal forward needed stitches in his shin after the win over France, but still hopes to play. He said, 'I've got a hole in my leg big enough to smuggle diamonds in. But everybody seems more worried about it than me. I've played with worse.'

Manager Alf Ramsey said, 'We will not know for another 24 hours whether Greaves will be fit.'

Defenders Jack Charlton and George Cohen, who have groin and ankle injuries respectively, are Ramsey's other injury concerns.

HOTEL WOMEN BUST-UP

ARGENTINA'S quarter-final preparations have been rocked after a man was caught trying to smuggle women into players' rooms.

A former Argentine football official has been barred from the Albany Hotel in Birmingham after he was spotted sneaking three women in through a side entrance.

Hotel assistant manager David Waite explained, 'A man turned up with three girls and attempted to take them through the goods entrance of the hotel. He was spotted by a porter and, at the same time, by an Argentine official. There was a heated argument.

'This man had no connection with the team, but he has been staying in the hotel on certain nights while the team has been here. As a result of the incident, he has been ordered to leave. We all know the man now. He is not wanted here and will not be admitted.'

Juan Santiago, leader of their World Cup delegation, was left fuming over the incident and thanked hotel staff for intervening.

He confirmed, 'A matter of discipline arose, which I had to deal with and which involved a person who had nothing to do with the official delegation.'

Santiago, who said the culprit was an ex-Argentine official, was furious that half the squad had been looking out of their bedroom windows at the women when they should have been resting.

WEMBLEY WAR CRY

PLAYING England in front of a partisan home crowd won't faze Argentina, according to manager Juan Carlos Lorenzo.

And he has told his players the hosts' players and the energy-sapping Wembley turf are nothing to worry about either.

Lorenzo – whose side will travel to London from their Birmingham base tomorrow – said, 'Wembley won't worry us. Everybody in the party is bang fit. The ball may get tired, but not the players.

'As for the crowd, we have beaten Brazil in Rio with almost everyone in the ground screaming for the home side. And, really, you can't do better than that.

'I'm not worried about the pro-English crowd. We expected that in England. England, whom I have seen twice, are good, but we have an equal chance of beating them.'

Two years ago Argentina won a four-nation tournament in Brazil dubbed the Little World Cup, beating the hosts in a stormy match and then edging Alf Ramsey's men 1-0 with a disciplined defensive performance.

Lorenzo was not in charge then, but said, 'I'm sure we'll have a strong psychological advantage from our victory over England in the Little World Cup.

'I have the players to do the job, so why should we have fears and doubts about the other side?

'England only have three good players – the two Charltons and Bobby Moore. The rest play without intelligence.

'We will have to be careful with Jack Charlton, because he is dangerous on corners, and Nobby Stiles because he starts incidents. What we really hope for is a referee who will not be pressured by the Wembley crowd.'

Lorenzo again defended his team's style, saying, 'I haven't passed on any warning to my players about rough play.

'I don't intend to issue instructions from what I read in the newspapers.'

SEMI STORM

A STORM is brewing over the choice of venues for next week's semi-finals.

With Wembley and Goodison Park already chosen as the grounds, FIFA delegates face a dilemma when they meet on Saturday to decide which match is played where.

FIFA knows that, if England get through, it could be criticised if the hosts again play at the national stadium, with Uruguay the only other quarter-finalists to have played there so far.

And there has been a widespread understanding on Merseyside that England would play at Everton if they were to win Group One and then reach the last four. The FA's official handbook suggests this.

The winners of the Portugal-North Korea quarter-final could regard Goodison as an unfair choice, as it would deny them a first chance to play at Wembley.

But FIFA assistant secretary René Courte said, 'There are many unanswered questions. If Portugal win their quarter-final, it could be argued that they have had all their games in the North-West and it would be wrong for them to play a semi-final there as well.'

England manager Alf Ramsey said after England's win over France that switching venues would not worry him, but he admitted Wembley DOES give his team an advantage.

He said, 'We have played three matches here. It's the ground which is used for international matches and the England players are used to it. I am not concerned where we play, but I think it is probably to our advantage to play at Wembley.'

IT'S ENGLAND 0 ARGENTINA 1

ARGENTINA have scored a pre-match victory – by winning the right to wear their first-choice colours.

FIFA felt TV viewers watching in black and white would be confused by both teams wearing light-coloured shirts and dark shorts.

So the two countries drew lots and England lost – meaning they will have to wear all white, while the South Americans can wear dark shorts as usual with their light blue and white-striped jerseys.

In the other quarter-finals, North Korea and Hungary will both have to switch from their usual red shirts to white.

FIFA also today confirmed the referees for the four matches. West German Rudolf Kreitlein – whose previous game was Russia's win over Italy – takes charge of the England-Argentina match. English referee Jim Finney has been given the West Germany-Uruguay game.

LATE KICK-OFF KO'D

FIFA today ruled out switching England-Argentina to a later kick-off time than the other three quarter-finals.

All four matches are scheduled for 3pm on Saturday and FIFA looked into putting back the hosts' tie to 7.30pm so that fans attending the other three games could watch it on television.

When England faced Mexico last Saturday, they DID have a later kick-off time than the other three group games played that day.

But today – after talks with Wembley chiefs, TV bosses and local authorities – it was decided a late switch for this Saturday would cause too many logistical problems.

BEAT THE RETREAT

ENGLAND will regret facing Argentina instead of West Germany in the last eight.

That is the verdict of Swiss FA assistant general secretary Edgar Obertüfer, whose team were outplayed by both.

England have avoided the Germans in the quarter-finals, but Obertüfer believes Alf Ramsey's men have drawn the short straw.

He said, 'West Germany scored five against us and Argentina only two, but most of our players felt the South Americans were the tougher side. How does one get through their retreating defence?'

The Swiss, who spent their last day in Sheffield buying gifts for loved ones, flew home without midfielder Richard Dürr after he had an emergency appendix operation. The 27-year-old is recovering at the Claremont Nursing Home in Sheffield.

A television has been set up in his room so he can watch the rest of the tournament and Dürr joked today, 'I told them I would go home unless I had one!'

BUNCH OF DOPES

WORLD CUP bosses today rubbished an Argentine radio station's report that England have been thrown out of the tournament for doping offences.

FIFA president Sir Stanley Rous confirmed, 'It's sheer nonsense. All dope tests taken on all players so far have proved negative.'

A FOUL EVERY THREE MINUTES

THE Soviet Union are the dirtiest team left in the competition, according to official statistics.

Argentina have been censured by FIFA over their foul play, but figures suggest the USSR have been the worst offenders, while the Argentinians have committed less fouls than England.

In the 2,160 minutes played so far, referees have blown for 693 fouls. That works out at an offence every three minutes, seven seconds. The foul count for the quarter-finalists is USSR 66, Hungary 48, England 45, Argentina 44, Uruguay 42, Portugal 37, North Korea 34 and West Germany 33.

Nobby Stiles, warned by FIFA over his conduct, tops the England fouls list with ten. He is followed by Roger Hunt (eight), Bobby Moore and Jack Charlton (six) and Martin Peters (four).

ITALIANS PELTED

ITALY'S flops were pelted with rotten tomatoes and eggs when they arrived home today.

The Italians – knocked out at the group stage by North Korea – needed police protection when they landed at Genoa Airport.

Manager Edmondo Fabbri and his squad had hoped to make a discreet return, but hundreds of supporters were waiting.

They ran a gauntlet of hate, with fans shouting 'assassins' and other insults. Police cars escorted the squad for the first few miles of their journey away from the airport.

Giacomo Bulgarelli, still limping as a result of the injury which forced him off against Korea, said, 'There is little to say. All I CAN say is that we ought to be ashamed.'

TEARS FOR SOUVENIRS

BRAZIL'S fallen champions said an emotional goodbye as they left their Cheshire base today.

Police held back around 200 well-wishers who gathered outside the Lymm Hotel and local schoolgirls among the crowd sobbed as Pelé and Co. boarded their coach.

Hotel manager Charles Watkin said, 'We'll miss them very much. They're a fine bunch of lads.

'They were terribly upset last night when they learned they were definitely out of the competition. Some of them were in tears. It was an emotional sight and I had a lump in my throat.'

KICK IN THE SHIN

NORTH KOREA defender Shin Yung-Kyoo has warned World Cup favourites Portugal not to underestimate them.

The Hornets were in confident mood as they relocated to a new base near Liverpool today ahead of Saturday's Goodison Park date with Eusébio and Co.

Speaking outside the Jesuit Spirituality Centre, a 19th-century country house in Rainhill, Shin Yung-Kyoo said, 'No one gave us a chance of achieving anything, but we have done well. We have beaten Italy and we are confident about facing the Portuguese.

'Our players are tremendously fit and can last the pace as well as any side left in the competition. We will give Portugal a good game.'

NO CLOWNS

PORTUGAL today insisted they don't regard North Korea's giantkillers as 'clowns'.

Reports in Italy claim that is how an Azzurri official described the Koreans after scouting them ahead of Tuesday's ill-fated meeting.

The Portuguese are expected to sweep aside the tournament's surprise team, but selector Manuel Afonso promised they won't make the same mistake as the complacent Italians.

He said today, 'Make no mistake, we respect the North Koreans. A team that qualifies for the last eight of the World Cup cannot be clowns.

'But we still plan to play as we have throughout the tournament. When a team has a magnificent forward line like ours, it is senseless to play defensively.'

SOVIET SUPERPOWER

HUNGARY coach Lajos Baróti admits Soviet Union strength could prove too much for his side on Saturday.

Baróti's men caused a huge upset when they beat champions Brazil on their way to the last eight.

But he admitted, 'The Russian physique is much stronger than the Brazilians'. I am satisfied with our displays so far, although I know Russia will be a hard side to beat. But after Korea have beaten Italy, who knows what can happen?'

Hungary – who were welcomed to their Gateshead hotel today just seven hours after Chile checked out – may be regretting their decision to bring only 18 of their 22-man squad to England. Four of their players are injured and Újpest Djóza full-back Kálmán Ihász is flying in as cover.

COPS GUARD GERMANS

WEST GERMANY have been given a police guard to keep fans out of their team headquarters.

Assistant coach Udo Lattek and official press officer Wilfried Gerhardt had to spend 90 minutes today turning away hundreds of well-wishers and autograph hunters at their Derbyshire country retreat. Police eventually took over, with a patrol car parked outside the gates of the Peveril of the Peak Hotel in Ashbourne.

A police spokesman said, 'Things are quieter now, but it's been pretty chaotic. We've had coach-loads of them and we've even had to haul one or two fans out of the players' rooms.'

After the group stage, the Germans chose to stay on in Ashbourne because they have enjoyed the peace and quiet there.

After today's disturbances, Gerhardt said, 'We did not want to defeat our object of having a peaceful stay and there were so many supporters that it could also have harmed the hotel's business. We must now have 100 per cent concentration for our next match.'

SUBS FOR 1970

SUBSTITUTES could be allowed at the 1970 World Cup in Mexico – and not just for injured players.

Replacements for injured players are permitted in some internationals and substitutions are becoming commonplace in club football. FIFA chiefs are now considering a change for the next World Cup after seeing injuries have a big impact on several matches.

Secretary general Helmut Kaiser said it was likely teams would be able to name two subs and use them for tactical reasons as well as injuries. A study group set up by FIFA will report back on the issue next year.

Kaiser said, 'We should do something about replacing injured players in World Cup matches. The trouble is that you can never be sure a player is really injured. That is why FIFA is proposing that a side should consist of 13 players and that a man could be replaced without having been injured.'

PORTUGAL FAVOURITES

ENGLAND'S win over France has failed to convince bookmakers that they should be World Cup favourites.

The bookies still fancy free-scoring Portugal at 3/1, with England 7/2, West Germany and Hungary 4/1, Argentina 8/1, the Soviet Union 9/1, Uruguay 20/1 and North Korea 100/1.

NET LOSS

ENGLAND 66 is still on course to be the lowest-scoring World Cup.

The last finals, in Chile, saw a record low of 89 goals in 32 matches at an average of 2.8 per game.

With 24 matches played this time, the goals total is 58 at an average of 2.4. Unless at least 32 goals are scored in eight knockout games, the tournament will set an unwanted record.

Group One, featuring England, saw just nine goals – the same number Portugal scored in the top-scoring Group Three, in which there were 21 goals.

Group Two was second with 16 goals – nine of them conceded by Switzerland – while Group Four, topped by the Soviet Union, was the second-lowest scoring with 12.

Friday 22 July
Rest Day Five

GREAVES IS OUT

JIMMY GREAVES is out of England's quarter-final showdown with Argentina.

The Tottenham Hotspur forward needed stitches in a gashed shin suffered against France on Wednesday.

England's record goalscorer had been confident he would be ready for tomorrow's Wembley clash, saying he had played with worse injuries.

But today he was ruled out after an examination by England medical staff.

He laughed off claims the injury was a cover story for him being dropped, saying, 'Honestly, I had no chance of playing. The bruise has come out right up my leg. I couldn't really think about being there.'

Alf Ramsey, who will delay naming his side until tomorrow, may draft in Alan Ball or George Eastham and push Bobby Charlton into an even more advanced role. Alternatively, he could bring in West Ham United forward Geoff Hurst.

ALF NOBBY BOOST

FA CHIEFS today threw their weight behind Alf Ramsey in the row over Nobby Stiles.

The England manager is under pressure to drop Stiles after FIFA issued a public warning to the Manchester United player.

Stiles faces disciplinary action if there is any repeat of his foul play against France, when he was booked and then left Jacky Simon writhing in agony with a late challenge. Ramsey is fuming that Stiles has been singled out by FIFA and today he won a significant battle when the FA issued a statement making it clear the decision over whether Stiles faces Argentina will be the manager's.

Until Ramsey took charge, a selection committee picked England teams, but the former Ipswich Town boss took the job on the understanding he would have total control.

The FA statement is a clear sign that Ramsey has received assurances there will be no interference in team selection.

It read, 'The sole responsibility for picking the England side rests in the hands of Mr Ramsey, as it has always done.'

GONE TO THE DOGS

ARGENTINA are unhappy at being barred from training on the Wembley pitch ahead of tomorrow's quarter-final.

The South Americans should have had a 20-minute workout on the pitch this afternoon.

But they were turned away because Wembley officials wanted to get the stadium ready for this evening's greyhound meeting.

Argentina manager Juan Carlos Lorenzo, who was at least able to inspect the pitch, said, 'We would have liked to have tried out the pitch. I will tell my team all about it instead.'

Lorenzo is predicting a tight game, adding cryptically, 'I have watched England and they are good. We are afraid of all of them – and none of them.'

In Argentina, newspapers today questioned FIFA's choice of referees for the quarter-finals, saying West German and English referees should not be involved while their countries are still in the competition.

A German will take charge of England-Argentina, while an English official has been appointed for the Germans' clash with Uruguay.

MARZ MISSION

ARGENTINA defender Silvio Marzolini believes they will hit peak form against England.

The Boca Juniors full-back was in the side beaten 3-1 by the Three Lions in the World Cup four years ago.

But he warned today, 'Our team hasn't yet reached its peak. We think that will come at Wembley.

'We had a depressing defeat in Italy before we came to England. Only now are we getting over the blow to our confidence and regaining our rhythm.

'England will find us vastly different to the side they beat in 1962. I was in that side and we thought only of attack. This time we shall remember the lesson and pay attention to defence.

'One thing is for certain. We would much rather play England than Uruguay. If we had played Uruguay and lost, there would have been a tremendous scandal in Argentina.

'But losing against England at Wembley would hardly be a disaster. And, if we win…oh boy!'

Argentina have been censured by FIFA over rough play, but Marzolini, 25, has been honoured for 'outstanding play and sportsmanship'. Midlands football writers voted him Group Two's best player and, after being presented with a silver tankard, he said, 'I'm most gratified, but I feel this is an honour for the team as a whole.'

KOREA 'INVENTED FOOTBALL'

A TOP North Korean official today boasted: We invented football and we will win the World Cup.

Responding to suggestions that the Hornets are the weakest nation in the last eight, North Korean FA vice-president Kim Deuk-Joon insisted they had stars 'without equal' and would beat tournament favourites Portugal.

He said, 'You think that the Portuguese will reach the final? That is your opinion. Our opinion is different. We think WE will go to the Wembley final. We expect to win the World Cup.

'We know all there is to know about football. After all, we invented the game.

'We don't expect any trouble from Portugal. We didn't come over here to reach the quarter-finals. We came here to win the World Cup.

'I repeat, we invented football. Nobody taught us football. We did it ourselves. We have a history going back 2,000 years and were playing football long before the British.'

He added, 'Park Seung-Jin is the greatest player in the competition. If he was taller, he would be the greatest in the world. We have many stars. Shin Yung-Kyoo, Pak Doo-Ik, who scored the goal against Italy, and goalkeeper Lee Chan-Myung are without equal.'

The Hornets squad's average height is 5ft 5in but their FA chairman Kim Eung-Sir says facing the likes of powerhouse forwards Eusébio and José Torres tomorrow won't be a problem.

He said, 'We do not think our lack of inches is a great disadvantage. We have met taller teams already. We were better than them. It is ability on the ground that counts.

'Italy were tall and we beat them. And we have special tactics to counter Eusébio.'

The Hornets got an extra ten minutes on the Goodison Park pitch today when their interpreter left to make a broadcast for Korean radio – and Everton officials were unable to get across the message that the official 20-minute training slot was over.

Since relocating from the North-East, the squad have been using Brazil's team bus, with a label saying 'Korea' stuck over that of the deposed champions.

LACK OF FAITH

NORTH KOREA'S chances against Portugal have been written off – by their Jesuit host.

The Hornets have been staying at the Jesuit Spirituality Centre in Rainhill in the build-up to tomorrow's quarter-final.

The retreat's superior, Reverend Peter Blake, has enjoyed putting them up, but has little faith in their hopes of another upset.

He said, 'They are a splendid crowd. I am afraid, however, that they will be beaten by Portugal. But, for the sake of the peace of nations, I hope they score a goal.'

EARLY NIGHT

PORTUGAL'S players were sent to bed at seven o'clock tonight ahead of the biggest match of their lives.

Eusébio and Co. can make history by reaching a first semi-final by beating North Korea and coach Otto Glória brought their bedtime forward three hours to make sure they will be at their sharpest.

He said, 'This is the best way before our biggest match in the competition. Sleep does the players good. It takes their minds completely off things that happen around them.'

Brazil complained about Portugal's rough play, but Glória insisted they would not bully the Koreans.

He added, 'We shall be far too prepossessed with trying to play good, match-winning football to try on any rough stuff. Portugal have never tried to be tough with anybody, so why should we start now?'

DEUTSCHLAND UDDER ALLES

HELMUT SCHÖN took his West German squad for an afternoon on a Derbyshire cattle farm today – then ordered them to butcher Uruguay's defence.

The German coach and his squad were invited by local councillor George Peach to visit his farm, where he breeds British Friesians.

Schön, who earlier gave his players only a brief morning workout, believes they are ready to tackle a Uruguayan defence which frustrated England.

Asked what his orders will be ahead of the Hillsborough clash, Schön said, 'Attack! Attack hard, attack fast and, above all, attack relentlessly. We learned much from our game with the similarly-difficult Argentine defence.

'But now Uruguay cannot afford to have the same faith and reliance on defence as they did in the match with England, when they were quite content with a point.

'We have reached the knockout stage and draws are of no use. Although we must not do anything foolish, it must be remembered that the team that gets through must score a goal.

'Forget all this talk about Uruguay playing only defensive football. I want my men to be prepared should they try to shock us by suddenly changing their tactics.

'Against England, the Uruguayans slowed down the game very cleverly and England allowed them to dictate the tempo. We must not make that mistake. We must seize the initiative.

'We have potential goal power all along the line and this is not the time for being ultra-cautious. It takes courage, as well as skill, to march on from here.'

Uruguay trainer Omar Borrás said, 'Germany are a strong side and, above all, we must play to contain them. But this is sudden death, so we must score goals too.'

Around 10,000 German fans will be at Hillsborough in a crowd of around 40,000. They will see Helmut Haller, left out against Spain for tactical reasons, return in midfield.

EUR LOOKING GOOD

SOVIET UNION coach Nikolai Morozov has hailed resurgent Hungary as one Europe's top teams.

The USSR take on the Magyars tomorrow and Morozov promised they won't take them lightly.

He said, 'Hungary play the same style as we do and it will be a difficult game. Six months ago they had a crisis in their team, but they have overcome this and now they are one of the best sides in Europe.'

If the Soviets get through, Morozov would rather face Uruguay than West Germany.

He added, 'The Uruguayans have a lot of technical ability, but they tend to keep the ball to themselves too long. Germany are very strong physically and have the technical ability to match it. Their strong finishing makes them dangerous opponents.'

YOUNG AND HUNGARY

HUNGARY coach Lajos Baróti has urged fans not to expect too much of his exciting young team.

Their qualification at the expense of world champions Brazil has sparked comparisons with the Magical Magyars team of Ferenc Puskás and Co., who dominated football in the 1950s.

But Baróti sounded a note of caution ahead of tomorrow's quarter-final meeting with the USSR.

He said, 'This team has an average age of 21, so it is unfair to compare them with the Puskás team, whose average age was 27. Perhaps in two years' time we shall know just how good they are.'

THAT'S YOUR LOT

WORLD CUP chiefs have confirmed tomorrow's quarter-finals will be decided by the drawing of lots if they are still level after extra time.

Organisers have ruled out hastily-arranged replays, with the first semi-final due to be played barely 48 hours after the quarters.

FIFA says that, if required, the referee will make the draw on the pitch in the presence of the match commissar and one delegate from each team.

BOSS DODGES FLAK

COACH Vicente Feola will dodge fan protests in Brazil by staying in Europe – while his wife is under police guard at home.

The knives are out for Feola, 56, after the champions' early exit and fans even burnt an effigy of him during riots in Rio de Janeiro after the defeat by Portugal.

Players and officials, making the long journey home, expect an angry reception when they touch down in Rio on Monday.

But Feola is still in England and today he revealed he will stay to watch the rest of the tournament before going to West Germany and Italy on business. He said, 'By that time I hope the fuss will have died down in my country. From what I have heard, our team can expect a rough reception when they get to Rio.

'The authorities have put a police guard on my wife and my house in Rio for fear that some fans might try to do them harm.'

Saturday 23 July
Matchday Eight

West Germany v Uruguay (quarter-final)
3pm, Hillsborough, Sheffield

Portugal v North Korea (quarter-final)
3pm, Goodison Park, Liverpool

USSR v Hungary (quarter-final)
3pm, Roker Park, Sunderland

England v Argentina (quarter-final)
3pm, Wembley, London

HOTHEADS CRASH OUT
**West Germany 4 (Haller 11, 83, Beckenbauer 70, Seeler 75)
Uruguay 0
Sent off: Horacio Troche (Uruguay, 49); Héctor Silva
(Uruguay, 54)
Quarter-final, Hillsborough, Sheffield (att: 40,007)**

HELMUT SCHÖN today slammed Uruguay for losing their heads
as West Germany ruthlessly ended their World Cup hopes.

The South Americans could face action from FIFA after having
two men sent off by English referee Jim Finney.

The Germans, already leading through an early Helmut Haller
goal, made them pay for the two second-half dismissals with three
goals in the last 20 minutes.

Germany coach Schön said, 'They have great talent, yet they appear to have no idea of how to tackle properly. They lose their heads and their regard for the rules and bring all the trouble on themselves.

'I'm proud of the way my players kept their heads and I was glad we had such a firm referee.'

Uruguay coach Ondino Viera was angry with ref Finney and fumed, 'We will never again play in England.'

Trainer Omar Borrás said, 'We must agree the referee was right in sending off both players. It would have been fairer, though, if one of the German players had gone off too.'

The Hillsborough crowd made their feelings clear over this ill-tempered clash – but their boos weren't reserved for the Uruguayans.

Haller was jeered for alleged play-acting following the clash which led to Héctor Silva's sending-off. He appeared to be seriously injured, but then rejoined the action – even tearing off a bandage the physio had applied to his leg.

Schön claimed, 'Haller didn't want the Uruguayans to realise how hurt he was.

'He is a player with a lot of courage.'

Uruguay's plan to defend deep and counter-attack was quickly undone when Haller diverted a Sigi Held shot into the net.

The match soon developed into a physical battle. Both sides put in some heavy tackles, but the Uruguayans – and the Sheffield crowd – were unimpressed with the Germans' theatrics.

Uruguay, also upset when Karl-Heinz Schnellinger appeared to get away with handling on the goal line, self-destructed after half-time.

Four minutes into the second half, captain Horacio Troche was dismissed for an off-the-ball clash with Lothar Emmerich. Troche then slapped Uwe Seeler in the face as ref Finney ushered him off.

And after 54 minutes, Silva was sent off when he and Omar Caetano combined to hack down Haller.

Silva, who angrily confronted Haller as the German received treatment, had to be escorted off by four policemen.

Germany destroyed the nine men in the closing stages. Franz Beckenbauer scored with a low shot after beating several players, Seeler rifled in from the edge of the box and Haller exchanged passes with Seeler to slot in the fourth.

WEST GERMANY: Hans Tilkowski, Horst-Dieter Höttges, Karl-Heinz Schnellinger, Franz Beckenbauer, Willy Schulz, Wolfgang

Weber, Lothar Emmerich, Helmut Haller, Uwe Seeler (capt), Wolfgang Overath, Sigi Held.

URUGUAY: Ladislao Mazurkiewicz, Luis Ubiña, Omar Caetano, Héctor Salvá, Jorge Manicera, Horacio Troche (capt), Julio César Cortés, Néstor Gonçálvez, Héctor Silva, Pedro Rocha, Domingo Pérez.

EUSÉBIO GOES 4 IT
Portugal 5 (Eusébio 27, pen 43, 56, pen 59, Augusto 80)
North Korea 3 (Park Seung-Jin 1, Lee Dong-Woon 22, Jang Sung-Kook 25)
Quarter-final, Goodison Park, Liverpool (att: 40,248)

CAPTAIN Mário Coluna claimed Portugal never doubted they would beat North Korea today – despite trailing 3-0 after 25 minutes.

Four-goal Eusébio inspired one of the great World Cup comebacks to leave his country just two wins from glory. His scoring spree – including two penalties – wrecked brave Korea's hopes of becoming the first Asian side to reach the semi-finals.

The Hornets' dream looked like becoming a reality as they raced into a commanding lead.

But Portugal skipper Coluna insisted, 'We weren't disturbed at any time. We knew we would beat Korea. We know it will be different with England. If *they* get a couple of goals in front, *they* won't lose.'

Coach Otto Glória said the thrilling victory summed up their football philosophy, saying, 'Attack is our best defence. We don't like to play on defence. We don't know HOW to play on defence.

'We made mistakes in defence, but the Korean attack was good. I wasn't surprised at their speed and the tactics they used.

'It's too early to say what our chances are of winning the cup, but we certainly have a good chance, with some luck.'

The Koreans had said they did not fear Portugal – despite the Europeans' obvious height and strength advantages – and quickly showed why.

They led inside a minute when captain Park Seung-Jin fired a pass from Han Bong-Jin into the top corner. The lead was doubled after 22 minutes when goalkeeper José Pereira could only palm a Jang Sung-Kook cross into the path of Lee Dong-Woon.

The Goodison Park crowd chanted 'We want three' and the Hornets obliged when Jang Sung-Kook skipped past a defender and drove the ball past Pereira.

Crucially, though, Portugal got a goal back just two minutes later when Eusébio lashed in a José Augusto pass.

Eusébio made it 3-2 from the spot just before half-time, after José Torres was fouled, and got his hat-trick 11 minutes after the break with a thunderous shot.

With the Koreans on the ropes, Eusébio got his fourth from a second spot-kick after his run into the box was ended by a reckless challenge.

Portugal wrapped it up when Augusto headed in after Torres nodded a Eusébio corner across goal.

Benfica star Eusébio – now hot favourite to be the competition's top scorer – said, 'I am still a humble man, you understand. We came here shy and afraid for our first World Cup – not to shine, but to watch other players and to learn.

'We still cannot really believe how well we have done. We were very nervous and we will go on the pitch on Tuesday still not believing, although West Germany, not England, are the side we have always feared the most.'

North Korean FA chairman Kim Eung-Sir admitted they ran out of steam. He said, 'It was a good match and both teams played fine football. Our players fought very hard and we are very grateful to the people of Liverpool, who gave us such good support.

'Perhaps it would have been better if we had saved enough energy for the later stages of the game to make more positive attacks.

'Portugal are a good team with an impressive attack. They might win the competition. No.13 (Eusébio) was a good player.'

PORTUGAL: José Pereira, João Morais, Alexandre Baptista, Vicente, Hilário, Jaime Graça, Mário Coluna (capt), José Augusto, José Torres, Eusébio, António Simões.

NORTH KOREA: Lee Chan-Myung, Shin Yung-Kyoo, Lim Zoong-Sun, Ha Jung-Won, Oh Yoon-Kyung, Im Seung-Hwi, Park Seung-Jin (capt), Han Bong-Jin, Pak Doo-Ik, Lee Dong-Woon, Jang Sung-Kook.

PORK CHOPS HUNGARY
USSR 2 (Chislenko 5, Porkujan 46) Hungary 1 (Bene 57)
Quarter-final, Roker Park, Sunderland (att: 26,844)

VALERY PORKUJAN made it three goals in his first two internationals as the Soviet Union took another step towards a first world crown.

Hungary coach Lajos Baróti's fears that the USSR would be too powerful for his young side today proved all too real.

And the Soviets have an exciting new talent of their own to thank after 21-year-old Dynamo Kiev forward Porkujan – fresh from scoring two on his debut against Bulgaria – netted the winner.

Goalkeeper József Gelei gifted the USSR an early lead when he dropped an Eduard Malafeyev cross and Igor Chislenko pounced.

The Soviets, who now face West Germany as they bid to add the world championship to their 1960 European crown, doubled their lead just after the break.

The Hungarians gave away a needless free kick when Kálmán Mészöly pushed Malafeyev. While they were still disputing the decision, Galimzian Khusainov found the unmarked Porkujan and he buried the chance.

Hungary responded well and Ferenc Bene continued his record of scoring in every game by shooting home Flórián Albert's pass. They pushed for an equaliser and USSR goalkeeper Lev Yashin, back after missing the final group game to rest his injured knee, had to make a brilliant save from captain Ferenc Sipos's free kick.

With ten minutes left, Hungary missed their best chance to level when winger Gyula Rákosi missed his kick with the goal gaping.

The USSR have just 48 hours before facing West Germany and coach Nikolai Morozov refused to speculate on their chances.

He said, 'I never make predictions. We shall have to wait and see what happens in the semi-finals.'

USSR: Lev Yashin, Vladimir Ponomaryev, Vasily Danilov, Valery Voronin, Albert Shesternev (capt), Iosif Sabo, Galimzian Khusainov, Igor Chislenko, Anatoly Banishevsky, Eduard Malafeyev, Valery Porkujan.

HUNGARY: József Gelei, Sándor Mátrai, Benõ Káposzta, Kálmán Mészöly, Ferenc Sipos (capt), Gusztáv Szepesi, Ferenc Bene, István Nagy, Flórián Albert, Gyula Rákosi, János Farkas.

ARGENTINE 'ANIMALS'
England 1 (Hurst 78) Argentina 0
Sent off: Antonio Rattin (Argentina, 35)
Quarter-final, Wembley, London (att: 90,584)

ALF RAMSEY today branded Argentina 'animals' after this Wembley war.

England booked a semi-final date with Portugal thanks to Geoff Hurst's header in an ill-tempered match.

The game was held up for seven minutes after Argentina captain Antonio Rattin was controversially sent off and there were ugly scenes at the end as the South Americans angrily confronted referee Rudolf Kreitlein.

England manager Ramsey said, 'It seems a pity that so much Argentine talent is wasted. Our best football will come against the team who come out to play football and not act as animals.'

The West German referee struggled to keep control from the start in a game littered with petty fouls and off-the-ball incidents.

England – who actually conceded 33 fouls to Argentina's 19 – were frustrated by the South Americans' defensive tactics.

It may have been a different story had Kreitlein given a penalty for a challenge on Alan Ball after only four minutes.

Instead, the match became a stop-start war of attrition and the flashpoint came after 35 minutes when Rattin was dismissed for dissent.

The Argentina captain repeatedly questioned the referee's decisions and eventually, after one particularly prolonged protest, Kreitlein's patience snapped and he ordered him off.

Rattin refused to go and play was held up as Argentine officials came on to the pitch and a heated debate ensued between them, the match officials and FIFA representatives. At one point, Argentina looked set to walk off in protest.

Eventually Rattin was persuaded to go, although even then police had to intervene to stop him taking a seat on the bench and, finally, he made a slow walk back to the tunnel.

Even with ten men, Argentina's defence held firm and, with both sides tiring in soaring temperatures, it took the Three Lions until 12 minutes from the end to break through.

Hurst – in for the injured Jimmy Greaves – had come close early in the second half when goalkeeper Antonio Roma brilliantly turned his effort over the bar after the West Ham United man found himself clean through.

But Hurst finally came up with the killer blow when he glanced a header beyond Roma's reach from Hammers team-mate Martin Peters's chipped cross.

For the first time, Ramsey picked no wingers and instead used Peters and the recalled Ball to provide the width in a 4-4-2 formation.

Ramsey said, 'We were patient and it paid off. England played to win and win we did. We are afraid of no one.'

Ramsey broke his usual habit of not singling out individuals for praise, hailing Nobby Stiles for holding up under the pressure of being warned by FIFA over his conduct.

'I was delighted with him in view of the criticisms made recently about his strong play.

'Stiles was magnificent in the way he played the ball and in his conduct. Onega was considered the dangerman and Stiles played him so well he was hardly in the game.'

At the end, Ramsey stormed on to the pitch and stopped George Cohen swapping shirts with Alberto González.

There were unpleasant scenes as the players headed for the tunnel, with a number of Argentine players and officials confronting referee Kreitlein and his linesmen. Police and tournament officials rushed to their assistance and Kreitlein was escorted off.

ENGLAND: Gordon Banks, George Cohen, Ray Wilson, Nobby Stiles, Jack Charlton, Bobby Moore (capt), Alan Ball, Geoff Hurst, Bobby Charlton, Roger Hunt, Martin Peters.

ARGENTINA: Antonio Roma, Roberto Perfumo, Silvio Marzolini, Roberto Ferreiro, Rafael Albrecht, Antonio Rattin (capt), Jorge Solari, Alberto González, Luis Artime, Ermindo Onega, Oscar Mas.

'STAR SPAT IN MY FACE'

A FIFA official claims Argentina star Ermindo Onega spat in his face after today's stormy Wembley clash.

In shocking scenes as the teams left the pitch, referee Rudolf Kreitlein was jostled by Argentine players and officials.

One appeared to aim a blow at the West German and a posse of policemen and tournament officials dashed over to shepherd him to safety.

Match commissar and FIFA vice-president Harry Cavan, the man with overall responsibility for the match, said, 'I ran to the assistance of the referee when he was being kicked and jostled by Argentine players and officials as he was leaving the field.

'I took one of their players by the shoulder to turn him round, so that I could note his number. It was number 20, Onega, and he spat in my face. I have seen players disappointed after losing – in tears even – but this was mass hysteria. It was frightening. The scuffles continued down the tunnel into the dressing rooms, with the police coming to our assistance.'

REFFIN' SHAMEFUL

ANGRY Argentina players today blamed referee Rudolf Kreitlein for their controversial defeat.

The West German official stunned the South Americans by sending off captain Antonio Rattin for dissent.

Midfielder Jorge Solari, among those booked as Kreitlein struggled to keep control of the match, complained, 'Who can win against a referee? It's impossible. We were the better team.'

Forward Oscar Mas said, 'It's incredible. I never thought they would eliminate us in this manner. I never thought this could happen in a World Cup.'

Earlier in the tournament, FIFA warned Argentina about their conduct after Rafael Albrecht was sent off in an ill-tempered group match against West Germany.

Defender Roberto Ferreiro said, 'I really can't believe it. The Germans kicked us all the time and nothing happened, but they sent off Albrecht. Now they sent off Rattin because he is correctly questioning a foul that only exists in the imagination of the referee.

'We played well. If Rattin had not been sent off, we would have won.'

Playmaker Ermindo Onega, the man accused of spitting at FIFA vice-president Harry Cavan in the ugly post-match scenes, said, 'Our plan was working to perfection. I'm sure we would have won if we had continued with 11.'

And defender Albrecht agreed, 'Until Rattin was sent off, we were controlling the game. They could only shoot from distance. They were no danger to us. Even with ten men we were the better team.'

BAD PENNY

ARGENTINA forward Alberto González has admitted they hoped to beat England on the toss of a coin.

The South Americans were forced to play for 55 minutes with ten men and their blanket defence held out until just 12 minutes from the end. There would have been no replay had the match remained level after extra time and González said, 'We were playing defensively hoping to last out for the toss of a coin.'

VERY CROSS, THE MERSEY

THOUSANDS of fans look set to boycott Monday's Goodison Park semi-final after FIFA confirmed the hosts will play at Wembley.

World Cup chiefs today decided England-Portugal will be held at the national stadium on Tuesday, while Goodison hosts the West Germany-USSR match.

FIFA secretary general Helmut Kaiser said the decision was taken so more fans could watch the England match. But thousands of fans in the North-West bought tickets for Monday on the assumption England would play there if they reached the last four.

Everton chairman Edward Holland Hughes said the decision was a snub to Northern fans and left organisers open to accusations of bias towards England.

He said, 'Naturally we are disappointed. We had been led to believe that, if England reached this stage, the privilege of receiving England would be ours.

'The football-loving public of the North have been ignored and deprived of seeing the England side.

'In Lancashire – and Liverpool in particular – we have a football-loving public who would have risen to the opportunity in a manner which London certainly will not be able to.'

He claimed the tie should have been staged at Goodison so 'it could not be suggested that England had received favoured nation treatment by apparently having the monopoly of Wembley'.

Fans reacted with anger. Francis Griffin, who has attended all four matches at Goodison, said, 'It's a very bad thing for England to play all their games on one ground. It does smack of a fiddle.'

And Trevor Skempton, another supporter who block-booked tickets for the Goodison fixtures, complained, 'A promise had been made that England would play at Goodison. This decision is the biggest insult that Liverpool has had for years.'

The confusion may have been fuelled by conflicting information in the FA and FIFA tournament handbooks and by schedules published in many newspapers.

The FA publication says, 'If successful in the quarter-finals, England will proceed to Liverpool to play the semi-final at the ground of Everton FC on July 25. The party will travel to Liverpool on July 24.'

Many newspapers have been running tournament schedules stating that the winners of Group One will play their quarter-final at Wembley and then, if they win that, play at Goodison. But the FIFA handbook states, 'The two semi-final matches will be played at Everton on July 25 and Wembley on July 26, but the actual allocation of grounds will not be made until the competing teams are known.'

Sid Rudd, secretary of the World Cup liaison committee in Liverpool, said, 'While I, like everybody else, would have liked to have seen England play here, at no time did FIFA issue any literature to say at which venue the teams would play the semi-finals.

'People have assumed things, but there has never been anything in writing from FIFA.'

PELÉ 1970 SNUB

PELÉ has sensationally revealed he WON'T play at the next World Cup.

The Brazil superstar is crestfallen over the brutal treatment he received as the world champions crashed out at the group stage.

And now he says he will retire at some point in the next two years because 'ideal football has become impossible'.

The 25-year-old, who suffered knee ligament damage as Brazil crashed out against Portugal, said, 'At the next World Cup in Mexico, I shall not be there. I'm not sad in defeat, only that I haven't been allowed to play football. Ideal football has become impossible.

'This is terrible for the spectators, who want a show. This has been obvious with the English crowds. They are not as fanatical as at home, but are more discerning. They appreciated good football, whichever the team.'

BUMPER TV DEAL

ENGLISH football chiefs have signed a lucrative new deal for domestic television coverage.

But the contract – worth £80,000 – includes tough restrictions on live coverage amid growing concern over the impact football on TV is having on attendances.

The Football League and FA, worried about dwindling domestic crowds, have noted the huge viewing figures for live World Cup matches, with some pushing 20m.

Under the new deal, the ONLY English club match to be screened live will be the FA Cup Final.

Midweek highlights coverage will be rotated between BBC and ITV, with up to 45 minutes to be shown, but not before 9.45pm.

ITV will screen highlights on Sunday afternoons, while the BBC will switch its experimental Saturday night show *Match of the Day*, which features one match played that day, from BBC2 to BBC1.

ONLY HERE FOR THE BEER

BEER is still a clear winner for English fans when it comes to World Cup tipples.

Wembley chiefs tried to add a touch of continental style by ordering in white and red wine for the tournament, but sales have been disappointing.

In contrast, sales nationwide of Watney's limited edition World Cup Ale have been so good that the firm may keep selling it after the tournament.

A Watney's spokesman said, 'It looks the same as our light ale, but it's just that little bit stronger.'

Sunday 24 July
Rest Day Six

ARGENTINA BAN THREAT

ARGENTINA were today told they will be banned from the next World Cup unless they promise to behave.

The ultimatum came after a meeting of FIFA top brass in Kensington over the ugly scenes which marred yesterday's defeat by England.

FIFA chiefs say Argentina will be refused entry for Mexico 70 'unless certain assurances are given as to the conduct of their team officials and players'.

Captain Antonio Rattin – who took seven minutes to leave the Wembley pitch after being sent off – has been banned for four internationals.

Team-mates Roberto Ferreiro and Ermindo Onega have both been hit with three-match suspensions and the Argentine FA has been fined the maximum £83 6s 8d.

FIFA said Onega had been banned 'for having spat in the face of the official commissar' Harry Cavan.

And the disciplinary committee found Ferreiro guilty of assaulting referee Rudolf Kreitlein as he left the pitch.

A FIFA statement said Argentina had 'by their misbehaviour brought the game into disrepute' and had ignored demands issued before the tournament and after their game against West Germany 'for displays of good football and conduct which would enhance the reputation of the competition'.

They were deemed guilty of 'flagrant breaches of the laws of the game' and had shown 'disregard for discipline and good order'.

The statement added, 'Other South American teams taking part in the tournament lost with dignity and without besmirching the reputation of the tournament or bringing the game into disrepute. The attack on the referee after the game by players – particularly number eight, Ferreiro – and by team officials was particularly regrettable.

'The referee would have been justified in bringing a charge against certain players for assault, but he informed the police that he did not wish to do so.'

England brothers Jack and Bobby Charlton – both booked on Saturday – have been warned about their future conduct.

FIFA vice-president Cavan said after the meeting, 'The fine may seem ridiculous when you consider that Argentina will be taking home about £20,000 from the World Cup.

'We couldn't do any more than impose the maximum fine because of FIFA regulations.'

ROUS 'MORON' SLUR

A TOP Argentinian official says FIFA president Sir Stanley Rous would be 'a moron' to ban them from the next World Cup.

The South Americans reacted with outrage today at being told they will be excluded from Mexico 70 unless they promise to behave.

Juan Santiago, leader of the Argentine World Cup delegation, said, 'We have been very unjustly treated. Words cannot express my anger. If we are refused entry, Sir Stanley Rous is rather a moron – that is my personal opinion. By saying Argentina cannot enter in 1970, maybe FIFA just want to make sure that England or other European countries always win the World Cup?

'The referee was absolutely to blame for all the fighting and for us threatening to leave the field. We will demand that he is expelled from the FIFA list. He is not up to international standards.'

Argentine FA vice-president Fernando Menéndez Behety insisted, 'It is impossible to give a guarantee in advance of the behaviour of a team and its officials.

'I do not approve of the conduct of our players and officials yesterday, but they were provoked by the referee. He was absolutely biased in favour of England.

'The referee and those who selected him were responsible for the trouble. He was against Argentina from the start.

'I apologise to the huge Wembley crowd for our not being able to show them that we can play skilful football. Antonio Rattin has told me he only insisted on asking for an interpreter in order to ask the referee why he was continually pulling up his men.

'Argentines are not dirty players. They have never broken opponents' legs. Who was badly hurt in the England side after yesterday's match? No one! I think this World Cup is probably a failure.'

ALF NOT WELCOME

ALF RAMSEY will be barred from entering Argentina as England boss after his 'animals' outburst.

The Three Lions manager infuriated the South Americans with his post-match comments following yesterday's quarter-final.

Today Argentine officials reacted by slapping a ban on Ramsey visiting the country in an official capacity.

Responding to Ramsey's comments, Argentine FA vice-president Fernando Menéndez Behety said, 'That is not very sporting from him, being an official of the home team.

'When I invite someone into my house, I do not treat him as an animal. Argentina has decided that Mr Ramsey will not be able to go to Argentina as an official. As a citizen he can go, but not as an official in football games.'

In a bizarre outburst, Juan Santiago, leader of the Argentine World Cup delegation, said, 'His charge of Wembley animals is beneath him and beneath us. Either he was not in a normal state of mind or drugged.'

Argentina manager Juan Carlos Lorenzo also condemned Ramsey, saying, 'What an incredible thing to say. This statement seems to be beneath Mr Ramsey. We are most downhearted over all this.

'Now all we want to do is get out of England and go home. The World Cup has been spoiled for us.'

REF: IT WAS A DISGRACE

REFEREE Rudolf Kreitlein today revealed he sent off Argentina captain Antonio Rattin for the way he LOOKED at him.

The West German, who does not speak Spanish, admitted he could not understand what Rattin was saying.

He explained, 'I sent Rattin off because he was following me and shouting at me. I had no option. He was trying to be the referee.

'I couldn't understand Rattin, but I could read in his face and actions just what he was saying. The look on Rattin's face was quite enough to tell me what he was saying and meaning. I do not speak Spanish, but the look told me everything.'

The Stuttgart tailor reacted angrily to claims he was biased towards England as part of a pro-European conspiracy.

'That is a ridiculous accusation,' he said. 'I have refereed matches all over the world and this was undoubtedly the roughest I've ever refereed. It was terrible – a disgrace.

'I have been told by FIFA that I could take out assault charges for what happened as I left the field. I shall not take any action against the Argentine players and officials who assaulted me. I just want to forget the whole dreadful experience.

'Some Argentinians pushed me about a little. The whole thing made me boiling mad, but now I just want to forget it.'

Kreitlein, a referee for 20 years, welcomed today's disciplinary verdict, saying, 'I am so happy FIFA have backed me up.'

RATTIN: REFS BIASED

ANTONIO RATTIN claims England will win the World Cup because referees are biased towards them.

The Argentina captain, banned after he was sent off by West German referee Rudolf Kreitlein, said today, 'The four-match suspension is savage. I would like to know what the judge of the court said – what he wrote down as his reason.

'I was sent off simply because I asked for one minute with an interpreter because the German referee could not understand me.

'After I was sent off, there were all kinds of kicks, bangs and tackles, but no one was sent off. So why was I sent off?

'The English people should erect a big monument to this referee. He was very, very good to England. All I can say is that England will win the World Cup because the referees are on their side.'

Argentina manager Juan Carlos Lorenzo said, 'I do not know why Rattin was sent off, so obviously I cannot understand the suspension. It is all completely unjust.'

BRIT EMBASSY ALERT

ARMED guards are protecting the British Embassy in Buenos Aires amid anti-English protests.

Embassy staff have been bombarded with hundreds of angry telephone calls and police have been stationed outside to protect staff.

Argentine newspapers have accused FIFA of a conspiracy against South American teams.

They pointed to the fact a West German refereed the England-Argentina game and sent off Antonio Rattin, while it was English official Jim Finney who dismissed two Uruguayans in their defeat by the Germans.

One Argentine newspaper, *Cronica*, raged, 'The English stole the game. They are still the pirates that pillaged the Caribbean and stole the Malvinas.'

Argentine President, General Juan Carlos Onganía, has issued a statement hailing the team as heroes. He told them, 'Your brilliant performance, your courage and fighting spirit have earned you the joyful welcome which awaits you from the people and government of the nation.'

NEW RATTIN TIFF

ARGENTINA narrowly avoided another row tonight – when they turned up 55 minutes late for a ministerial reception.

The government laid on the event as a thank you to the losing quarter-final nations, with the Earl of Harewood presenting each country with a crystal trophy. But the reception, hosted by Minister for Sport Denis Howell, almost became the centre of a new controversy when the Argentine party initially failed to show up.

They apologised when they eventually arrived nearly an hour late, saying their coach driver had got lost on the journey from their hotel in Welwyn Garden City, Herts.

Minister Howell shook hands with captain Antonio Rattin, whose sending-off against England sparked the Wembley controversy.

SIGN OF BAD LOSERS

A PAIR of young autograph hunters got a nasty surprise after getting the signatures of two Uruguay players.

Sheffield kids Jean Blagden, 12, and brother John, nine, waited outside the Hillsborough dressing rooms after West Germany's 4-0 win yesterday.

And they were thrilled when two Uruguayans signed their autograph books. But when they had the players' messages translated from Spanish, delight turned to surprise.

One read, 'The referee is a thief.' The other said, 'German thieves stole the game from Uruguay.'

FIFA disciplinary chiefs meet tomorrow to discuss the dismissals of captain Horacio Troche and Héctor Silva in their defeat by the Germans.

HOTSHOT 'UNSTOPPABLE'

PORTUGAL selector Manuel Afonso has tipped Eusébio to destroy semi-final rivals England.

The Benfica forward hit four goals in the comeback win against North Korea and Afonso warned, 'No one can stop Eusébio the way he is playing now.'

But England manager Alf Ramsey believes his defence can shackle Eusébio and the aerial threat of José Torres.

Ramsey said, 'You can be sure of one thing – Eusébio will not be scoring four goals on Tuesday. And Jackie Charlton is capable of looking after Torres.'

HERO IS NO ALI

EUSÉBIO insists he won't follow the example of boxing superstar Muhammad Ali by using his fame in the battle against racism.

The American fighter – in England to defend his world heavyweight title against Britain's Brian London – frequently speaks out on race issues and even changed his name from Cassius Clay because he believes that was his 'slave name'.

But Portugal forward Eusébio insisted, 'I do not approve of Cassius. I have never had to fight a colour bar, but even if I were urged to, I would never make a racial platform of my sport.

'It would spoil it for me. I am a simple man, born to kick a ball. This is my happiness and it is enough. I want nothing more.'

MOORE THAN A GAME

BOBBY MOORE says England's win over Argentina has convinced the players they are destined to win the World Cup.

The Three Lions captain said, 'In every cup competition, there is always a game that everybody knows is *the one*. This was *the one*. All the lads thought the same about this match.

'They were the toughest team I have seen and with great players, too. But we have done it. Roll on the next one.'

BETTER THAN PELÉ

BOBBY CHARLTON is harder to stop than Pelé, according to the man who has had to man-mark both.

Portugal midfielder Vicente has faced the Brazilian superstar on numerous occasions, but he admits he fears the England ace more going into Tuesday's semi-final.

The Belenenses player, who has twice come up against Charlton in internationals, said, 'He is more difficult to mark than Pelé.

'Pelé goes only one way – forward. Charlton will go back 50 yards to gain two. He is the man to draw you out of position.'

However, Portugal coach Otto Glória today admitted Vicente may not be fit for the Wembley showdown.

He said, 'The question of how Vicente might play against Bobby Charlton depends on whether he can play at all.'

Portugal are also sweating on the fitness of João Morais – the defensive hardman whose brutal hack on Pelé rendered him virtually lame.

Glória will ask FIFA to allow Portugal extra time training at Wembley. The rules usually only allow a 20-minute visit.

He said, 'Wembley is the cathedral of football and we are happy to play there. We are more concerned about playing England than worrying about Wembley.

'England have played four successive matches at Wembley and that is obviously to their advantage. We would like to go there twice before Tuesday. If it is not possible, then we want to train on this famous pitch for longer than 20 minutes.'

SOVIET WALL OF SILENCE

SOVIET UNION chiefs are hiding their stars behind an iron curtain of silence ahead of tomorrow's semi-final with West Germany.

Access to the USSR players has been limited during the tournament and there was no change today for reporters hoping for interviews at the Lymm Hotel in Cheshire.

Soviet Vice-Minister for Sport Leonid Nikonov gave a brief press conference alongside coach Nikolai Morozov.

Nikonov said reporters might be able to speak to players tomorrow morning, but added, 'Please, not at any other time. No talking to the players or anything like that.'

Nikonov, who said the team won't be named until tomorrow, admitted the Germans posed a major threat to Soviet hopes.

'They play very beautifully,' he said. 'They are physically very well prepared. They are very strong. They are all good technically, very skilled. They are also good tactically. Therefore this game will be very serious.'

Asked if the USSR would win the World Cup, Nikonov would only say, 'The French have a saying. That it is a bad soldier who does not think of being a marshal.'

West Germany coach Helmut Schön has had the Soviets scouted and believes his side can reach the final.

He said, 'One of our trainers saw their quarter-final with Hungary and reported back. Russia are a very good team. But we have the technical ability to win and we believe in ourselves.'

179

KEEPER'S CATCH

LEV YASHIN today showed he is still a big fish for the Soviet Union.

The goalkeeper joked when he arrived in England clutching a fishing rod that he was only here for the angling.

And when the USSR relocated to the Lymm Hotel, Cheshire, he wasted no time in trying his luck at nearby Lymm Dam.

Soviet Vice-Minister for Sport Leonid Nikonov revealed, 'It was his first fishing expedition in England and he caught two big fish.'

Monday 25 July
Matchday Nine

West Germany v USSR (semi-final)
7.30pm, Goodison Park, Liverpool

GERMANS MARCH ON
West Germany 2 (Haller 43, Beckenbauer 67)
USSR 1 (Porkujan 88)
Sent off: Igor Chislenko (USSR, 44)
Semi-final, Goodison Park, Liverpool (att: 38,273)

WEST GERMANY are one step from a second world title – with Soviet Union legend Lev Yashin blamed for wrecking his nation's chances of their first.

Goals from Helmut Haller and Franz Beckenbauer downed a USSR side hampered by a sending-off and a player handicapped by a serious injury.

But USSR coach Nikolai Morozov insisted a blunder by Yashin was the decisive moment.

Morozov moaned, 'The first goal was totally unexpected, but I feel, and I have told Yashin this, that he was to blame for the second goal.'

The match was a disappointing spectacle and Italian referee Concetto Lo Bello had his work cut out as the teams went toe-to-toe in a physical battle.

Influential Soviet midfielder Iosif Sabo was a passenger for much of the match after twisting his ankle in an early challenge with Beckenbauer. And two disastrous minutes for Igor Chislenko just before the break really put the Soviets on the back foot.

Chislenko was left hobbling by a tackle from Karl-Heinz Schnellinger, who then charged forward to set up Haller for the opener. Moments after the Soviets kicked off again, the limping Chislenko blatantly fouled Sigi Held and he became the first European to be sent off in the competition.

Chances were at a premium after the break, but the Germans were given breathing space when Beckenbauer fired in from the edge of the box as Yashin stayed rooted to the spot.

Valery Porkujan did give the USSR hope when he pounced after goalkeeper Hans Tilkowski spilled the ball. That meant the forward, who only made his debut in the final group game, has scored in all three of his international appearances.

But, despite a half-chance when Anatoly Banishevsky headed over, the Germans held on to reach a first final since their 1954 triumph.

USSR coach Morozov admitted, 'We have no objection to the referee's sending-off decision.

'There was no deliberate kicking. You must understand that the Germans were so good technically that our players had difficulty with their tackles.'

Of the injury to key man Sabo, he added, 'He had a pain-killing injection during the interval, but his injury was still a handicap.'

West Germany coach Helmut Schön denied his side were guilty of gamesmanship in the sending-off, saying, 'There is no provocation from my team. Everybody could see what happened tonight. Chislenko was injured by a fair tackle and he ran after our player and committed a bad foul.'

He added, 'I think it was not a good game, but occasionally there was some good football played.

'We are very glad we have reached the final and we hope we can refresh ourselves in the next five days.

'It is very difficult to play an important quarter-final and then the semi-final with only two days' rest. Uwe Seeler has shoulder and back injuries and goalkeeper Hans Tilkowski is also injured.'

Schön will be hoping key man Beckenbauer faces no further action after he was booked again.

WEST GERMANY: Hans Tilkowski, Friedel Lutz, Karl-Heinz Schnellinger, Franz Beckenbauer, Willy Schulz, Wolfgang Weber, Lothar Emmerich, Helmut Haller, Uwe Seeler (capt), Wolfgang Overath, Sigi Held.

USSR: Lev Yashin, Vladimir Ponomaryev, Vasily Danilov, Valery Voronin, Albert Shesternev (capt), Iosif Sabo, Galimzian Khusainov, Igor Chislenko, Anatoly Banishevsky, Eduard Malafeyev, Valery Porkujan.

FANS SNUB SEMI

FED-UP fans gave tonight's semi-final the cold shoulder amid anger over England's match being played at Wembley.

Merseyside supporters wanted England-Portugal to be staged at Goodison Park and thousands boycotted West Germany's win over the USSR.

Only 38,273 turned out, with many who had tickets not bothering to show up. More than 58,000 had watched Portugal beat Brazil in a group game at the same stadium.

Touts gave away batches of tickets and Everton Supporters' Club chairman George Bailey said, 'It's a good job the England semi-final wasn't on television tonight at the same time as this game – the ground would have been empty.'

Some fans inside the ground showed their anger by displaying banners condemning the decision for England to play in London.

Police removed banners saying 'Down with FIFA. England for the cup' and 'Fix. Insult. Best fans'.

REF-KICK STAR BANNED

URUGUAY midfielder Julio César Cortés was today banned for SIX internationals for kicking English referee Jim Finney.

FIFA's disciplinary committee dished out the punishment after finding him guilty of committing the offence at the end of Uruguay's quarter-final defeat by West Germany.

Sent-off duo Horacio Troche and Héctor Silva will serve three-match suspensions.

CRISIS SUMMIT

A SOUTH AMERICAN crisis meeting tomorrow could spark a major split in world football.

Officials from Argentina, Chile, Uruguay and Brazil will meet in London to discuss their claims of pro-European refereeing bias.

All four countries are out – three of them in controversial circumstances – with the semi-finalists all coming from Europe.

Four of the five players sent off in the competition have been South Americans and there has been criticism of the appointment of English and West German referees for each other's quarter-finals.

FIFA has threatened Argentina with expulsion from the next World Cup after the scenes which overshadowed their defeat by England, but one Buenos Aires newspaper claimed today, 'England made a deal with the referee to sell us out.'

Newspapers in Italy, France, Spain and Switzerland have all criticised FIFA, saying referees from England and Germany should not have been involved when the two countries were still in the competition.

Now South American football chiefs are ready to take on FIFA in a battle that could throw the international game into turmoil.

Brazilian Confederation of Sport president Dr João Havelange, speaking in Lisbon, claimed he had never seen a World Cup so badly organised.

Havelange said, 'In Brazil, my guests travel first-class, but in England the Brazilian team had sometimes to travel second-class. FIFA should review their methods and have more respect for us.'

He also criticised what he claimed was 'the abrupt change of the playing of the semi-finals from Liverpool to London, making Portugal travel, while England stayed where they were'.

Uruguayan newspapers have slammed English referee Finney for sending off two of their players against West Germany.

One, *El Dia*, wrote, 'Because of the excesses and very bad performance of the referee, Uruguay's good start was undermined.'

The Peruvian Football Federation today promised to back Argentina, Brazil and Uruguay in what it called 'the battle against FIFA'.

RAMSEY FIFA RAP

ALF RAMSEY has been warned by world football bosses over his controversial 'animals' outburst.

He said after the win over Argentina that England would play better against opponents who 'come out to play football and not act as animals'.

The comment infuriated Argentine officials and, at a meeting in Liverpool today, FIFA chiefs called on the English FA to have words with Ramsey.

The world governing body has written to the FA to 'bring their attention to the unfortunate remarks made by Mr Ramsey'.

GREAVES SEMI KO

JIMMY GREAVES will miss out on the chance to shoot England into their first World Cup Final.

A shin injury kept England's record goalscorer out of the quarter-final win over Argentina.

West Ham United forward Geoff Hurst was drafted in for the Tottenham Hotspur man and scored the winner.

Doubts remain over former Chelsea and AC Milan star Greaves's fitness, so Alf Ramsey will field an unchanged team for the biggest game in England's history.

CLASH OF STILES

EUSÉBIO today pleaded for protection from England midfield hardman Nobby Stiles.

The Manchester United player is walking a disciplinary tightrope after FIFA warned him last week over his future conduct.

And Portugal sensation Eusébio cranked up the pressure ahead of tomorrow's semi-final when he said, 'I hope it is not too physical, but that is up to the referee. I hope the referee is fair to both sides.

'Stiles is a hard man. I don't mind playing against him – I am not afraid. But the referee must watch him very, very carefully.

'He has been allowed to get away with too many things. I have watched England's games on television and seen Stiles going in a bit hard. If we do these things, we have our numbers taken. But Stiles has too often been left alone by referees.'

Eusébio, shackled by Stiles in both legs of Benfica's European Cup quarter-final defeat by United this season, added, 'I am used to being closely marked. All I hope is that the referee is firm and fair.

'I didn't think this was so in England's match against the Argentine. The referee saw the worst fouls of the Argentine players, but ignored those of England. England gave away more fouls, but it was Rattin who was sent off.

'Why was he sent off? He didn't do anything and the referee, a German, couldn't speak Spanish, so how could he say that Rattin said something to him? The referee must have been guessing and Rattin was entitled to speak as captain.'

The Mozambique-born forward, top scorer with seven goals, believes the burden of expectation on the hosts will help Portugal at Wembley. He added, 'The public have been wonderful to me. I like the English people very much. I feel that, with luck, we can beat England. They have so much pressure on them and cannot afford to lose. They will never have another chance like this to win the World Cup.

'Winning is not so important to us, so we can play our natural game. I prefer playing in front of a big crowd, whichever side they support, because the atmosphere is better.

'England, it is true, have a good defence, but we haven't seen England's defence tested yet. The teams they have played against only defended, so England weren't under pressure.

'With us, it will be different. We are an attacking team and we will be attacking tomorrow.

'The strain will be on England, because they are at home and the crowd want them to win. For us, there is nothing to lose. I hope to score one or two, but I cannot make any forecasts. How many I score is up to God.'

BRAZIL DON'T GO NUTS

BRAZIL'S World Cup flops got off lightly today as fans stayed away when they arrived home.

Armed police were posted at Rio de Janeiro and Sao Paulo airports to protect the players and officials from expected protests.

But no fans turned up and the cops were able to stand by and watch as the deposed champions were greeted by their loved ones.

HUNGARY BOSS QUITS

HUNGARY coach Lajos Baróti today revealed he is quitting to spare his 'frayed nerves'.

The long-time Magyars boss wanted out before the tournament, but he was persuaded by the nation's football chiefs to carry on.

Baróti took his side to the last eight before their run was finally ended by the USSR. He said, 'For me, my duties came to a close with this World Cup.

'I have been in charge since 1957 and my nerves have been frayed for the past nine years. We have been unlucky in top international tournaments like the World Cups in Chile and England.'

BOOKIES BACK GERMANS

WEST GERMANY were tonight installed as the new World Cup favourites after booking their place in Saturday's final.

Bookmakers rate them 6/5 favourites, with Portugal 2/1 and England 3/1 ahead of tomorrow's second semi-final.

Tuesday 26 July
Matchday Ten

England v Portugal (semi-final)
7.30pm, Wembley, London

BOBBY DOUBLE DELIGHT
England 2 (B. Charlton 30, 80) Portugal 1 (Eusébio pen 82)
Semi-final, Wembley, London (att: 94,493)

ALF RAMSEY tonight hailed this his 'greatest' victory after England reached the World Cup Final for the first time.

The usually-reserved England manager's delight was obvious after two-goal Bobby Charlton set up a Wembley showdown with West Germany on Saturday.

Ramsey – burdened by the expectations of a nation and his own promise that England will win the World Cup – described reaching the final as 'the most important thing in our lives'.

He said, 'There is nothing quite like it. This is undoubtedly the greatest victory since I took over. The team did everything that could be asked of it. Portugal have played very good football in reaching the semi-finals, but I think tonight they probably played better than ever. It is a pity anyone had to lose.'

Ramsey paid tribute to the crowd – with a nod to fans on Merseyside, who were left disappointed when the semi-final wasn't staged there.

He said, 'The crowd gave us great incentive. It was as if Liverpool had transferred some of their supporters to Wembley.'

The England manager admitted he was concerned when his side took so long to extend their lead in the second half after Charlton sent them in at the break 1-0 ahead.

'We lost a little of our composure in the second half,' he said. 'But I believe this was understandable following our punishing match on Saturday.

'Some of the players were in distress in the second half against Argentina because of the heat and occasionally we saw the effects of this tonight.'

The aftermath of that ill-tempered quarter-final had dominated the build-up to this match.

Yet England and Portugal brought a smile back to the face of this World Cup with an open, attacking match in which the first foul didn't come until 22 minutes were on the clock.

The hosts lived up to Ramsey's promise of playing their best football against another team who were willing to attack.

An injury meant Vicente, the man who would have man-marked Charlton, was ruled out and the Manchester United playmaker was outstanding.

England looked dangerous throughout the first half and they got the opener after half an hour when Roger Hunt beat defender José Carlos and, when goalkeeper José Pereira slid in to block him, the ball broke for Charlton to slot it home.

It wasn't until ten minutes from the end that England doubled their lead when Geoff Hurst laid the ball back for Charlton to slam a powerful shot high into the net.

If the England fans thought it was all over, they were mistaken. Just two minutes later, Jack Charlton blatantly handled on the line to keep out a José Torres header after goalkeeper Gordon Banks was beaten. Eusébio sent Banks the wrong way from the spot.

There was still time for two heart-stopping moments. Torres beat Jack Charlton in the air to set up António Simões, but he shot wide. And in the dying seconds, Banks produced a superb save when captain Mário Coluna thundered in a dipping shot.

England held on to spark joyous and relieved celebrations. Now Ramsey will turn his attention to West Germany.

No German team have ever beaten England and Ramsey's men have won home and away against West Germany in the past 14 months.

Ramsey said, 'This should be an extremely good match. Germany are a very good and well-balanced side. But I do not expect them to provide a bigger challenge to us than Portugal did tonight.

'We have seen several of Germany's matches on television and we shall watch some more before Saturday.'

The manager said he was hopeful Jimmy Greaves's shin injury 'should heal in the next few days'.

ENGLAND: Gordon Banks, George Cohen, Ray Wilson, Nobby Stiles, Jack Charlton, Bobby Moore (capt), Alan Ball, Geoff Hurst, Bobby Charlton, Roger Hunt, Martin Peters.

PORTUGAL: José Pereira, Alberto Festa, Alexandre Baptista, José Carlos, Hilário, Jaime Graça, Mário Coluna (capt), José Augusto, José Torres, Eusébio, António Simões.

ALF AND SAFETY

ALF RAMSEY was watching his words tonight as he tried to draw a line under the Argentina 'animals' row.

The England manager infuriated the South Americans with his outburst in a TV interview shortly after the quarter-final win.

FIFA has written to the FA drawing its attention to Ramsey's comments and disciplinary action against the Three Lions boss could follow.

Tonight he was at pains to avoid any further trouble, saying, 'I had better be careful what I say, as every word will be recorded.

'My choice of words on the previous occasion was unfortunate, but it is more unfortunate that I should be subjected to this pressure.

'But that does not excuse my choice of words. Perhaps the least said about it, the better.'

OTTO TIPS ENGLAND

PORTUGAL coach Otto Glória is backing England to go on and win the World Cup.

After watching England end his side's dream of glory in their first finals, Glória has no doubts they will be too good for West Germany.

He said, 'Play like you did tonight and the World Cup is yours on Saturday. This was the REAL final.

'The Germans are very strong in their play, but they are technically inferior to England. England play football as it should be played. England play with the heart. Germany are apt to rely on physical force.

'England are the best team we have met in the tournament. Hungary have a very balanced attack and are as good as England, except in the closing stages of the build-up towards goal.'

FIFA has been criticised for allowing England to play again at Wembley, but Glória added, 'I don't think it affected the result.

England's public gave them terrific support and I feel it would have been the same wherever in England we had met them.'

FAME GAME

ENGLAND'S defence are so good that Eusébio would have needed to be 'a god' to have got the better of them.

That was the verdict of Portugal coach Otto Glória after seeing the Three Lions tame the star of the tournament.

The World Cup's top scorer took his tally to eight, but his only success came from the penalty spot.

Glória said, 'Eusébio paid the price of fame tonight. He was marked closely and only a god could have done better than he did.'

Eusébio had appealed for protection from England hardman Nobby Stiles, but the officials had a quiet night as the two sides played out a thrilling and sporting contest.

Stiles – on a warning from FIFA for alleged rough play – was on his best behaviour and manager Alf Ramsey said, 'I gave no special instructions to Nobby Stiles about the marking of Eusébio. He was instructed to play his normal game. I do not wish to pick out any individuals. They all did a wonderful job for England.'

England – now unbeaten in 15 matches, including 13 wins – equalled the World Cup record of Uruguay in 1930 and Hungary in 1938 of reaching the final while conceding only one goal.

Even that came from a penalty and England have played two more games than the Uruguayans and Hungarians did when setting the record.

BOSS FEELS BUBBLY

DISCIPLINARIAN Alf Ramsey let his guard down tonight as England's heroes toasted their victory with a glass of bubbly.

Bosses at the Hendon Hall Hotel laid on a champagne reception when the players returned from Wembley and Ramsey relaxed his usual no-booze rule to mark the occasion.

BOYCOTT THREAT

ARGENTINA flew home today with a warning they are ready to lead a South American split from FIFA.

Officials from seven countries were represented at a two-hour emergency meeting of the South American Football Federation executive committee. Finalists Argentina, Brazil, Uruguay and Chile were joined by Bolivia, Venezuela and Peru in talks over alleged bias against South America. They emerged with a demand that a conditional ban on Argentina for Mexico 70 be lifted and there are even suggestions that South American nations could quit FIFA and set up a rival competition to the World Cup.

Before jetting back to Buenos Aires, Argentine FA vice-president Fernando Menéndez Behety said, 'I am not in a position to say we will split with FIFA and organise our own competition, but we are definitely in favour of this move.

'We felt that England were favoured. This became obvious as the competition developed. Why, for instance, were we forced to play with only ten men against West Germany and England?'

Behety said Argentina would not enter the next World Cup unless they received 'assurances that referees will be impartial and honest so that the shameful events of the present World Cup will not be repeated'.

South American Football Federation vice-president Juan Goñi, of Chile, said it had been agreed they would write to FIFA demanding the ban threat be lifted.

FIFA has told the Argentinians they will be excluded unless they guarantee the good conduct of their players and officials.

But Goñi said, 'It is impossible to predict what players and officials Argentina will have in 1970. How then can Argentina give any undertakings about their behaviour? FIFA are judging the 1970 team and officials by the 1966 team and officials. They cannot do that.'

Goñi conceded the disciplinary committee was within its rights to punish players, but delegates felt the committee overstepped the mark with its 1970 ultimatum.

He explained, 'We think that decision number five [regarding Argentina and 1970] cannot be given by that committee, because it exceeds their powers. We recognise the absolute power of the disciplinary committee to judge the incidents that have happened between England and Argentina and to punish anybody who could be responsible for those incidents.

'We have not spoken about the decisions against Rattin, Onega or the other players or officials. We only complain about the decision number five.'

England manager Alf Ramsey tonight tried to bring a close to the Argentina 'animals' row by admitting there was no excuse for his post-match comments.

But the South American nations are demanding an investigation, with Goñi calling on the FIFA disciplinary committee – rather than the English FA – to deal with Ramsey.

Goñi added, 'We think that the disciplinary committee is not only the right body, but the proper body, to take care of that and judge it.

'We are not asking the committee to punish Mr Ramsey, but we are going to ask it to take care of the matter instead of the FA.

'Our rules and articles in FIFA show that the disciplinary committee must take care of ALL the unfair moves of the players, officials, managers and everybody.

'I emphasise we are not asking for Mr Ramsey to be punished. We are asking for the same proper body and procedure to deal with Mr Ramsey. Rattin was dealt with by FIFA. They did not ask his national association to consider his case. Why should Mr Ramsey's case be different?'

Argentina goalkeeper Antonio Roma, reflecting on their controversial exit, said, 'It was a hard match, but I don't think you could call England dirty. Still, I can't see England winning the World Cup.'

REF SWAP PLAN

REFEREES from Europe and South America should do a job swap to avoid trouble at future World Cups.

That was the call today from South American Football Federation vice-president Juan Goñi amid the fallout from Saturday's quarter-finals. The Chilean believes many of the disciplinary problems during the tournament have been caused by confusion over the different refereeing styles in Europe and South America.

He said, 'I think 30 of our referees should change with 30 of your referees to get to know each other's way of interpreting the laws of the game. Perhaps we could then get one interpretation.'

GERMANY FALLING

WEST GERMANY have denied accusations they cheat to get players sent off.

Four of the five dismissals in the tournament have come for teams facing the Germans, with the latest coming in their semi-final win over the Soviet Union.

But coach Helmut Schön today defended his players, saying, 'It was not our fault that the four players were sent off. All four incidents were clear-cut, deliberate fouls and the players just had to be sent off.

'I am most upset at suggestions that we have provoked our opponents into retaliating. It is very bad sportsmanship to imply this and I don't see why people should try to spoil the atmosphere of the final before even a ball has been kicked. There is no acting when one of my players goes down. Take a player like Uwe Seeler, for instance. He has taken countless knocks in his career without complaining. Everyone must know that he does not lie down.

'If Germany are accused of being responsible for the players being sent off, then I must say that the referees who have handled our matches so far must all be bad ones.

'To blame West Germany is a most unsporting and unfair way of interpreting the incidents. We are just as fair-minded as the English and cannot understand why such rumours are started against us.

'We don't deserve the insinuations and I hope they are forgotten. My players know I won't tolerate provoking the opposition and that I will take action against offenders.'

FRANZ BAN FEAR

FINALISTS West Germany are sweating over a ban for wonder-kid Franz Beckenbauer.

The 20-year-old Bayern Munich midfielder, one of the stars of the tournament, could be ruled out after being booked against the Soviet Union – his second caution of the tournament.

His case will be on the agenda at the latest meeting of FIFA's over-worked disciplinary committee tomorrow.

The Germans complained after the Argentina group match that Beckenbauer had wrongly been listed as having been booked, saying it was a case of mistaken identity.

They could now live to regret not appealing at the time.

KO NOT OK

KNOCKOUT matches could be scrapped under radical new plans for future World Cups.

Hungarian Sports Authority vice-president Árpád Csanádi today claimed FIFA president Sir Stanley Rous is considering a switch to an eight-team round-robin formula.

Confederations including Africa are already upset that more finals places are not open to nations from outside Europe and South America. But Csanádi is backing a cut from 16 teams to just eight.

He said there was not enough time between matches and claimed, 'The system is not good enough. I understand that Sir Stanley Rous is looking for a new system.

'Some of the leading experts think it would be a good idea to have eight teams in a final table, playing each other. The winner would be the team with the most points.'

The World Cup has been played under the current system of a group stage followed by knockout matches since 1954.

In Brazil, in 1950, the four winners of the first-round groups played out a four-team final pool stage to decide the champions, but that experiment was abandoned.

MEARS MEMORIAL

SIR STANLEY ROUS was among the congregation at a memorial service today for FA chairman Joe Mears.

Mears died from a heart attack in Norway while he was away with the England touring party on the eve of the World Cup.

The service at City Temple in London was attended by a host of notables from the football world including Rous, a long-time friend and colleague.

Wednesday 27 July
Rest Day Seven

ALF WIEDERSEHEN, JIMMY?

ALF RAMSEY is facing one of the toughest decisions of his England reign – whether to recall Jimmy Greaves for the final.

The Three Lions manager looked deep in thought as he watched the men who did not feature in yesterday's semi-final take part in a training game against Arsenal players at the Gunners' London Colney training centre in Herts. Greaves is back in full training after missing the last two matches with a gashed shin and Ramsey must decide whether to stick with forwards Geoff Hurst and Roger Hunt. With Ramsey switching to a 4-4-2 formation, the pair have done well.

The Tottenham Hotspur man has been the national team's undisputed number one goalscorer since making his debut in 1959 and is regarded by foreign coaches and fans as the superstar of English football. But Ramsey has shown in the past that he is not afraid to leave him out, dropping him against Scotland in 1964 and again as recently as May last year against Sweden.

Despite insisting he is fully over a bout of hepatitis, the former Chelsea and AC Milan star has been in poor form at the finals.

And pundits have speculated for some time that Ramsey feels Greaves's individual style does not fit into the highly-organised team pattern he has developed.

ENGLAND SEE RED

ENGLAND have been told they can't wear their traditional white shirts against West Germany.

A FIFA meeting today decided the hosts must switch to their 'away' strip – red shirts, white shorts and red socks – to avoid a clash with the Germans' white shirts, black shorts and white socks.

CHARLTON'S FINAL GOAL

BOBBY CHARLTON has told his England team-mates: Don't blow it now.

The Manchester United man was the semi-final hero as he floored Portugal with two goals.

But Charlton says the Three Lions cannot celebrate until they pass the final test against West Germany.

He said, 'You tend to think after such a good result that we have won it, but we have got one more hurdle to go and we just hope we can get over that one and then we can really start to celebrate.'

Charlton's joy was clear when his first goal went in last night – and he revealed he celebrated so enthusiastically because he knew England's rock solid defence would see them to victory.

He added, 'Our defence has been playing so well that we only have to get one goal and you can really look forward to a win.

'When we got the first one I thought, "They'll have to play very well now to beat us." I couldn't see any other result.'

With England 2-0 up, Portugal did pull a goal back – the first Alf Ramsey's side had conceded in the tournament – to make it a nervous last few minutes.

Charlton's brother, Leeds United defender Jack, admitted he felt 'terrible' as England hung on after he handled on the line for the penalty which gave Portugal a lifeline.

Big Jack said, 'When you are two goals up and you have got about five minutes to go, which we knew, and you have got to give a penalty away, which I considered I had to do, it put them right back in the game again. You know you are in for a hiding in the last five minutes. It was terrible.'

MINER INCONVENIENCE

THE Charlton brothers' dad missed their semi-final heroics – because he was down a coal mine.

Bobby Charlton Snr is a miner in Ashington, Northumberland, and worked his shift as normal on the night his lads Jack and Bobby helped England beat Portugal.

A Coal Board spokesman said today, 'He missed Bobby's two superb goals and he missed Jackie's outstanding performance. It seems a real pity.'

When the Coal Board heard what had happened, Bobby Snr was given time off to watch a TV re-run of the match. He and his wife, Cissie, WILL be at the final on Saturday.

ARISE, SIR BOBBY

NEWSPAPERS across Europe have praised England for their win over Portugal – with one calling on the Queen to knight Bobby Charlton.

Defeated Portugal received plaudits for their performance, with Charlton's outstanding display cited as the difference between the teams.

Lisbon-based *Diario de Noticias* said, 'England owed their victory in an extremely even match to their excellent, well-drilled defence. Stiles did an excellent job in marking Eusébio, while Bobby Charlton, the player of the highest class in the England team, had his day of glory.'

And another Lisbon newspaper, *A Voz,* asked, 'Why tears, boys, unless they are out of emotion? You carried out your mission bravely and we are as proud of you in this defeat as we were proud of you in your triumphs.'

In France, where the newspapers had ridiculed England earlier in the tournament, *Paris-Jour* admitted, 'At last some good football. Playing as they did here, England can very well win the cup they have coveted for so long.'

Another French publication, *L'Equipe,* wrote, 'The English certainly played their best match since the World Cup series began. They were alert, agile and always first on the ball. Their success is well merited.'

And *France Soir* wrote, 'More than ever, all England is now convinced that genial, balding Bobby Charlton will give them their first World Cup.'

In West Germany, newspapers had mixed views. *Bild-Zeitung* claimed, 'The English fans care more for their team's victory than for good play. The Portuguese defence gambled away victory. England scored a lucky win.'

But Hamburg-based *Die Welt* warned, 'The English forward line is something to be reckoned with.'

Moscow news agency *Tass* proclaimed, 'The match came like a spring of clear water breaking through the murky wave of dirty football which has flooded the championships.'

There was almost unanimous praise of Bobby Charlton, with Milan-based *Corriere Della Serra* raving, 'At Wembley they were expecting Eusébio – instead they saw Bobby Charlton. He was the hero.'

Swedish publication *Aftonbladet* insisted, 'If Queen Elizabeth II can knight Stanley Matthews, then it is her duty to give Bobby Charlton a knighthood too.'

And Stockholm-based *Expressent* went one further, adding, 'If Nelson's statue was not so firmly based on its foundations in Trafalgar Square, there would be a risk today that Bobby Charlton would be in his place.'

Despite the fallout over the treatment of South American teams, England even won praise in Uruguay, where *La Manana* conceded, 'Wembley was the scene of the best game of the tournament and vibrated with a clean victory that takes the favourites to the final.'

PARADE PANIC

ENGLISH FA chiefs admit they haven't even thought about a parade to celebrate the Three Lions' success.

West German officials have arranged a welcome procession in Frankfurt, whether their team win the final or not.

But FA secretary Denis Follows was caught on the hop when quizzed over what plans were in place to honour Alf Ramsey and his men.

'I suppose this is what we could call our English reserve, but this sort of thing had not even occurred to us,' he said.

'It seems to be a good idea. We will probably announce our route and the time of our journey when we move out of the Hendon Hall Hotel to the Royal Garden Hotel at Kensington for the official FIFA reception on Saturday night.'

QUEEN U-TURN

THE Queen WILL be at the World Cup Final after all.

It was originally thought the Queen's speech at the opening ceremony might be her only direct involvement in the World Cup.

But following England's march to the final, Buckingham Palace today confirmed the monarch will now attend Saturday's showpiece and present the trophy to the winning captain. However, the monarch will not go on to the field at the end of the match.

Officials are keen to avoid embarrassing scenes similar to those in 1958 when Brazil players pulled the King of Sweden into their post-match celebration photos and teenager Pelé broke down in tears and sobbed on the King's shoulder.

ELECTRIC SHOCK

ELECTRICITY bosses today revealed how they had to cope with a record-breaking power surge when the final whistle blew on England's semi-final win.

Output jumped by an unprecedented 1.7m kilowatts as householders turned on lights, kettles and other appliances at around 9.25pm.

Usage was 14.8m kilowatts at 9.15pm, but ten minutes later it soared to 16.5m.

A Central Electricity Generating Board spokesman said, 'It seems that TV viewers were so engrossed in the match that they didn't even bother to switch on lights until the match was over.

'But we were expecting a sudden, thumping increase. In estimating demand for power, our engineers keep a close eye on forthcoming TV programmes because of the big effect they can have on electricity supply.'

FRANZ FINAL LET-OFF

WEST GERMAN officials spoke of their relief tonight after Franz Beckenbauer was cleared to play in the final.

The Bayern Munich midfielder faced the threat of suspension after receiving his second booking of the tournament in the semi-final win over the USSR.

But FIFA today confirmed he can play on Saturday after the disciplinary committee accepted German pleas that he was the victim of mistaken identity over a caution against Argentina.

The Germans complained after that match that the referee had got it wrong, but they had chosen not to appeal at the time.

West German FA secretary Herman Joch said tonight, 'We were worried, but we thought his first caution was an error.

'Possibly the referee confused him with Wolfgang Overath, but he did not protest at the time because we do not encourage our players to do so.'

Beckenbauer said, 'I'm delighted and very glad I can play in the final. I had a clear conscience. I had no idea I had been cautioned by the referee in the first match.'

HONOUR, NOT CASH

WEST GERMANY'S stars have been told to win the World Cup for honour rather than cash.

A bonus of £22,000 is on offer to the England squad if they claim the Jules Rimet Trophy.

But the West Germans have been told they will not get a penny for winning the nation's second title. West German press officer Dr Wilfried Gerhardt said, 'The honour of representing West Germany is enough. I'm sure our players could not try any harder if they received a big bonus.'

REF'S DREAM DATE

SWISS referee Gottfried Dienst says his 'secret hope' has become a reality with the news he is to take charge of the World Cup Final.

The 47-year-old postal worker was enjoying a visit to Lord Bath's lion park at Longleat, Wiltshire, when FIFA confirmed his appointment.

Dienst, who posed for photographs while holding a lion cub which was dressed in a Union Jack waistcoat, said, 'Every man has his secret hopes. Mine was to referee the World Cup Final.'

The official's previous big-game assignments have included the 1961 and 1965 European Cup finals.

West Germany welcomed his appointment, with press officer Dr Wilfried Gerhardt saying, 'We are most happy about the choice, because he speaks English and German. But we are determined not to get into trouble – we shall say nothing. Our players will not argue or dispute decisions given by Mr Dienst.

'People say our team are actors and feign injury. This is like saying the victim is responsible for murder. It is as far-fetched as that.'

EUSÉBIO'S SHOT AT A GRAND

EUSÉBIO insists he is not taking anything for granted in the race to be top scorer.

The Portugal hero has eight goals going into tomorrow's third-place play-off against the Soviet Union and is hot favourite for the £1,000 prize put up by a London casino.

West German Helmut Haller is his nearest challenger with five and would have to become the first man to score a hat-trick in a final just to draw level.

But Eusébio will go all-out tomorrow to put the race beyond doubt and secure a third-place finish for Portugal.

Speaking at their hotel in Harlow, Essex, he said, 'Football is full of surprises. Another player could still catch me. One or two goals against Russia will clinch it. For me, however, the satisfaction will be if Portugal win – and win well – and, above all, if we can satisfy that wonderful Wembley crowd with some more good football.'

Reflecting on yesterday's defeat by England, he added, 'We are all proud to have taken part in a game which the world acclaims as a credit to football.'

The Soviets will be without Igor Chislenko after he was today suspended for three matches for his sending-off in the defeat by West Germany.

ROUS HAILS FAIR PLAY

UNDER-FIRE world football chief Sir Stanley Rous today thanked England and Portugal for launching 'the rehabilitation of football'.

The FIFA president praised the sportsmanship shown in yesterday's semi-final after the controversies which have rocked the tournament.

He said, 'It was a game of football as it should be played. I did not see one deliberate foul. The film of this match will go around the world and I trust it will mean the rehabilitation of football.'

BUENOS HEROES

ARGENTINES today hailed their team as unofficial world champions when the squad arrived home to a heroes' welcome.

Thousands of fans, some carrying banners depicting senior FIFA officials as donkeys, ignored heavy rain to greet the squad at Buenos Aires Airport.

Supporters chanted 'Argentina champions' and fans broke through police cordons to welcome the players, with a number of women hugging and kissing captain Antonio Rattin.

The squad were taken by bus to meet the President, General Juan Carlos Onganía, at his official residence.

BETTING BONANZA

WORLD CUP fever has sparked a massive gambling boom.

A punt of £1,250 on Portugal winning the third-place play-off has taken the total staked on the tournament with top bookmaker William Hill past the £100,000 mark.

A Hill's spokesman said, 'The interest in betting on this World Cup series has been quite fantastic. Bets have poured in from every country which had a team in the series, except North Korea, and from other countries such as Denmark and Sweden.

'It looks as though by the time the whistle blows on Saturday's final we'll have taken more on the World Cup in ante-post bets than we'd expect to take ante-post on the Derby.'

Thursday 28 July
Matchday Eleven

Portugal v USSR (third-place play-off)
7.30pm, Wembley, London

PORTUGAL TAKE BISCUIT
Portugal 2 (Eusébio pen 12, Torres 89)
USSR 1 (Malafeyev 43)
Third-place play-off, Wembley, London (att: 87,696)

PORTUGAL signed off their World Cup adventure tonight by taking third place and a special award for sportsmanship.

The England squad were at Wembley to see the match, having earlier watched a special screening of West Germany's group-stage win over Spain.

And they saw Eusébio end any doubts about who will be the tournament top scorer by netting his ninth goal.

The crowd were on Portugal's side after their thrilling semi-final clash with England and their status as the nation's second-favourite team was recognised when biscuit company Carr's presented them with a silver salver inscribed with the message 'For good sportsmanship'.

Portugal struck early when Murtaz Khurtsilava's handball gifted Eusébio the chance to score from the penalty spot.

But the teams went in level at half-time after a blunder by goalkeeper José Pereira. He failed to hold a long-range strike from Slava Metreveli and Eduard Malafeyev pounced.

The match was an anti-climax, raising fresh questions about the point of a third-place play-off.

It appeared to be heading for extra time until José Torres put the USSR – and the crowd – out of their misery when he volleyed past Lev Yashin in what will surely be the veteran goalkeeper's final World Cup appearance.

Portugal coach Otto Glória apologised for his team's disappointing display, explaining, 'We have been through some hard matches, so we knew we had to pace ourselves through the 90 minutes.'

PORTUGAL: José Pereira, Alberto Festa, Alexandre Baptista, José Carlos, Hilário, Jaime Graça, Mário Coluna (capt), José Augusto, José Torres, Eusébio, António Simões.

USSR: Lev Yashin (capt), Vladimir Ponomaryev, Aleksei Korneyev, Georgy Sichinava, Murtaz Khurtsilava, Vasily Danilov, Viktor Serebrianikov, Valery Voronin, Anatoly Banishevsky, Eduard Malafeyev, Slava Metreveli.

ALF CASE CAN WAIT

FA CHIEFS have no immediate plans for a disciplinary hearing over Alf Ramsey's 'animals' outburst.

South American federations have called for FIFA to deal with the issue, but the world governing body has instead written to the English FA drawing its attention to his comments about Argentina.

FA secretary Denis Follows said today that no special hearing was planned and it was likely the issue would only be discussed some time next season once there were domestic cases to deal with too.

Follows said, 'Mr Ramsey's case, like all others, will be reported to the FA disciplinary committee for discussion in the normal way.'

ALI KO'S ENGLAND

MUHAMMAD ALI'S trainer apologised today after the boxing superstar missed a meeting with England's football heroes.

Captain Bobby Moore, the Charlton brothers, Jimmy Greaves and Ray Wilson visited his North London gym to watch him working out ahead of his world heavyweight title defence against Brian London on Saturday week.

But Ali and trainer Angelo Dundee were two hours late, by which time the players had already had to leave for training at Highbury.

Dundee said, 'This is the first time we've ever been late for training. It bugs us, because training is what we are here for. But we got caught up with so many interviews, autographs and traffic. We're really sorry we missed your soccer players.'

Ali, who plans to be at Saturday's final, said, 'I'll catch up with them at the ball game at Wembley.'

Dundee said Ali would be able to go, as he was taking two days off. The trainer said, 'Muhammad is in real shape right now and can afford to take a rest, because we don't mean to leave his fighting edge in the gym. The Wembley tickets are being fixed for us. We've been watching the games on TV and the champ has got very interested.

'Sure, we know all about Bobby Charlton – almost as much as we know about Brian London.'

Of the title fight, Ali said, 'London will have a chance if he comes with a pistol, a big club and two police dogs to help him find me in the ring.'

HOME WINNERS

JACK and Bobby Charlton's home town today revealed plans for a civic reception to salute their most famous sons.

The brothers will be honoured with a parade in the mining town of Ashington, Northumberland.

Their mum, Cissie, said, 'We're all delighted our town should acknowledge Jack and Bobby. They're delighted to learn what Ashington Council propose.'

CHARLTON A DIDI MAN

WORLD CUP winner Sepp Herberger has singled out Bobby Charlton and Franz Beckenbauer as the men who could decide the final.

The coach who led West Germany to glory in 1954 today predicted they will win a second world crown.

But he admitted he feared the 'wonderful' Charlton and compared him to brilliant former Brazil playmaker Didi.

Herberger said, 'We have a real chance. We shouldn't get too anxious. England are a stronger and speedier side, but West Germany will win. I cannot say what I base that on, but you will see in the game on Saturday.

'Bobby Charlton is like Didi of Brazil, a wonderful player. He controls the tempo of the game from midfield.

'He is everywhere and, as he showed against Portugal, he scores goals as well. He is a beautiful player, classic in style. A similar player on our side is Franz Beckenbauer. He is good too.'

Herberger also questioned England's tactics, with the 4-2-4 formation used early in Alf Ramsey's reign becoming 4-3-3 by the start of the tournament and then 4-4-2 in the last two matches.

Herberger said, 'England are very fast and fit, but I don't think 4-3-3 is best for English teams. That is a problem for Mr Ramsey.'

West Germany coach Helmut Schön has urged people not to compare the 1954 and 1966 sides. He said, 'Football has changed and they played in a different style.'

GERMANS ARE BUZZING

WEST GERMANY coach Helmut Schön today predicted his players are in the mood for glory.

The Germans have had to come through bruising battles against Argentina, Uruguay and the USSR.

But after supervising a training session at Bragbury End, Herts, Schön said the squad looked fresh and ready for action.

'You could see that today in training,' he said. 'They are still calling for the ball all the time and that is the right mood and the right spirit.'

Schön's biggest worry is the fitness of goalkeeper Hans Tilkowski. Second-choice Sepp Maier has a broken bone in his hand and number three Günter Bernard has won only four caps. The manager added, 'Tilkowski's shoulder injury has improved greatly over the past two days. He was able to train today and we're very hopeful he will be fit.'

REPLAY PLANS REVEALED

TOURNAMENT chiefs today told fans not to throw away their final ticket stubs in case there is a replay.

Organisers have revealed the ticket sales arrangements in the event of a replay, which would take place at Wembley on Tuesday.

Tickets would go on sale straight after Saturday's game to fans who produce ticket stubs. Any tickets still unsold after the weekend would then go on general sale on Monday.

FA HIT JACKPOT

THE English FA is set to make a profit of around £500,000 from a tournament that has smashed World Cup cash records.

Saturday's final will be watched live on TV by 400m people worldwide and a 90,000-plus Wembley crowd, bringing in gate receipts of more than £200,000. That ticket income shatters the previous record of £147,700 for the 1962 final in Chile.

And it tops off a tournament which has generated around £2.5m in ticket sales, TV rights fees and merchandising.

The FA will get more than £1m and should make a profit of around half that once its share of organising costs is deducted.

WORLD TUNES IN

ENGLAND'S final showdown with West Germany will be screened live in 29 countries.

And another 30 countries have bought the rights to broadcast delayed coverage.

In England, Lancashire County Cricket Club are setting up televisions at Old Trafford for fans who want to break away from the Roses match with Yorkshire to watch the football.

Five racecourses are making similar arrangements. Warwick's clerk of the course, Malcolm Hancock, said, 'I feel it's the right thing to do in view of the great interest in the match.'

ROUS 'FIX' SLUR

WORLD football chief Sir Stanley Rous faced another stinging attack today – this time from Brazil.

South American nations have blasted tournament organisers, claiming they have been victims of a pro-European conspiracy.

Today Brazilian Confederation of Sport president João Havelange again took a swipe at FIFA president Rous, saying of the Englishman, 'Ask him and he will give you the final result of the World Cup.'

TOUTS CASH IN

TICKET touts are set to make thousands of pounds from Saturday's final.

With the countdown on to the big match, one tout today explained how scalpers had lost money on earlier matches, but would make a killing on England v West Germany.

Bruce Davies, 21, said, 'On the previous games, we have lost quite a lot of money. I was giving tickets away for nothing for the semi-final and all the previous games.

'Some people will make hundreds, even thousands, of pounds, I suppose, if they have got enough tickets.

'I've got about 60 left. At the moment I'm charging about £20 for a £3 seat. Somebody has told me there are thousands of Germans coming over without tickets, so I suppose it's all a question of supply and demand. Possibly tomorrow and Saturday outside the ground they'll be fetching £30, £40.'

Asked if fans were 'mugs' to pay inflated prices, he added, 'Well, they are mugs to the extent that when the tickets were first advertised, if they were that keen to go they should have applied then. If they want to go now, they have got to pay, obviously.'

Friday 29 July
Rest Day Eight

GAME OF YOUR LIVES

ALF RAMSEY has told his team they will have to play the game of their lives tomorrow.

England are just one win from an historic first world title and have never lost to a German team.

But manager Ramsey has warned that no one should take victory for granted, despite having beaten them at home and away in the past 14 months.

He said, 'This is a very fine German team and the only thing I can say is that it helps that we know their players and their style perhaps better than any other team in the tournament.

'But, for England to win, it must mean every Englishman playing better than he has ever played in his life. I believe they will.'

Ramsey and captain Bobby Moore believe their '12th man' can lead them to glory – the Wembley crowd.

The home supporters, sometimes criticised by Ramsey in the past, have stuck by their team throughout the tournament – even when England were struggling.

Ramsey said, 'The fans have been magnificent. Their cheers and encouragement have been an unforgettable inspiration.

'Their support is one thing I will always remember with gratitude and, I must say, with pride.'

Skipper Moore added, 'Our fans are the greatest. In fact, the lads call them the 12th man. When we play in the final, it is the ambition of every player to repay their support in the best possible way by winning the World Cup. From the bottom of my heart, I say "thank you".'

Moore is going for a unique Wembley hat-trick tomorrow. As West Ham United captain he lifted the FA Cup there in 1964 and then, last year, the European Cup Winners' Cup.

He admitted, 'I always thought we had a chance of winning the World Cup, but it is hard to believe we are actually in the final.

'The wonderful thing is that our success has been a real team effort and the crowd has played a part too.

'We know it will be a hard game, but all the boys are confident of bringing the World Cup to England.'

Three years ago, Ramsey promised victory and when he was asked today if he stood by his prediction, he replied, 'I see no reason to change my opinion.'

Ramsey insists fatigue after five hard matches won't be a problem, adding, 'They are professional footballers and I see no reason why they should be tired. Everything possible has been done for them.

'I think, having got to the final, the players are as relaxed as they possibly can be and certainly the tension and problems they have are no greater than those confronting the Germans.

'One of our objects has been to relieve the players from this tension and no one knows how successful we have been until we see their performance tomorrow.

'We know we have a very good side to beat. They are very efficient, a very strong side, very well organised. It is going to be a difficult match, but all matches are difficult as far as I'm concerned.'

JIMMY RIDDLE

ALF RAMSEY is keeping West Germany guessing over whether Jimmy Greaves will play in the final.

England's record goalscorer is back in full training after the shin injury which kept him out of the last two matches.

And today the Tottenham Hotspur forward insisted, 'I am 100 per cent fit.'

Ramsey, who will delay naming his team until four hours before kick-off tomorrow, must decide whether to stand by the XI who beat Argentina and Portugal. The manager was giving no clues today, but if he does choose to recall Greaves, the question will be who he leaves out and whether he sticks with what has evolved into a 4-4-2 system.

Greaves could replace Roger Hunt or Geoff Hurst, but Ramsey could even opt to go with three out-and-out forwards in a 4-3-3 formation.

MUCH MOORE RELAXED

BOBBY MOORE says England have gone from 'trembling jellies' to the most relaxed team he has ever played in.

The Three Lions captain will have no worries about his players choking on the biggest stage of all when he leads them out at Wembley tomorrow.

He said, 'Before the opening game against Uruguay it was a job to fasten your bootlaces. We trembled like jellies on a rough crossing.

'After that, there hasn't been a trace of nerves. The boys joke and gag and I think we are a length in front when we join the other team in the tunnel for the march out and our lads are still laughing.

'I can't remember any team that has enjoyed their football so much.'

CHARLTON ATHLETIC

ENGLAND'S players relaxed on the eve of tomorrow's historic match – with a game of cricket.

And the athletic Bobby Charlton showed he's as sharp in the field as he is on the football pitch when he took a catch high above his head when Nobby Stiles miscued a shot off the bowling of Jimmy Greaves.

Captain Bobby Moore, watching from the sidelines, reacted by saying, 'Man, that was real cool.' Asked if England would be just as 'cool' tomorrow, he replied, 'But, of course.'

DEFEAT NO DISGRACE

HELMUT SCHÖN has told his West German players not to be held back tomorrow by the fear of defeat.

The Germans got a taste of the Wembley pitch today in a 20-minute training session – just as a thunderstorm hit London.

After putting his rain-soaked men through their paces, coach Schön said, 'I'm sure that now our players are here, in the final, they will feel freer, less nervous, than at any time.

'Now, win or lose, there can be no disappointment after what we have already achieved. To be second will be no disgrace.

'But our players should be under less tension than the English. Our players are physically and mentally fit and are ambitious to do well.'

OUT TO SEELER VICTORY

UWE SEELER believes he is destined to score West Germany's winner 'in the den of the lion'.

The 30-year-old German captain says he has come up with vital winners on the road to the final and is ready to finish the job.

'We are in the den of the lion, but we are not afraid,' he said. 'We qualified for the finals by beating Sweden 2-1 and I got the deciding goal. We reached the quarter-finals by beating Spain 2-1. Again I got the deciding goal. Now I would like to score the goal that wins the World Cup.'

The Germans have never beaten England and the most recent meeting, in February, saw Alf Ramsey's men win 1-0 in a Wembley friendly.

But Seeler warned, 'The last time England beat us, we didn't have Helmut Haller and Karl-Heinz Schnellinger. This time we have our strongest team and it will be different.

'We are not worried about Nobby Stiles. He can only take one man. We are an all-round team. We do not have a Eusébio, a special star. But in Emmerich we have the man who can score a goal when people are least expecting it.'

The Germans' official press officer Dr Wilfried Gerhardt praised Seeler for the way he keeps bouncing back for more, however roughly opponents treat him.

Gerhardt said, 'It's amazing how he shrugs off the treatment he receives. Against Russia in the semi-final, he was kicked in the mouth. I thought he would be minus a few teeth when he came in, but no, everything was intact!'

The Germans won't receive a financial bonus for winning, but star midfielder Haller, who plays in Italy with Bologna, said, 'The most important thing for me is not the money, but the honour of playing in a World Cup Final.'

MATTHEWS CAR CRASH

DOCTORS hope England legend Sir Stanley Matthews will be well enough to watch the final on television after he was injured in a car crash today.

Port Vale general manager Matthews, 51, was taken to Stoke-on-Trent Hospital with head, knee and rib injuries suffered in the accident in Staffordshire.

The former Stoke City and Blackpool winger, whose illustrious England career only came to an end at the age of 42, was driving to training when the crash happened.

His passengers – Vale player-manager Jackie Mudie and three young players – escaped serious injury.

Hospital secretary Ernest Taylor said today, 'At the moment, Sir Stanley's condition is rather poorly. He will obviously have to be detained, although his condition is not too serious. It should be possible for him to sit up in bed tomorrow and watch the final.'

THREE LIONS ON PARADE

ENGLAND fans WILL get a chance to salute their heroes on the streets of London tomorrow – win or lose.

The FA today revealed hastily-arranged plans to involve supporters in the post-final celebrations.

Alf Ramsey and his men will leave their Hendon Hall Hotel base by coach at 6.15pm and the public will be able to cheer them along the route as they are driven to the Royal Garden Hotel in Kensington High Street for the official FIFA reception.

The Three Lions will also make an appearance on the balcony of the Royal Garden Hotel at 8.30pm.

'WAGS' STOOD UP

WIVES and girlfriends of England's World Cup stars have been sidelined in plans for two lavish post-final celebrations.

The WAGS are not invited to a government cocktail party or a FIFA banquet tomorrow.

Four hundred guests will be at the banquet at the Royal Garden Hotel in Kensington – but the players' other halves will have to make do with a hen party on another floor.

Asked why the women weren't invited, an FA spokesman said, 'Quite honestly, I don't know, but it has been hectic arranging this. We are not by any means slighting the players or their wives.'

Bobby Charlton's wife, Norma, today laughed off the snub, saying, 'It doesn't worry me – those things are usually full of boring old speeches.'

Asked who she thought would win the final, she said, 'Oh, England, of course. I think it's going to be close. I think there will only be a goal in it. I think West Germany will play much better than when they played Russia.'

Norma was one of a group of WAGS who enjoyed a trip to see *The Black & White Minstrel Show* at the Victoria Palace Theatre in London's West End tonight.

Once the official celebrations are over tomorrow, she is looking forward to the players and their partners enjoying a night out after barely seeing each other during the tournament.

She added, 'We're going to go on the town and have a really good time and make up for the last three weeks.'

MISSUS BANKS ON ENGLAND

GORDON BANKS'S West German wife says she will be cheering on England against her homeland.

Ursula Banks faces a case of divided loyalties ahead of tomorrow's final when her goalkeeper husband goes for glory.

The 27-year-old, who met the Leicester City player when he was based in Helmstadt on National Service, said today, 'I shall be torn, but definitely shouting for an England victory.

'I'm also proud that my country has reached the final, but I hope they finish runners-up.'

PROUDEST PARENTS

THE proudest mum and dad in England will be at Wembley for tomorrow's final – Bobby and Cissie Charlton.

Jack and Bobby's parents travelled down to London from Ashington, Northumberland, today.

Cissie, 53, revealed she had brought some good luck charms with her – 11 medallions sent to her for the team by a group of nuns in Durham.

She said, 'The nuns sent the medals with a letter. It was so kind it had me in tears. They said they had watched all the games and were praying for England to win.'

SICK AS A DOG

THE owner of the dog which found the Jules Rimet Trophy is 'hurt' at not being given a ticket to the final, his sister has claimed.

Londoner David Corbett and his pet, Pickles, became national heroes when they found the trophy after it was stolen from an exhibition in March.

Corbett's sister, Eileen, said today, 'David didn't bother looking for a ticket for the final, as he felt so sure the Football Association would send him one. He's hurt and disappointed.'

An FA spokesman said, 'We never promised Mr Corbett a ticket.'

CROWN JULES

THE whereabouts of the Jules Rimet Trophy will be kept a closely-guarded secret until the last possible moment ahead of the final.

Tournament chiefs are taking no chances with security after the theft of the cup earlier this year.

Asked where the trophy was, FIFA secretary general Helmut Kaiser said, 'I don't know and I don't want to know! All I can say is that the cup will be at Wembley at the precise moment when I have to hand it over to our president, Sir Stanley Rous.'

BAN U-TURN

FIFA president Sir Stanley Rous today promised to review the threat of a 1970 World Cup ban on Argentina.

The South Americans reacted furiously when the world governing body warned they would be excluded from Mexico 70 unless they guaranteed the good conduct of their officials and players.

But today Rous led a FIFA delegation in peace talks with the South American Football Federation.

A summit of South American nations earlier this week led to talk of a split from FIFA and the launch of a competition to rival the World Cup.

Emerging from today's talks, Rous confirmed the Argentina ban threat would be reconsidered.

And FIFA secretary general Helmut Kaiser said, 'The meeting was a very friendly one at which we discussed the incidents and their reaction.

'The South American delegation told us "We are all one family and should live together".

'Everyone seemed happier after the discussion. No decision was taken except that there would be another review of the matter at our next executive meeting in November.'

Saturday 30 July
Matchday Twelve

England v West Germany (final)
3pm, Wembley, London

HURST TREBLE WINS CUP
England 4 (Hurst 18, 101, 120, Peters 78)
West Germany 2 (Haller 12, Weber 89)
After extra time (2-2 at 90 mins)
Final, Wembley, London (att: 96,924)

ENGLAND are the world champions.

Geoff Hurst today became the first man to score a World Cup Final hat-trick to spark joyous celebrations at Wembley.

And Alf Ramsey insisted the historic win was never in doubt – even when a last-gasp West German equaliser forced extra time.

Ramsey – the calmest man in the stadium as the drama unfolded – said, 'I had no fears after 90 minutes or during the whole of the game.

'We created many chances in the last ten minutes before extra time and I think we created more goalscoring attempts and movements than we did during the other five matches we played.

'I thought that extra time would prove which side would be fitter. It takes two teams to make a match of this nature. The Germans played very well and it is most unfortunate that there had to be a losing team.'

Ramsey, whose decision to play Hurst and leave out Jimmy Greaves paid off, promised three years ago that England would win the Jules Rimet Trophy for the first time in their history. He has fulfilled that pledge by rebuilding the side to such an extent that only two of today's XI – Bobby Moore and Bobby Charlton – were in the team beaten by France in his first match.

And Ramsey said today's victory had proved once and for all that England are now a great team.

He added, 'I'm delighted we won. It has been a great satisfaction to me. Winning the World Cup has become a desire. The desire has rubbed off on the players. It was not generally appreciated that the English players were good players. They were underestimated players. I said that it would take a great side to beat us, because we are a great side.'

Ramsey had warned it would be a tight match, but even he could not have realised just how tight it would be.

England fell behind after only 12 minutes when full-back Ray Wilson headed a hopeful ball into the box straight to Helmut Haller and his low shot beat goalkeeper Gordon Banks.

But the omens were on England's side as no team had won a post-Second World War final after scoring first.

Captain Moore set about getting England back in the game. His run forward was halted by Wolfgang Overath's trip. Quick-thinking Moore took the free kick almost instantly and Hurst, reading his West Ham United team-mate's mind, headed home the captain's chipped cross.

With Bobby Charlton and Franz Beckenbauer cancelling each other out in midfield, the game became a nervous stalemate until England finally went ahead late in the second half.

Alan Ball's corner was half-cleared to Hurst on the edge of the box. His mis-hit shot was blocked by Horst-Dieter Höttges and, when the ball dropped to Martin Peters, he lashed it into the net.

England were now just 12 minutes from victory. It seemed they would hold on but the Germans were given one last chance by Swiss referee Gottfried Dienst. He felt Jack Charlton had climbed on Sigi Held to win a header – a decision the Leeds United defender bitterly disputed.

Lothar Emmerich drove the ball into the crowded penalty area and, after a series of ricochets, it skidded across the six-yard box for Wolfgang Weber to stab it beyond Banks's desperate dive.

There was barely time to restart before Dienst blew for full time. As the Germans collapsed to the ground and received massage treatment before the start of extra time, Ramsey urged his team to send a psychological message to their opponents by staying on their feet.

One man whose energy was never in doubt was Alan Ball. The Blackpool midfielder, England's youngest player, had run his heart out throughout and his industry led to a breakthrough ten minutes into extra time. He chased down a pass from Nobby Stiles and crossed into the box, where Hurst controlled the ball and hit a shot on the turn. The ball thudded against the underside of the crossbar and bounced down before Weber headed it clear.

Roger Hunt, following in after Hurst's shot, appealed for a goal and there was confusion as referee Dienst at first awarded a corner, before consulting Soviet linesman Tofik Bakhramov.

Bakhramov hadn't run back to the halfway line to signal a goal but, to the Germans' astonishment, he told the referee it HAD crossed the line. Despite heated protests, the goal was given.

The Germans, clearly running out of steam, rarely threatened to find a way back in the remaining 19 minutes.

And any doubts about the result were blown away in the dying seconds when Moore picked out Hurst with a superb long pass and the forward, ignoring a handful of fans who had run on to the field thinking the match had already finished, unleashed an unstoppable shot into the top corner.

Moments later, the England players were celebrating as the final whistle confirmed their victory. Ramsey sat impassively on the bench as those around him jumped up in delight.

As the celebrations began, the non-playing members of the squad – led by former captain Jimmy Armfield – rushed on to shake hands with the victorious XI.

Ramsey waited at the bottom of the steps leading up to the Royal Box and shook hands with every member of the team before they made their way up to receive the trophy and their medals.

Moore gave his manager a hug and Ramsey patted him on the back as he set off to climb the famous 39 steps.

When he reached the Royal Box, Moore had the presence of mind to wipe his dirty hands on a velvet drape before shaking hands with the Queen, who was flanked by FIFA president Sir Stanley Rous.

After receiving his medal and the trophy, the West Ham United man lifted the World Cup one-handed above his head to huge cheers.

Hat-trick hero Hurst was next to receive his medal, while Bobby Charlton wept tears of joy as he took his turn.

With fans eager to shake their heroes' hands and hug them as they made their way back down the steps to the pitch, policemen helped clear the way. With the presentation over, the crowd joined in a rousing rendition of *God Save The Queen* and sang *When the whites go marching in* as Moore led his players on a lap of honour.

Players including Stiles and Jack Charlton urged the non-playing members of the squad to join them in parading the trophy, but the reserves waved them on their way, clearly not wanting to steal any of the glory.

Skipper Moore, raising the trophy above his head, was lifted shoulder-high by team-mates as the team posed for photographers and a grinning, gap-toothed Nobby Stiles delighted the crowd as he did a jig of joy beside the pitch while waving the World Cup above his head.

The scenes topped anything the famous stadium had seen and captain Moore paid tribute to the fans, saying, 'On behalf of all the lads, I'd like to say that our supporters have been really marvellous. We just had to repay them by winning.'

ENGLAND: Gordon Banks, George Cohen, Ray Wilson, Nobby Stiles, Jack Charlton, Bobby Moore (capt), Alan Ball, Geoff Hurst, Bobby Charlton, Roger Hunt, Martin Peters.

WEST GERMANY: Hans Tilkowski, Horst-Dieter Höttges, Karl-Heinz Schnellinger, Franz Beckenbauer, Willy Schulz, Wolfgang Weber, Lothar Emmerich, Helmut Haller, Uwe Seeler (capt), Wolfgang Overath, Sigi Held.

GIVE US MOORE CREDIT

BOBBY MOORE believes England won because they had the best team – not because they were at home.

The Three Lions captain admitted that playing at Wembley was an advantage, but he is convinced talent was the key factor.

He said, 'The team has grown more and more confident as the tournament progressed. Teams have always done well in their own country, but apart from this home advantage, which was obviously a great help, we always felt we had capable enough players to win it.

'We always felt we had an outstanding opportunity and, as the time to the World Cup got nearer and nearer, we felt more and more confident and, well, we have answered it today.'

Moore said his team were upset over the free kick which led to Germany's late equaliser. But the players realised they needed to forget any sense of injustice and dig deep to finish the job.

He added, 'It was a wonderful game and we're so happy to have won, that everything else is forgotten.

'We were all tired towards the end. I think the Germans were about as tired as we were. In extra time, we realised that glory was just around the corner and we all had to make that extra effort.'

OH BROTHER!

BOBBY CHARLTON feared referee Gottfried Dienst had 'robbed' England of glory.

The Swiss official penalised Bobby's brother, Jack, for climbing on Sigi Held to win a header and that free kick led to West Germany's late equaliser.

The Manchester United star was clearly relieved as well as delighted as he said, 'It's the greatest feeling in the world – and to think we were nearly robbed.

'That should never have been a free kick they gave against Jackie. In the first period of extra time, he did exactly the same and the referee waved play on. Still, who cares? What a day!'

'PHANTOM GOAL' ROW

WEST GERMANY coach Helmut Schön says England's vital third goal should never have been allowed.

The German players argued furiously with referee Gottfried Dienst that the ball hadn't crossed the line when Hurst's shot bounced down off the underside of the crossbar.

Hat-trick hero Hurst admitted he hadn't had a clear view, but said team-mate Roger Hunt had told him it was a goal.

Hurst said, 'I was about the only one who didn't see it because, as I hit the shot, I turned and I didn't see any of it.

'I didn't see whether the keeper had touched it on to the bar or anything. Roger Hunt, who was very near me, said it was definitely in, that there was no doubt about it at all. I'm happy to accept Roger's view. He was right there and he's certain the ball crossed the line.'

But Germany boss Schön said, 'All my players agreed that the shot bounced down outside the line.

'However, we are satisfied as a whole with the result. England deserved to win. England will make fine world champions.

'We can be proud of the good game. We had worked out the English tactics and we were right, because their dangerman, Bobby Charlton, was blotted out.'

NOBBY SMILES

ENGLAND hardman Nobby Stiles today thanked Alf Ramsey for standing by him.

The England manager faced calls before and during the tournament to dump a player written off by critics as a clogger.

But Ramsey kept faith in the Manchester United midfielder, even when Stiles had to walk a disciplinary tightrope in the knockout rounds after a public warning from FIFA.

Gap-toothed Stiles was all smiles today as he delighted the Wembley crowd with a victory jig on the pitch.

And he said, 'What a manager, what a bloke, what an achievement. They can call me what they like from now on, but they can't take this triumph away from any of us.'

BALL BUSTER

RELIEVED Alan Ball admitted West Germany had pushed England to the limit with two hammer blows in today's final.

The Blackpool midfielder – England's youngest player – got a reality check when the Germans took an early lead. Ball said: 'I thought we were invincible until they scored the first goal!'

And, speaking as the players left Wembley, Ball revealed how devastated the Three Lions had felt when Wolfgang Weber's late equaliser forced extra time.

'It broke our hearts,' said Ball. 'I thought we would win, but you don't know in football until the final whistle, do you?

'In extra time, my legs said I couldn't run any more. My heart said I had to, so I did.'

ROYAL SEAL OF APPROVAL

SIR STANLEY ROUS has revealed how the Queen was swept up in the excitement of today's drama.

The FIFA president sat next to Queen Elizabeth II in the Royal Box and he said, 'The Queen enjoyed it enormously and was obviously thrilled during the final part of extra time. She kept asking, "How much longer to go?"'

BOBBY DAZZLED

CAPTAIN Bobby Moore tonight raised a champagne toast to England's glory and admitted: We still can't believe it.

Thousands of fans turned out to salute the squad as they arrived at a celebration banquet attended by Prime Minister Harold Wilson.

A smiling Moore, enjoying a glass of bubbly with his wife, Tina, before the banquet, said, 'It's marvellous. It's magnificent. A wonderful day and we still can't believe we've won. I'm so tired I can hardly grasp it all.'

Traffic in the streets around the Royal Garden Hotel in Kensington was brought to a standstill as fans turned out in force with Union Jacks and banners as the team coach made its way to the banquet.

Thousands who gathered around the hotel gave a huge roar as the squad emerged on to the hotel balcony and Moore held aloft the Jules Rimet Trophy.

The biggest ovation was reserved for manager Alf Ramsey when he took his turn to lift the trophy.

Prime Minister Wilson, who had flown back from Washington yesterday, had greeted the players at the reception, telling skipper Moore, 'Congratulations Bobby, very well done.'

As the banquet got under way, Moore cut a yard-long cake which had been iced to look like a football pitch.

The players' wives and girlfriends were seated together at a table in a separate room for the banquet.

While the official celebrations were going on, thousands of flag-waving fans partied in London.

In Trafalgar Square, supporters jumped into the fountain and there were joyous chants of *England, England, We won the cup* and *When the whites go marching in*.

The traffic-packed streets came to a standstill as motorists hooted their horns in celebration.

And an AA spokesman said tonight, 'It's like VE Night, election night and New Year's Eve all rolled into one.'

BOSS GETS PM'S VOTE

FOOTBALL-MAD Prime Minister Harold Wilson tonight made sure reluctant hero Alf Ramsey got his moment in the limelight.

When England stepped on to the Royal Garden Hotel balcony to lap up the adulation of the crowd below, the manager appeared reluctant to take his turn lifting the trophy.

But Wilson, who flew back from government business in the USA in time to attend the final, took Ramsey's arm and ushered him forward. He told him, 'It's only once in a lifetime, you know.'

The Labour Party leader revealed how the Germans' late goal had wrecked his big-match prediction.

He said, 'It was a marvellous game. I was a bit shattered when it went into extra time. I had said that it would be 2-1 in England's favour and I was only one minute out!'

Wilson was introduced to Jack and Bobby Charlton's mother, Cissie, and quipped, 'I was wishing you had more children when the match was in the balance.' She joked, 'So did I. We could have done with 11.'

NATIONAL ALF SERVICE

ALF RAMSEY tonight dropped a big hint he is ready to stay as England manager until at least after the Three Lions defend their crown in Mexico.

Today's triumph is sure to make the former Ipswich Town manager one of the world's most sought-after bosses and there is already speculation he could be tempted to take a big-money job abroad.

Ramsey was reluctant to discuss his future plans, but he said, 'Everyone seems concerned about what I'm going to do.

'But it would be good to have another go. Don't forget we have now qualified for the next World Cup in Mexico. It's good to have won at home – it would be good to win there.'

He admitted the pressure during the tournament had been worse than he expected, adding, 'I did not think the strain would be so great.

'Even trivial things became a chore. The constant demands for autographs and the hundreds of letters telling me who to play and how to play.

'I have disagreed with people, I've been furious with people, but if you carry these troubles on your shoulders you find that you get into soup.

'I always remember, after a year as manager of Ipswich, the chairman said to me "As a football club manager you must learn to grow a few extra skins". This was sound advice and this I have done.'

Former manager Walter Winterbottom is thrilled his successor has achieved something he failed to do in four tilts at the World Cup.

He singled out Alan Ball for special praise, saying, 'He never stopped chasing. This was a big factor throughout.'

JIMMY GRIEVES

JIMMY GREAVES skipped tonight's official celebrations after admitting he had mixed emotions over England's triumph.

The nation's record goalscorer failed to net in three group games and, after an injury kept him out of the quarter-final win, Alf Ramsey stuck with Geoff Hurst.

After seeing the West Ham United man grab the glory with a hat-trick, Greaves insisted, 'Who cares who scored the goals – so long as they were England's.'

But the Tottenham Hotspur forward admitted, 'I am the most disappointed, but proudest, man in the world.'

WE WANT OUR BALL BACK

BOBBY MOORE tonight pointed a finger at West Germany over the mysterious disappearance of the final match ball.

Despite the usual custom of a player keeping the ball when he scores a hat-trick, England hero Geoff Hurst did not come away with it at the end. It is not clear what happened to the ball, but captain Moore claimed, 'One of the Germans pinched it, I'm told.'

YES! MINISTER

SPORTS MINISTER Denis Howell tonight insisted winning the World Cup was worth every penny of taxpayers' money spent on the tournament.

Howell, who won a long-running battle for public funds to be spent on stadium improvements, said, 'I told the Chancellor of the Exchequer that this has been the best half-million pounds the government has ever spent.'

He watched the final from the Royal Box and admitted the drama of West Germany's late goal and extra time left him on the edge of his seat.

'To be honest, I wouldn't have given the free kick against Jackie Charlton which led to the Germans scoring just before the end of normal time.

'I think there was more tension in the Royal Box than on the field.'

PAWS IN CELEBRATIONS

ENGLAND'S celebrations tonight included a special guest – the dog who saved the World Cup.

Black and white mongrel Pickles shot to fame in March by finding the stolen Jules Rimet Trophy in Norwood, South London, while out walking with his owner, David Corbett.

Corbett's sister hit out ahead of the final, saying it was unfair that her brother hadn't been sent a ticket by the FA as a 'thank you'.

Thames lighterman Corbett and his hero pet watched the final on TV, but they WERE part of today's historic events after all.

They were invited to tonight's official celebrations in Kensington and Pickles was the centre of attention as he was introduced to the players and other guests at the Royal Garden Hotel.

Sunday 31 July
The Day After The Final

EYE DON'T BELIEVE IT

HAT-TRICK hero Geoff Hurst looked back on his dream World Cup and admitted: I didn't think I'd play a single game.

The West Ham United forward, who made history as the first man to score three in a final, was today nursing a black eye from a collision with West Germany goalkeeper Hans Tilkowski.

And he joked, 'At least this proves I played yesterday – and I'm finding that pretty hard to believe at the moment.

'I honestly didn't think I would get a single game. I thought I would just be around as a reserve.

'I had a bad game on England's tour and, when Roger Hunt and Jimmy Greaves played against Uruguay, I reckoned that was it. I certainly didn't expect things to work out the way they did.

'I felt really sorry for Jimmy when he injured his leg, but it gave me the chance I had been dreaming of. I played in two cup finals for West Ham at Wembley, but I've never known anything quite like this game. The fans were magnificent.

'Things went well when I came in against Argentina and I was lucky enough to score the only goal. But I still thought Jimmy would get the place for the final.'

Hurst – who has only three days off before West Ham's pre-season European tour – added, 'I felt really proud being in the team with my club-mates Bobby Moore and Martin Peters.

'Bobby, of course, brilliantly set up my first goal with a great free kick. Then Martin scored with a marvellous shot.

'There has been a lot of argument about my second goal. I was unsighted after hitting the ball, but Roger Hunt was closest to the goal and says it definitely crossed the line.

'There was even confusion over my last goal. I didn't know whether the final whistle had blown before I shot into the net.

'But the boys grabbed hold of me and pointed to the scoreboard which showed "England 4 West Germany 2". It was great, just great.'

ROUS'S GOAL PLEA

SIR STANLEY ROUS hopes to settle the argument over England's controversial third goal once and for all.

The FIFA president today contacted ITV and asked them to provide the clearest possible slow-motion footage of Geoff Hurst's disputed strike. West Germany claim the whole of the ball did not cross the line, but Rous said, 'It will be wonderful to prove to the world that this was a valid goal.'

ALF'S BIG DEAL

FA CHIEFS are drawing up a new deal to stop Alf Ramsey being lured away from the England job.

The man who masterminded England's triumph has been linked with Arsenal and will be the subject of lucrative offers from abroad.

Ramsey's contract runs out in May, but the FA are set to pay him a £5,000 bonus for winning the trophy and increase his salary, which is currently £4,500 a year. However, FA secretary Denis Follows admitted today that England chiefs cannot compete financially with the offers Ramsey is expected to receive.

Follows said, 'Everyone now looks again to England to lead the world and to Alf Ramsey to show them the way. Now the offers to him will come in from wherever football is played.

'He has a job for life with the Football Association. We know we could never pay Alf the money he might command elsewhere. If, for example, Inter Milan offered him £30,000 a year, how could we stand in his way? This is a decision for the individual. But we can offer him a secure professional position, a job that must bring satisfaction and pride. These are our weapons, but the decision rests with Alf.

'Whether he stays or goes, no one will ever be able to repay him for the riches he has brought to English – no, British – football.'

Ramsey was today playing his cards close to his chest over his plans, saying, 'I will have a few days at home, opening all the letters which have been sent to me, some rest and then a holiday.'

Asked whether England can win again in four years, he said, 'There is no reason why not.' But would he be in charge in Mexico? 'I would not like to say.'

Quizzed over possible interest from top European clubs, he said, 'I don't think I would go abroad. After all, I am an Englishman. I prefer it here.'

The former Ipswich Town manager would only say he wanted to work in 'a job that satisfies me', adding, 'It would be fun to build a team again in the way that I built Ipswich and England.'

100 YEARS OF FAILURE

ALF RAMSEY today said it had taken English football 100 years to learn how to play the right way.

For decades England were regarded as masters of the game, but the myth was exploded by four World Cup flops and painful defeats such as two beatings by Hungary in the early 1950s.

Ramsey, who was in the team crushed 6-3 at Wembley by Hungary in England's first home defeat by a nation from outside the British Isles, has remoulded the team and tactics since taking over in 1962.

He quickly abandoned the long-accepted 3-2-5 formation and his tactics evolved from 4-2-4 to 4-3-3 and, for the final three matches of the tournament, 4-4-2.

Analysing England's development, he said, 'I was a little worried before the series began that English football was still behind the rest of the world. But obviously we were not. From the fact that we won the World Cup, it can be taken that we have caught up.

'It has taken English football 100 years to realise that football can be played differently from the way it was when it was originated.

'What has English football got to offer the world? Good football, played strongly and within the rules of the game.

'We were the strongest and fittest team in the World Cup, so I don't think we have to concentrate on that.

'But there are certain technical points, like ball control, at which we can never hope to beat South American or Latin European sides. We Englishmen are built differently. We play a different kind of football.'

HOO-RAY FOR WILSON

RAY WILSON is looking forward to a well-earned rest after completing a famous cup double.

The England full-back was in the Everton side which won the FA Cup Final against Sheffield Wednesday in May. And he followed that up with the 'wonderful experience' of playing every game in England's World Cup campaign, appearing six times in 20 days.

Former Huddersfield Town defender Wilson, 31, said, 'World Cup matches are so different from the FA Cup, where you have two or three weeks between rounds.

'I think you get used to the pressure in the World Cup. You have no time to relax between games. No sooner have you finished one match than you have to be ready for the next.'

TOTAL DEDICATION

ONE of Alf Ramsey's right-hand men says total commitment on and off the pitch from the England squad was the key to success.

Trainers Harold Shepherdson and Les Cocker worked alongside Ramsey throughout the tournament and put the squad through a punishing 'boot camp' in the build-up to the finals.

Shepherdson said the 22-man party were united in a common cause throughout the preparations and tournament.

He said, 'These fellows were away from their homes for virtually two months and they did everything we demanded of them without a grumble and with no dissension.

'And, in the final, they showed their character after Germany's second goal forced extra time.

'Little Alan Ball was so disappointed that he was nearly in tears, but he and the others picked themselves up and got on top again.'

BIG SCREEN STARS

ENGLAND re-lived their Wembley heroics by watching a specially-arranged colour screening of the final at a Soho cinema today.

Captain Bobby Moore and the Charlton brothers enjoyed it so much they asked to watch it again.

EUSÉBIO GIFT TO IDOL

PORTUGAL star Eusébio today made a touching tribute to his idol Bobby Charlton.

The World Cup's top goalscorer turned up at the cinema where a screening of the final had been arranged for the England players – and handed Charlton a dozen bottles of port.

As Eusébio waited patiently outside with his gift, he said, 'It is for that great footballer Bobby Charlton. It is because he scored two goals against my team.'

TROPHY UNDER WRAPS

ENGLISH FA secretary Denis Follows was today taking no chances with the Jules Rimet Trophy.

Follows joined Alf Ramsey and the England squad at a televised champagne lunch held in their honour at ATV Studios in Boreham Wood, Herts.

And he kept a tight grip on a small black leather case containing the famous trophy.

The trophy, insured for £30,000, was stolen while on display in Westminster in March, but was later found after being dumped in South London.

'Obviously we have been affected by what happened when it was stolen,' said Follows. 'It will remain in my own sticky little hand. I brought the cup here myself and I cannot move fast enough to get it back under lock and key.'

Asked where the trophy would be kept while in the FA's stewardship over the next four years, he joked, 'I'm not going to tell anyone!'

He did, however, say he expected the trophy would go on public display at 'selected events'.

HE'S THE GREATEST

ENGLAND captain Bobby Moore paid tribute to Alf Ramsey today with a toast to 'the greatest manager in the world'.

Ramsey – flanked by his wife Vicky and daughter Tania, 20 – looked shocked when Moore made the toast at a televised lunch at ATV Studios.

Addressing the guests, the England manager apologised if he gave the world the impression of being unemotional – not least when he remained unmoved amid wild celebrations at Wembley yesterday.

He explained, 'I am sorry that I present this picture to everyone, but it is not intentional, I assure you. But it was important that someone remained sane within the England party. That was me.'

GIMME MOORE

BOBBY MOORE wants to carry on his amazing Wembley trophy run.

The England captain, who now looks set to agree a new deal to remain with West Ham United, has lifted the FA Cup, European Cup Winners' Cup and World Cup at the national stadium in successive seasons.

Asked today whether he could keep up the sequence next season, Moore joked, 'We'll think of something. How about the League Cup – is that held at Wembley?'

GRAND STAN FINISH

INJURED England legend Sir Stanley Matthews DID watch Alf Ramsey's men win – eventually.

Former Three Lions winger Matthews, recovering in hospital in Stoke-on-Trent after a car crash on the eve of the final, caught most of the action live on television.

But a hospital spokesman revealed today that Matthews had fallen asleep in the final minutes and had to watch the end of the game when it was re-run later.

OH BABY!

JACK CHARLTON'S heavily pregnant wife found extra time too stressful to watch on TV.

Pat Charlton, 29, did not attend the final because she is expecting their third child at any time.

And Leeds United defender Big Jack explained today, 'My wife told me on the telephone that she was feeling fine, but that she could only watch 90 minutes of the match. She went up to bed and rested during extra time. It was too much for her, poor love.'

Pat said, 'During the match, I kept my fingers crossed, hoping the baby wouldn't choose an inconvenient moment for its entry into the world. When I stopped watching, Jack had just given away the free kick which led to the second Germany goal.

'I went upstairs while the rest of the family watched the rest of the match. When I heard we had won, I just wept with joy.'

Asked about possible names for the baby, she joked, 'If it's a boy, you can be sure of one thing – we're not calling him World Cup Willie, even in fun.'

HERR-RAISING

WEST GERMANY'S nearly men received a heroes' welcome today when they arrived home.

Tens of thousands of people greeted them at Frankfurt Airport and thousands more lined the ten-mile route into the city centre.

Frankfurt mayor Willi Brundert cut short his holiday in Austria to receive them at the city's Guildhall.

Fans held up banners proclaiming 'You won all the same' and 'We greet our world champions'.

Before leaving England, coach Helmut Schön said, 'England were magnificent. We are proud to have played in such a dramatic final. I have no regrets about anything. I am a happy man, because this was a victory for football. People said it would be a defensive game. It was not. With six goals, how could anyone say it was defensive?

'Your crowds, too, were magnificent. All the way from our hotel to the reception on Saturday night, the route was lined with thousands of people cheering and waving. You would have thought that we, not England, had won the World Cup.'

OWN GOAL

ENGLAND 66 will go into the record books as the joint lowest-scoring World Cup so far.

Only the six-goal final saved the tournament from becoming the outright holder of the unwanted record.

The last finals, in Chile, produced 89 goals in 32 matches at an average of 2.8 per game and the goals scored in yesterday's final at least meant this year's tournament equalled that total.

After the group stage, the average stood at a lowly 2.4, but some free-scoring matches in the knockout stages, particularly Portugal's 5-3 win over North Korea, boosted the ratio.

'LUCKY PIRATES' JIBE

ENGLAND were today hailed around the world as worthy champions – except in Argentina.

Press reports in most nations said Alf Ramsey's men deserved to win, but a headline in *The Argentine* newspaper branded the final 'a farce' in an article headlined 'Lucky pirates'.

Otherwise, though, the only real dissent came over the controversial third England goal.

One West German newspaper, *Die Welt am Sonntag,* ran the headline 'Linesman decides world championship'.

The goal was described in Spain by *Marca* as 'a phantom goal', but the same newspaper said the hosts deserved the win, saying, 'The key was England's fighting spirit and physical efforts.'

And in Portugal, Lisbon-based *Diario de Noticias,* wrote, 'The victory of the English, though their third goal may have aroused many doubts, was fair.'

In Uruguay, *El Pais* reported, 'England's most glorious day – champions of the world for the first time. Uruguay was the only team the champions could not defeat. The masters of football are now undisputed.'

Swedish newspaper *Aftonbladet* claimed, 'The cup is at home and deservedly so. England deserved victory, not only yesterday, but in the entire tournament, for they were the best team.'

Soviet Sports wrote, 'England were worthy winners, gaining victory convincingly and attractively.'

That view was echoed in France, where Paris-based *L'Humaite Dimanche* said, 'England well deserved the World Cup. It was a triumph of strength and determination.'

While English newspapers today greeted the hosts' success with triumphant headlines, the fact the match went to extra time posed a problem for last night's editions of regional evening papers.

The usual Saturday deadline time meant the *Liverpool Echo* had to send its sports supplement to press at the end of 90 minutes – with the unfortunate front page headline 'Disappointing final goes to extra time'.

CLUBS V COUNTRY

ENGLAND'S hopes of future glory could be wrecked by a clubs-v-country battle.

New Football League president Len Shipman today issued an ominous warning over co-operation with the national team.

Manager Alf Ramsey has fought hard over the last three years for greater access to his players and this season clubs did release their stars more readily for World Cup warm-up matches.

The Football League has an agreement with the FA that players must be made available for four matches a season.

The FA would like to increase this number, with England building towards the 1968 European Championships and 1970 World Cup.

But Leicester City chairman Shipman, who takes over from long-time League president Joe Richards, said, 'We cannot let England have our players more freely.

'League clubs have done everything they can to help England win the World Cup. But the players are the clubs' assets.

'Now, for a change, the clubs will want first call on the players' services for club games and summer tours. It simply must be this way.'

His view is at odds with that of FA secretary Denis Follows, who said, 'I expect to be flooded with invitations for England to play abroad. We are restricted by our agreement with the League to four internationals in each season. That is one of the things that will certainly be discussed.'

Follows, though, promised the FA won't cash in by demanding huge fees for England to play overseas friendlies.

He added, 'I don't think we shall be out to commercialise the World Cup. Brazil, I believe, asked guarantees of 20,000 US dollars to play after their World Cup victories.'

Follows said the success of the tournament could spark a boom in football at domestic level and urged the Football League to make the most of the opportunity.

He said, 'The playing of the World Cup in England, apart from England's victory, has given the game a fantastic new impetus.'

BRAZIL WANT CUP BACK

BRAZIL are already plotting how to win back the World Cup – and want to tap into Alf Ramsey's secret formula for success.

The two-time champions' bid for a third successive world title ended in disaster as they crashed out at the group stage.

Brazilian FIFA representative Luís Murgel said today, 'Brazil salutes England – you are worthy champions. You had fire, discipline and the will to win. Others teams may have played better in single matches, but you were the most consistent and never had a bad game.

'We are determined to regain the world crown from you and we are now rebuilding to do so.

'We have better individual players than you, but how is it that you play better as a team? What has Alf Ramsey imparted to the players which lifts them above teams with a greater total of individual skill?'

The next World Cup will be held in Mexico and the hosts are already promising it will be bigger and better than 1966.

Mexican FA president Guillermo Cañedo said, 'This is the best organised World Cup so far, but we will surpass you in Mexico in four years' time.

'Your crowds, grounds and administration were wonderful. We will take the best ideas from the two previous tournaments to make sure we do better.'

PETERS CAR CRASH

WEMBLEY goal hero Martin Peters tonight escaped injury in a car crash.

The midfielder, 22, and his wife Kathleen, 21, were passengers in a chauffeur-driven car which was involved in a collision with another car 100 yards from England's Hendon Hall Hotel headquarters.

Kathleen suffered a bruised back and shock, but she did not require hospital treatment. Peters and two other men in the car were unhurt.

Peters even managed to sign autographs for a group of youngsters who approached him as he surveyed the damage to the vehicle.

Monday 1 August
Two Days After
The Final

MOORE VOTED NUMBER ONE

BOBBY MOORE today picked up his prize as the World Cup's best player and said: We've turned a dream into reality.

The England captain was presented with a cheque for £750 and a silver salver after he was chosen by an international panel of journalists and broadcasters.

His West Ham United team-mate Geoff Hurst, who scored four goals in his three games, picked up £250 as England's top scorer.

Speaking at a lunch hosted by sponsor Radox, Moore said, 'The England team and all the final 22 players felt capable of making Alf Ramsey's words, "We will win the World Cup", come true. A bright dream became a reality.'

Hurst added, 'Everybody gave of their best and, thank goodness, that was enough.'

RESERVES SHARE BONUS

ENGLAND'S forgotten men will get an equal share of the players' cash bonus.

Seven of the squad did not feature in the tournament, but those who did play have agreed the £22,000 pot should be split equally.

Fulham full-back George Cohen, who played in all six matches, said, 'We hadn't really discussed it before Saturday, but it was unanimous among the team that the others shouldn't be cut out.

'Bobby Moore went to Mr Ramsey yesterday and asked if the money could be shared 22 ways. I am delighted that it will be.'

FA secretary Denis Follows said, 'When the question was raised that there might be a system of bonus awards based on the number of games in which they took part, the players would not even consider that.

'They insisted that everyone in the party had done a great job, either in preparation or in action on the field.

'There were regrets that some were more fortunate than others in being able to play, but there was definitely no question of anything else but an equal share.'

The seven who did not feature were goalkeepers Ron Springett and Peter Bonetti, plus outfield players Gerry Byrne, Jimmy Armfield, Norman Hunter, Ron Flowers and George Eastham.

POLICE HUNT

ROGER HUNT today thanked hundreds of fans who gave him a 'marvellous' welcome home.

The Liverpool striker drove home from London last night and was stunned to find around 600 well-wishers waiting to greet him in Culcheth, near Warrington.

Police, aware that a large crowd had gathered, were waiting to give Hunt an escort into the village.

And the player arrived home to find his street decked out in bunting, with flag-waving fans waiting to cheer him.

Hunt, who has to report for pre-season training with Liverpool on Thursday, said, 'I got the shock of my life. I never expected anything like this. It was marvellous.

'I expected a quiet homecoming to a celebration with a few relatives and friends, but there must have been 500 or 600 people outside our house and apparently many had been waiting for hours because they expected me to arrive earlier.'

BOBBY FLEES

BOBBY CHARLTON today hit the road with his family to escape World Cup pandemonium.

The Manchester United man arrived back in Flixton, Greater Manchester, last night – but he soon headed off again in search of some peace and quiet.

Before driving off with wife Norma and daughters Suzanne, three, and Andrea, 15 months, Charlton said, 'I don't know where we are going.

'We just want to be by ourselves for a few hours.

'The telephone started ringing early this morning and many people have asked if they could come round to see me.

'They were most understanding when I explained and said that I would have to make some public appearances which will cut into my private life again during the next few days.'

Reflecting on England's triumph and the pressure the players faced, Charlton added, 'At one time in the competition it seemed as if we would never make it, but when we went on to the field at Wembley we were full of confidence.'

FRIENDS RE-UNITED

MANCHESTER UNITED trio Bobby Charlton, Nobby Stiles and John Connelly could be back in action just seven days after England's final win.

Red Devils manager Matt Busby today confirmed he expects them to report back for pre-season training on Thursday.

They will be joining United's tour of Germany and Austria – and could even feature in a friendly at Celtic this Saturday.

Busby said, 'Charlton, Stiles and Connelly will rest until Thursday and I shall see how things are then. But you can take it they will be going on tour with us.'

TAKING THE PEE

JACK CHARLTON returned home with another World Cup 'trophy'...a potty!

FIFA drug testers presented the England defender with the joke award after he was randomly selected for a dope test on Saturday – the FOURTH time in six matches he had to give a urine sample.

'ELLO, 'ELLO

EUSÉBIO arrived back in Portugal today wearing a special souvenir – a British policeman's helmet.

The tournament top scorer explained, 'I will keep it forever. A British police sergeant insisted that I keep it. What a very nice fellow. I hope he won't be punished.'

The Portugal squad had to spend last night in a London Airport lounge when, having turned up at 4pm for their flight home, a technical fault grounded the aircraft.

Thousands of fans were waiting to greet them in Lisbon, many having waited 12 hours because of the delay.

BACK TO REALITY

FIVE England stars are facing uncertain club futures after the World Cup triumph.

Out-of-contract captain Bobby Moore will have make-or-break talks with West Ham United manager Ron Greenwood before the club's pre-season European tour.

Moore, now expected to agree a new deal, said, 'I shall talk everything over with them this week. It should all be sorted out soon.'

Alan Ball today made it clear he wants to leave Blackpool, despite returning to training today.

He said, 'I want to keep right in trim for the new season. I asked the manager if I could train with the boys – but I still want to leave.'

Blackpool have offered Ball a new four-year contract worth £30,000, but Leeds United have bid £100,000 for him and Stoke have topped that with a £110,000 offer.

Stoke are coached by his father, Alan Snr, and he said today, 'Most people agree Alan played his heart out for the whole of Saturday's final. He showed what he is really worth.

'He has proved that he is a world-class footballer. Stoke are very keen to get him. It's up to him.'

Goalkeeper Peter Bonetti, a target for West Ham, still wants to leave Chelsea. 'I was taken off the transfer list without being told a thing about it by my club,' he claimed today.

'Now they are insisting I join them on their tour of Germany immediately. This is too much. I have returned my air ticket to them and told them I'm taking a week's holiday, like it or not.

'For just once I'm going to put my family before football. I've written to the directors demanding an interview. I shall tell them I want to go back on the transfer list.'

Arsenal have had no offers for transfer-listed Eastham, while Manchester United winger Connelly wants talks with manager Matt Busby after being dropped at the end of last season.

Busby said today, 'John was a little upset at being left out, but I believe everything will be all right.'

FAN-TASTIC CHANCE

NEW Football League president Len Shipman today urged clubs to make the most of World Cup fever.

Shipman says the successful tournament can help the domestic game reverse a worrying decline in attendances and wants to make football a sport for the whole family.

He said, 'The World Cup has given British football its greatest opportunity and we must not let it slip.

'I'm going to call a meeting of the League management committee to discuss whatever ways and ideas there are to keep the English football public interested and satisfied.

'I know everyone in the Football League is tremendously keen to keep football number one in the public eye. Football has had a magnificent platform these last few weeks. We have won the public over and we must keep it.

'As far as I'm concerned, one of the biggest features of England's success was the tremendous interest shown by the women – the mothers, daughters and even grandmothers of the land.

'If we're able to keep their interest, we'll go a long way towards pulling back the thousands who have deserted football.

'We've always wanted football to be a family sport. It was during the World Cup. It can be again in the future.

'Even if the women don't come to every game, it is reasonable to think they'll be less resentful of their husbands and sons going to games.'

TIRED OF GOOD LOSERS

ENGLISH football should not be afraid of winning – after too many years of being good losers.

That is the view of FA secretary Denis Follows, who says England should be proud it finally has a team of winners.

He said, 'I may appear proud, arrogant and ostentatious – and I mean to do that very thing. Too often England has been afraid of winning and going down at the last minute. I'm tired of good losers.

'This is an occasion when we've been magnificent winners and I'm tremendously proud of the team and manager. I'm grateful to have played even a small part in this great triumph.'

The Aftermath
(Part One)

Autumn 1966
The man behind the mask

ALF'S 'WONDERFUL' FEELING

ALF RAMSEY has revealed the true depths of feeling he hid behind an emotionless mask of calm when England won the World Cup.

The Three Lions manager kept his excitement in check when the final whistle blew on the victory over West Germany.

And once the official celebrations were over, he went into hiding at his Ipswich home to escape well-wishers and the clamour for interviews.

But Ramsey, emerging back into the spotlight for the new international season, has lifted the lid on what the World Cup win really meant to him.

He insists he was 'just as thrilled as anybody' by England's triumph, but that the day left his mind in 'a jumble'.

And Ramsey says he will lead England all the way to Mexico 70 buoyed by the 'wonderful' feeling of bringing pleasure to the nation.

Ramsey, whose team play their first match as world champions against Northern Ireland in Belfast, said, 'The World Cup in 1970 will be a tremendously exciting challenge.

'It is a challenge for me, the players and English football. It is a challenge we must all look forward to. The objective for the England team while I am in charge will be to win every game we play.

'The thing that has pleased me most about our winning of the World Cup is the pleasure it has brought to so many people in and out of football.

'Everybody feels part of this success. It is a wonderful thing and I am honoured to have been in charge of such a great team of players.'

Ramsey, who has snubbed interest from club sides at home and abroad, appeared to be the coolest man in England during the final drama on 30 July.

He faced the ultimate test when the Germans forced extra time with a late goal, but he calmly issued his instructions before sending out his players to complete a 4-2 victory.

He reflected, 'I don't remember feeling any emotion at all. I was so busy carefully watching and noting every movement of the play that I had no time to experience any tenseness or excitement.

'Yet, when Germany equalised and I knew we had to play for another half-hour, I can remember my thoughts very clearly.

'I was absolutely furious because I knew exactly how many chances of scoring we had missed, but I knew I must not show my anger.

'I also realised that I must not indicate, either by word or expression, the least degree of sympathy for the team, because they had to go on playing.

'I knew they could do it – they knew they could do it. But even a casual "hard luck" might have put a doubt in their minds.'

When the final whistle blew, everyone around Ramsey on the England bench leapt to their feet in celebration, but the manager did not show a hint of emotion.

Yet he insists, 'I was just as thrilled as anybody, but for a while everything was confusing.

'There was a press and television conference. When I got away from that and went into the dressing room, I don't think I have ever in my life heard such a noise.

'There were far more people in there than there should have been and everyone was talking at once. You couldn't have any impression but noise. Just so much noise.'

After the match, the England party returned to the Hendon Hall Hotel before travelling into central London for the official celebrations.

Ramsey revealed, 'Someone had given me a terrifically large bottle of champagne. It really was terrific. I promised that we would share it before we went to the official reception and that is what we did.

'We had a lot of laughter and fun before we piled into the coach again.'

Ramsey admitted he was taken aback by the outpouring of emotion as the squad were driven from their hotel into London.

'The police were outside the hotel because they thought we might need help in getting away – and they were right.'

The mass celebrations and traffic chaos they brought to London that evening were described by the AA as 'like VE Night, election night and New Year's Eve all rolled into one'.

And Ramsey recalled, 'Never in my life will I forget that journey into London. Everywhere there were people lining the pavements and waving and shouting.

'One man stood in the middle of the road with his arms in the air and ran towards us until we had to stop. Then he climbed up, put his head through a window and all he could say was "I love you all" over and over again. He was quite a chap!

'Further along, our way was barred by a car parked slap across the road like a barricade and a young girl in a very bright red mini-skirt danced on the top of it.

'And there was a public house with about 40 customers outside – every one of them holding up a pint mug of beer in a toast. I felt the excitement then – and there is nothing quite like it.'

Ramsey said he had only seen his wife, Vicky, on four days in the two months before the tournament and the three-week-long finals.

The couple were reunited at the Hendon Hall Hotel after the official celebrations and Ramsey recalled, 'All the boys went off to celebrate after the reception, but I went back there to meet her.

'I didn't arrive until two o'clock and it was four o'clock when we went to bed. Until then we talked and drank – we couldn't stop talking. I don't know what I thought as I lay in bed that night.

'I had to be at a meeting at ten o'clock the next morning. That was badly arranged, but there it is! I know I didn't sleep much. I can't remember my thoughts – they were just a jumble. I kept wondering if it were really true and if we had really done it.'

The Ramseys locked themselves away at home for seven days to escape the post-tournament fuss.

Ramsey added, 'We put the telephone in a little room where it was difficult to hear it and determined that we wouldn't answer it for a week.

'We probably lost a lot of calls we would have liked, but it couldn't be helped. It was the only way we could get any peace.'

Now the dust has settled on the World Cup triumph, Ramsey is eager to launch a new chapter in his England career.

The next four years will see his team challenge for a first European Championship title, a competition which reaches its climax in 1968.

Then Ramsey hopes to mastermind a successful defence of the world crown in 1970.

He has no doubt his players deserved their World Cup success and believes they have the ability to scale even greater heights.

Ramsey added, 'There have been many reasons offered for our success in the World Cup. As far as I am concerned, we won because we had the best players – and we still have the best players.

'All of them are aware what the world expects of them. They know they are targets for every one of our competitors to aim at.

'But that is all part of the business of being champions. It should make them raise their game even further.'

If England do go on to even greater glories, Ramsey says one person will play a vital role – his wife.

Paying tribute to the part she has played in his career, he added, 'I don't know much about women and the only women I know are footballers' wives. But I do know what an essential place they have in our lives and this is particularly true of footballers.

'A footballer's wife needs to run the home completely so that he has no worries – give him the sort of food he likes and should have and to work only for his good and the good of his career.

'A footballer could be ruined by a wife who let him have all the household responsibilities, fed him the wrong diet and gave him no peace of mind. My wife has been splendid. I am very lucky.'

The Aftermath
(Part Two)

What happened to…

SIR STANLEY ROUS was FIFA president for another eight years. In 1974, Brazilian João Havelange, an outspoken critic in 1966, ousted him in a bitter election battle. Havelange won on a pledge to expand the world game and the tournament itself. The number of teams at the finals was increased to 24 in 1982 and later to 32. European influence in FIFA waned as Havelange's policies earned him widespread support from developing football nations in Asia, Africa, North America, Central America and the Caribbean. Sepp Blatter was elected to succeed him in 1998 and, although he is Swiss, Europe's influence continued to erode as Blatter steered FIFA on a similar path to Havelange.

THE FA disciplinary committee met on 6 September 1966, to discuss Alf Ramsey's 'animals' comment about Argentina. FIFA had written to the FA calling on it to ask Ramsey to explain himself. The FA disciplinary committee considered a letter from Ramsey in which he apologised for his remark. The committee agreed to accept his written apology and forward the letter to FIFA.

ENGLAND failed to add the 1968 European Championship crown to their world title when they lost in the semi-finals to Yugoslavia. Their reign as world champions was ended by West Germany, who beat them 3-2 after extra time in the quarter-finals of Mexico 70. It was the first time England, who led 2-0, had lost to the Germans in a competitive match. Reaching the semi-finals at the 1990 World Cup and 1996 European Championships is the closest England have come to winning another major title.

ALF RAMSEY was knighted in 1967 and continued as England manager until he was sacked in May 1974, after failure to qualify for that year's World Cup. The last of his 113 matches was a 0-0 draw in Portugal. After a break of three years, he briefly managed Birmingham City, but he left after an early upsurge in results petered out. He never returned to management. Sir Alf died in 1999.

ARGENTINA were allowed to take part in the 1970 World Cup, but failed to qualify. FIFA chose Argentina as hosts for the 1978 tournament and they won on home soil – ironically amid claims, notably from Brazil, that a crucial 6-0 win over Peru was fixed to help them reach the final. They also won the World Cup in 1986, beating England in the quarter-finals in controversial circumstances when Diego Maradona punched the ball into the net for their opener. He rubbed it in by saying, 'That goal was scored a little bit with the hand of God and a little bit with Maradona's head.'

WEMBLEY did not host Argentina again until 1974, when the South Americans met England in a friendly shortly after Sir Alf Ramsey was sacked. They insisted on having an Argentine referee. The home fans chanted 'animals' throughout and the 2-2 draw was marred by an ugly flare-up in which England captain Emlyn Hughes was felled by a punch from Ruben Glaria.

ENGLISH CLUBS were, as Football League president Len Shipman warned, reluctant to release players more often for England duty and the problem frustrated Sir Alf Ramsey for the rest of his reign. When nine players pulled out of the squad for his final match in 1974, he complained, 'We have to establish who runs football. In some way, the clubs have to be punished. I know of one club who can produce medical certificates declaring a player unfit at a moment's notice. The manager has a bundle of them in his desk.' That and the question of postponing domestic matches ahead of internationals would continue to infuriate England managers for decades.

BOBBY CHARLTON was voted European Footballer of the Year in December 1966, beating Eusébio by one vote. Charlton went on to break Billy Wright's England caps record, making the last of his 106 appearances in the 1970 World Cup quarter-final defeat by West Germany. Sir Alf Ramsey controversially substituted him with England leading 2-1 and the move backfired as the Germans equalised and went on to win 3-2 in extra time. Ramsey never picked him again. Charlton finished his England career with 49 goals, a record which stood until Wayne Rooney overtook it in 2015. After leaving Manchester United in 1973, Charlton had an unsuccessful spell as Preston North End manager. He was knighted in 1994.

BOBBY MOORE did agree a new contract with West Ham United and stayed with them until joining Second Division Fulham in 1974. He captained England at the 1970 World Cup and won 108 caps to overtake

Bobby Charlton's record. His international career was effectively ended by a 2-0 World Cup defeat in Poland in June 1973, in which his shocking mistake gifted the Poles their second goal. He was dropped for the decisive return match with the Poles in October 1973 when England failed to reach the 1974 finals. Sir Alf Ramsey recalled Moore for a friendly against Italy a month later, but it proved to be his final match. Moore, who had an unsuccessful spell as manager of Southend United and later worked in the media, died in 1993. A statue of him stands outside the new Wembley.

GEOFF HURST became a fixture in the England team, winning 49 caps and scoring 24 goals. He had made his debut against West Germany in a friendly in February 1966, and his final cap also came against the Germans as they beat England 3-1 in a European Championship quarter-final first leg at Wembley in 1972. That same year he ended his long association with West Ham United when he moved to Stoke City. He had an unsuccessful stint as Chelsea manager between 1979 and 1981, failing to win them promotion from the Second Division. He was part of Ron Greenwood's England coaching team between 1977 and 1982. Hurst was knighted in 1998.

JIMMY GREAVES won only three more England caps after the 1966 finals, scoring just once more. The last of his 57 caps came in May 1967 and he finished his international career with 44 goals, a record which was later overtaken by Bobby Charlton. Sir Alf Ramsey resisted pressure to recall Greaves, claiming the player had said he did not want to be considered unless he was guaranteed a starting place. Having joined West Ham United from Tottenham Hotspur in 1970, he retired in 1971. After successfully battling alcoholism, he became a TV pundit, forming the popular Saint & Greavsie double act with former Scotland international Ian St John.

ALAN BALL left Blackpool in August 1966 with Everton paying £112,000 to beat Leeds United and Stoke City to his signature. He later played for Arsenal and Southampton. The youngest member of England's World Cup-winning XI, he also became the last of that team to win a cap when he captained the Three Lions to a 5-1 win over Scotland in 1975. He was controversially dropped by Don Revie at the start of the 1975/76 season and never played for his country again. Ball, who later managed clubs including Portsmouth, Southampton and Manchester City, died in 2007.

GORDON BANKS won 72 England caps, the last of which came in 1972. At the 1970 World Cup he made what is widely regarded as the greatest save of all time when he somehow clawed out a Pelé header during England's 1-0 group stage defeat by Brazil. He was taken ill ahead of England's quarter-final against West Germany and his absence was seen as a major factor in the Three Lions' defeat. Banks, who left Leicester City for Stoke City in

1967, suffered a serious eye injury in a car crash in 1972. He retired from professional football in 1973, although he did later go on to play in the USA and the Republic of Ireland.

GEORGE COHEN was the first of the World Cup-winning XI to lose his place as a Ramsey regular, winning the last of his 37 caps in 1967. He remained with Fulham throughout his career but injury forced him to retire aged just 29 in 1969.

RAY WILSON remained England's first-choice left-back during the 1968 European Championship campaign, but he did not win another cap after playing in the third-place play-off win over the USSR. Wilson won 63 caps.

NOBBY STILES won only eight more caps, although he featured in the 1968 European Championships and was included in the 1970 World Cup squad. He won the last of his 28 caps shortly before Mexico 70, but did not play at the finals. Stiles, who won the European Cup with Manchester United in 1968, played for the Red Devils from 1960 to 1971 before finishing his career with Middlesbrough and Preston North End. Having retired in 1975, he went on to manage Preston, as well as Vancouver Whitecaps and West Bromwich Albion. He later worked as a youth coach with Manchester United.

JACK CHARLTON won 35 England caps, the last of which came at the 1970 World Cup finals. His only appearance in Mexico came in the final group-stage match against Czechoslovakia when Sir Alf Ramsey rested many of his first-choice side ahead of the quarter-finals. Charlton, who stayed with Leeds United throughout his playing career, went on to manage Middlesbrough, Sheffield Wednesday and Newcastle United. Touted as a possible England boss, he was overlooked by the FA when it appointed Ron Greenwood in 1977 and Bobby Robson in 1982. Charlton instead became Republic of Ireland manager in 1986. During his ten-year reign he masterminded a 1-0 win over England at the 1988 European Championship finals and drew his other three competitive meetings with his homeland.

MARTIN PETERS remained an England regular after the World Cup, winning the last of his 67 caps in 1974. He scored 20 goals for his country. Peters left West Ham United in 1970 for Tottenham Hotspur and later played for Norwich City and Sheffield United. He briefly managed Sheffield United in 1981, retiring as a player to take up the job, but he left after failing to stave off relegation to the Fourth Division.

ROGER HUNT featured in the 1968 European Championship campaign, playing in the semi-final defeat by Yugoslavia and the third-place play-off win over the USSR. However, he won just two more caps and the last of his 34 appearances came against Romania in 1969. He scored 18 goals for England. He remained with Liverpool until 1969 before playing for Bolton Wanderers for three years.

PETER BONETTI settled his differences with Chelsea, who sold their 1966 summer signing Alex Stepney to Manchester United only a few months after buying him. Other than a brief spell in North America in 1975, Bonetti stayed with them until 1979. He continued as Gordon Banks's England understudy and was widely criticised for his performance when called in as a late replacement when Banks fell ill before England's 1970 World Cup defeat by West Germany.

IAN CALLAGHAN, the Liverpool winger who won his second cap in the 2-0 group-stage win over France, had to wait until September 1977, for the next of his four caps. Recalled at the age of 35 by Ron Greenwood, his wait of 11 years and 49 days between international appearances set a new record. John Connelly and Terry Paine, the other two wingers tried at the finals, never played for England again.

SEVEN members of England's 22-man squad did not play a single minute at the World Cup – goalkeepers Peter Bonetti and Ron Springett, defenders Jimmy Armfield, Ron Flowers, Norman Hunter and Gerry Byrne and forward George Eastham. Only the XI who played in the final received winners' medals. In 2009, the other 11 members of the squad were finally presented with medals in a ceremony at 10 Downing Street after FIFA decided on a similar honour for players from all the World Cup-winning countries from 1930 to 1974.

TERRY VENABLES never added to the two England caps he won in the build-up to 1966. The player, who used the tournament to carry out his own scouting missions on the international teams on show, went on to become one of the world's top coaches. He managed club sides including Barcelona and coached England for two years, culminating in the 1996 European Championships held on home soil. Venables's team were hailed as possibly the best since Ramsey's era and reached the semi-finals at Euro 96 before losing on penalties to Germany.

WEST GERMANY – and later the reunified Germany – went on to become one of football's most consistently successful nations, winning the World Cup in 1974, 1990 and 2014 and the European Championships in 1972, 1980 and 1996. Having never beaten England until a friendly in 1968, the Germans have become a bogey team for the Three Lions, inflicting semi-final defeats on them in the 1990 World Cup and 1996 European Championships. They also progressed at England's expense in the 1970, 1982 and 2010 World Cups, as well as the 1972 European Championships.

HELMUT SCHÖN was West Germany coach until 1978, leading them in another three World Cup finals campaigns. After gaining revenge over England in 1970, his team lost to Italy in the semi-finals. Schön finally lifted the trophy in 1974 when the Germans won it as hosts. He also led them to the 1972 European title. Schön died in 1996.

FRANZ BECKENBAUER played in two more World Cup finals tournaments, scoring in West Germany's revenge win over England in 1970 and captaining West Germany to their triumph on home soil in 1974. He also captained the Germans to their first Wembley win over England, a 3-1 European Championship quarter-final first leg victory in 1972. He managed the national team between 1984 and 1990, taking them to the World Cup Final in 1986 and then winning the trophy four years later, beating England in the semi-finals.

HELMUT HALLER was eventually revealed as the West German player who left the field with the match ball at the end of the final. He was pictured with the ball under his arm after the final whistle and, in 1996, he agreed to hand it over to Sir Geoff Hurst. The ball is now on show at the National Football Museum in Manchester. Haller died in 2012.

PELÉ announced he would never play in another World Cup after the brutal treatment he received in 1966. However, he was persuaded to change his mind and was the outstanding player at the 1970 finals as an exciting new team made Brazil the first nation to win the Jules Rimet Trophy for a third time. He won the last of his 92 caps in 1971, finishing with a total of 77 goals. Pelé played for Santos from 1956 to 1974 before finishing his career with the New York Cosmos in the North American Soccer League, which also attracted the likes of Bobby Moore and Franz Beckenbauer.

BRAZIL were allowed to keep the Jules Rimet Trophy in 1970 after winning the World Cup for an unprecedented third time. However, the gold trophy, which had been stolen and recovered in London in the build-up to the 1966 finals, was stolen again in 1983 in Rio de Janeiro and was never recovered. Brazil also won the World Cup in 1994 and 2002.

EDU, the 16-year-old tipped as the new Pelé, did not play in the 1966 finals, but he did go on to win 42 caps and was in the squads for the 1970 and 1974 tournaments, playing once at each.

NORTH KOREA did not feature at the World Cup finals again until 2010, when they were knocked out at the group stage after losing all three of their matches. Their neighbours and bitter rivals South Korea have featured at every finals since 1986, finishing fourth as joint hosts in 2002.

ITALY'S failure in England cost manager Edmondo Fabbri his job and the Azzurri restored their pride by winning the 1968 European Championships and then reaching the final of the 1970 World Cup, where they lost to Brazil. The Italians went on to win the World Cup in 1982 and 2006, as well as reaching the final in 1994.

PORTUGAL qualified for only one of the next eight World Cup tournaments. That came in 1986 when they beat England 1-0 in the opening match under manager José Torres, one of the stars of their 1966 team. The Portuguese have never won the World Cup, but did reach the semi-finals again in 2006 and knocked out England at the quarter-final stage in that tournament and the European Championships in 2004. They also beat England in the group stages of Euro 2000.

EUSÉBIO played for Portugal for another seven years, but never got the chance to appear at another major international tournament. He scored 41 goals in 64 appearances for his country and stayed with Benfica until 1975. Having seen Bobby Charlton wreck his World Cup hopes at Wembley in 1966, Eusébio suffered more Wembley disappointment at the hands of Charlton in 1968 when Benfica lost there to Manchester United in the European Cup Final. Eusébio died in 2014.

GEORGI ASPAROUKHOV put his disappointing World Cup behind him and his superb performances for Levski Sofia and Bulgaria made him a target for top clubs including Benfica. He remained with Levski, though, and went on to feature in all three of Bulgaria's matches at the 1970 World Cup. He died in a car crash in 1971 aged just 28. In a 2000 poll, Bulgarians voted him the country's greatest player of all time, beating 1994 World Cup hero Hristo Stoichkov into second place.

OMAR BORRÁS, Uruguay trainer in 1966, later became head coach and his Mexico 86 team went down in World Cup history as one of the dirtiest ever. In a decisive group game against Scotland, José Batista was sent off after just 56 seconds, but Uruguay held out for the 0-0 draw they needed. Borrás was banned by FIFA for branding the referee 'a murderer', while the Scots claimed 21 minutes of the 90 had been lost to time-wasting. Scotland coach Alex Ferguson accused Borrás of 'lying and cheating and uttering a lot of rubbish'.

FIFA again attempted to crack down on rough play at the 1970 World Cup and introduced a system of yellow and red cards, the brainchild of former English referee Ken Aston, for bookings and dismissals. The tournament in Mexico did not feature a single sending-off.

DRUG TESTING became common in sports worldwide after FIFA's ground-breaking programme in 1966. Officially, Ernst Jean-Joseph was the first player to fail a drugs test at the World Cup finals when, in 1974, he tested positive after Haiti's defeat by Italy. However, in 2011, historians in Berlin discovered a letter sent in November 1966 by Professor Mihailo Andrejevic, the Yugoslav in charge of FIFA's anti-doping committee at the finals, to the president of the West German Athletics Federation in which he said that tests on three West German players had shown up small traces of the banned stimulant ephedrine. Andrejevic speculated in the letter that the results were probably the result of the players using cold remedies.

SUBSTITUTIONS were introduced for the 1970 World Cup finals as FIFA addressed concerns that the outcome of a number of matches in 1966 had been influenced by teams being handicapped by a serious injury to one or more of their players. Each team was allowed to make two subs for injury or tactical reasons. This was eventually increased to three.

GOAL DIFFERENCE replaced goal average at the 1970 World Cup as the system used to separate teams who had the same number of points in the group stage. FIFA decided the new system was simpler to understand and would encourage attacking play.

BRIAN LONDON failed in his bid to add the world heavyweight boxing title to the crown won by England's footballers. On Saturday 6 August – exactly a week after the World Cup Final – the Blackpool fighter was stopped inside three rounds by Muhammad Ali at Earls Court.

THE BBC switched its experimental BBC2 show *Match of the Day,* a football highlights programme which had been drawing viewing figures of only 20,000 since its launch in 1964, to a Saturday night slot on BBC1 at the start of the 1966/67 season. The hugely popular programme is still going strong and celebrated its 50th anniversary in 2015.

PAT CHARLTON was true to her word when she gave birth to her and Jack's third child, a son. He wasn't named Willie after the World Cup mascot. The couple chose the name Peter instead.

Appendix

HOW RAMSEY'S TEAM EVOLVED
27 February 1963–5 July 1966
Players listed in bold went on to play at least once during the finals

27 FEBRUARY 1963 (PARIS)
EUROPEAN NATIONS CUP, PRELIMINARY ROUND, SECOND LEG
France 5 (Wisnieski 3, 75, Douis 32, Coussou 43, 82)
England 2 (Smith 57, Tambling 74)
(France won 6-3 on aggregate)
Ron Springett, Jimmy Armfield (capt), Ron Henry, Brian Labone, Ron Flowers, **Bobby Moore, Bobby Charlton, John Connelly,** Bobby Tambling, Bobby Smith, **Jimmy Greaves.**

6 APRIL 1963 (WEMBLEY)
HOME INTERNATIONAL CHAMPIONSHIP
England 1 (Douglas 79) Scotland 2 (Baxter 28, pen 30)
Gordon Banks, Jimmy Armfield (capt), Gerry Byrne, Maurice Norman, Ron Flowers, **Bobby Moore,** Bryan Douglas, Jimmy Melia, **Bobby Charlton,** Bobby Smith, **Jimmy Greaves.**

8 MAY 1963 (WEMBLEY)
England 1 (Douglas 86) Brazil 1 (Pepe 18)
Gordon Banks, Jimmy Armfield (capt), **Ray Wilson,** Maurice Norman, **Bobby Moore,** Gordon Milne, Bryan Douglas, **Bobby Charlton,** George Eastham, Bobby Smith, **Jimmy Greaves.**

29 MAY 1963 (BRATISLAVA)
Czechoslovakia 2 (Scherer 52, Kadraba 72)
England 4 (Greaves 18, 81, Smith 45, B. Charlton 71)
Gordon Banks, Ken Shellito, **Ray Wilson,** Maurice Norman, **Bobby Moore (capt),** Gordon Milne, **Terry Paine,** George Eastham, **Bobby Charlton,** Bobby Smith, **Jimmy Greaves.**

2 JUNE 1963 (LEIPZIG)
East Germany 1 (Ducke 24) England 2 (Hunt 45, B. Charlton 70)
Gordon Banks, Jimmy Armfield (capt), **Ray Wilson,** Maurice Norman, **Bobby Moore,** Gordon Milne, **Terry Paine, Bobby Charlton,** George Eastham, Bobby Smith, **Roger Hunt.**

5 JUNE 1963 (BASLE)
Switzerland 1 (Bertschi 42)
England 8 (B. Charlton 19, 55, 83, Byrne 30, 50, Douglas 42, Kay 69, Melia 75)
Ron Springett, Jimmy Armfield (capt), **Ray Wilson, Bobby Moore,** Ron Flowers, Tony Kay, Bryan Douglas, Jimmy Melia, **Bobby Charlton, Jimmy Greaves,** Johnny Byrne.

12 OCTOBER 1963 (NINIAN PARK, CARDIFF)
HOME INTERNATIONAL CHAMPIONSHIP
Wales 0 England 4 (Smith 5, 68, Greaves 67, B. Charlton 86)
Gordon Banks, Jimmy Armfield (capt), **Ray Wilson,** Maurice Norman, **Bobby Moore,** Gordon Milne, **Terry Paine,** George Eastham, **Bobby Charlton,** Bobby Smith, **Jimmy Greaves.**

23 OCTOBER 1963 (WEMBLEY)
England 2 (Paine 65, Greaves 90) Rest of the World 1 (Law 82)
Gordon Banks, Jimmy Armfield (capt), **Ray Wilson,** Maurice Norman, **Bobby Moore,** Gordon Milne, **Terry Paine, Bobby Charlton,** George Eastham, Bobby Smith, **Jimmy Greaves.**

20 NOVEMBER 1963 (WEMBLEY)
HOME INTERNATIONAL CHAMPIONSHIP
England 8 (Paine 2, 38, 61, Greaves 20, 30, 60, 65, Smith 46)
Northern Ireland 3 (Crossan 42, Wilson 53, 85)
Gordon Banks, Jimmy Armfield (capt), Bobby Thomson, Maurice Norman, **Bobby Moore,** Gordon Milne, **Terry Paine,** George Eastham, **Bobby Charlton,** Bobby Smith, **Jimmy Greaves.**

11 APRIL 1964 (HAMPDEN PARK, GLASGOW)
HOME INTERNATIONAL CHAMPIONSHIP
Scotland 1 (Gilzean 72) England 0
Gordon Banks, Jimmy Armfield (capt), **Ray Wilson,** Maurice Norman, **Bobby Moore,** Gordon Milne, **Terry Paine, Bobby Charlton,** George Eastham, Johnny Byrne, **Roger Hunt.**

6 MAY 1964 (WEMBLEY)
England 2 (Byrne 43, 52) Uruguay 1 (Spencer 78)
Gordon Banks, George Cohen, Ray Wilson, Maurice Norman, **Bobby Moore (capt),** Gordon Milne, **Terry Paine,** George Eastham, **Bobby Charlton,** Johnny Byrne, **Jimmy Greaves.**

17 MAY 1964 (LISBON)
Portugal 3 (Torres 18, 47, 53)
England 4 (Byrne 21, 57, 88, B. Charlton 29)
Gordon Banks, George Cohen, Ray Wilson, Maurice Norman, **Bobby Moore** (**capt**), Gordon Milne, Peter Thompson, George Eastham, **Bobby Charlton, Jimmy Greaves,** Johnny Byrne.

24 May 1964 (DUBLIN)
Republic of Ireland 1 (Strahan 41)
England 3 (Eastham 9, Byrne 22, Greaves 55)
Tony Waiters, **George Cohen, Ray Wilson,** Ron Flowers, **Bobby Moore** (**capt**), Gordon Milne, Peter Thompson, George Eastham, **Bobby Charlton, Jimmy Greaves,** Johnny Byrne.

27 May 1964 (NEW YORK)
USA 0 England 10 (Hunt 4, 22, 53, 64, Pickering 6, 47, 74, Paine 49, 68, B. Charlton 67)
Gordon Banks, George Cohen, Bobby Thompson, Maurice Norman, Ron Flowers (capt), Mike Bailey, **Terry Paine,** George Eastham (**Bobby Charlton 33**), Peter Thompson, **Roger Hunt,** Fred Pickering.

30 MAY 1964 (RIO DE JANEIRO)
Brazil 5 (Rinaldo 35, 59, Pelé 63, Julinho 68, Roberto Dias 88)
England 1 (Greaves 48)
Tony Waiters, **George Cohen, Ray Wilson,** Maurice Norman, **Bobby Moore** (**capt**), Maurice Norman, Peter Thompson, George Eastham, **Bobby Charlton, Jimmy Greaves,** Johnny Byrne.

4 JUNE 1964 (SAO PAULO)
England 1 (Hunt 58) Portugal 1 (Peres 42)
Gordon Banks, Bobby Thomson, **Ray Wilson,** Maurice Norman, **Bobby Moore** (**capt**), Ron Flowers, Terry Paine, Peter Thompson, **Jimmy Greaves,** Johnny Byrne, **Roger Hunt.**

6 JUNE 1964 (RIO DE JANEIRO)
England 0 Argentina 1 (Rojas 66)
Gordon Banks, Bobby Thomson, **Ray Wilson,** Maurice Norman, **Bobby Moore** (**capt**), Gordon Milne, Peter Thompson, George Eastham, **Bobby Charlton, Jimmy Greaves,** Johnny Byrne.

3 OCTOBER 1964 (WINDSOR PARK, BELFAST)
HOME INTERNATIONAL CHAMPIONSHIP
Northern Ireland 3 (Wilson 52, McLaughlin 55, 67)
England 4 (Pickering 7, Greaves 12, 16, 24)
Gordon Banks, George Cohen, Bobby Thomson, Maurice Norman, **Bobby Moore** (**capt**), Gordon Milne, **Terry Paine,** Peter Thompson, **Bobby Charlton,** Fred Pickering, **Jimmy Greaves.**

21 OCTOBER 1964 (WEMBLEY)
England 2 (Pickering 32, Hinton 70)
Belgium 2 (Cornelis 22, Van Himst 42)
Tony Waiters, **George Cohen**, Bobby Thomson, Maurice Norman, **Bobby Moore (capt)**, Gordon Milne, Peter Thompson, Terry Venables, Alan Hinton, **Jimmy Greaves**, Fred Pickering.

18 NOVEMBER 1964 (WEMBLEY)
HOME INTERNATIONAL CHAMPIONSHIP
England 2 (Wignall 17, 60) Wales 1 (C. Jones 75)
Tony Waiters, **George Cohen**, Bobby Thomson, Ron Flowers (capt), Gerry Young, Mike Bailey, Peter Thompson, Alan Hinton, **Roger Hunt**, Johnny Byrne, Frank Wignall.

9 DECEMBER 1964 (AMSTERDAM)
Holland 1 (Moulijn 77) England 1 (Greaves 85)
Tony Waiters, **George Cohen**, Bobby Thomson, Maurice Norman, Ron Flowers (capt), Alan Mullery, Peter Thompson, **Bobby Charlton**, Terry Venables, Frank Wignall, **Jimmy Greaves.**

10 APRIL 1965 (WEMBLEY)
HOME INTERNATIONAL CHAMPIONSHIP
England 2 (B. Charlton 24, Greaves 34)
Scotland 2 (Law 40, St John 59)
Gordon Banks, George Cohen, Ray Wilson, Jack Charlton, Bobby Moore (capt), Nobby Stiles, Peter Thompson, **Bobby Charlton,** Johnny Byrne, **Jimmy Greaves,** Barry Bridges.

5 MAY 1965 (WEMBLEY)
England 1 (Greaves 17) Hungary 0
Gordon Banks, George Cohen, Ray Wilson, Jack Charlton, Bobby Moore (capt), Nobby Stiles, Terry Paine, George Eastham, **John Connelly,** Barry Bridges, **Jimmy Greaves.**

9 MAY 1965 (BELGRADE)
Yugoslavia 1 (Kovačević 15) England 1 (Bridges 22)
Gordon Banks, George Cohen, Ray Wilson, Jack Charlton, Bobby Moore (capt), Nobby Stiles, Terry Paine, John Connelly, Alan Ball, Jimmy Greaves, Barry Bridges.

12 MAY 1965 (NUREMBERG)
West Germany 0 England 1 (Paine 37)
Gordon Banks, George Cohen, Ray Wilson, Jack Charlton, Bobby Moore (capt), Ron Flowers, **Terry Paine, Alan Ball,** George Eastham, Derek Temple, Mick Jones.

APPENDIX

16 MAY 1965 (GOTHENBURG)
Sweden 1 (Eriksson 25) England 2 (Ball 9, Connelly 72)
Gordon Banks, George Cohen, Ray Wilson, Jack Charlton, Bobby Moore (capt), Nobby Stiles, Terry Paine, Alan Ball, George Eastham, John Connelly, Mick Jones.

2 OCTOBER 1965 (NINIAN PARK, CARDIFF)
HOME INTERNATIONAL CHAMPIONSHIP
Wales 0 England 0
Ron Springett, **George Cohen, Ray Wilson, Jack Charlton, Bobby Moore (capt), Nobby Stiles, Terry Paine, Bobby Charlton, John Connelly, Jimmy Greaves,** Alan Peacock.

20 OCTOBER 1965 (WEMBLEY)
England 2 (B. Charlton 3, Connelly 59)
Austria 3 (Flögel 53, Fritsch 73, 81)
Ron Springett, **George Cohen, Ray Wilson, Jack Charlton, Bobby Moore (capt), Nobby Stiles, Terry Paine, Bobby Charlton, John Connelly, Jimmy Greaves,** Alan Peacock.

10 NOVEMBER 1965 (WEMBLEY)
HOME INTERNATIONAL CHAMPIONSHIP
England 2 (Baker 19, Peacock 73) Northern Ireland 1 (Irvine 21)
Gordon Banks, George Cohen, Ray Wilson, Jack Charlton, Bobby Moore (capt), Nobby Stiles, Peter Thompson, **Bobby Charlton, John Connelly,** Joe Baker, Alan Peacock.

8 DECEMBER 1965 (MADRID)
Spain 0 England 2 (Baker 8, Hunt 58)
Gordon Banks, George Cohen, Ray Wilson, Jack Charlton, Bobby Moore (capt), Nobby Stiles, Alan Ball, George Eastham, **Bobby Charlton, Roger Hunt,** Joe Baker (Norman Hunter 35).

5 JANUARY 1966 (GOODISON PARK)
England 1 (Moore 74) Poland 1 (Sadek 42)
Gordon Banks, George Cohen, Ray Wilson, Jack Charlton, Bobby Moore (capt), Nobby Stiles, Alan Ball, George Eastham, Gordon Harris, **Roger Hunt,** Joe Baker.

23 FEBRUARY 1966 (WEMBLEY)
England 1 (Stiles 41) West Germany 0
Gordon Banks, George Cohen, Keith Newton (**Ray Wilson 45**), Norman Hunter, **Jack Charlton, Bobby Moore (capt), Alan Ball, Nobby Stiles, Bobby Charlton, Roger Hunt, Geoff Hurst.**

2 APRIL 1966 (HAMPDEN PARK, GLASGOW)
HOME INTERNATIONAL CHAMPIONSHIP
Scotland 3 (Law 41, J. Johnstone 62, 81)
England 4 (Hurst 18, Hunt 34, 47, B. Charlton 73)
Gordon Banks, George Cohen, Keith Newton, **Jack Charlton, Bobby Moore (capt), Nobby Stiles, Alan Ball, Bobby Charlton, John Connelly, Roger Hunt, Geoff Hurst.**

4 MAY 1966 (WEMBLEY)
England 2 (Greaves 9, B. Charlton 34) Yugoslavia 0
Gordon Banks, Jimmy Armfield (capt), **Ray Wilson, Jack Charlton,** Norman Hunter, **Martin Peters, Terry Paine, Bobby Charlton,** Bobby Tambling, **Jimmy Greaves, Geoff Hurst.**

26 JUNE 1966 (HELSINKI)
Finland 0 England 3 (Peters 42, Hunt 44, J. Charlton 89)
Gordon Banks, Jimmy Armfield (capt), **Ray Wilson, Jack Charlton,** Norman Hunter, **Martin Peters, Ian Callaghan, Bobby Charlton, Alan Ball, Roger Hunt, Geoff Hurst.**

29 JUNE 1966 (OSLO)
Norway 1 (Sunde 4)
England 6 (Greaves 20, 24, 44, 74, Connelly 22, Moore 40)
Ron Springett, **George Cohen,** Gerry Byrne, Ron Flowers, **Bobby Moore (capt), Nobby Stiles, Terry Paine, John Connelly, Bobby Charlton, Roger Hunt, Jimmy Greaves.**

3 JULY 1966 (COPENHAGEN)
Denmark 0 England 2 (J. Charlton 44, Eastham 61)
Peter Bonetti, **George Cohen, Ray Wilson, Jack Charlton, Bobby Moore (capt), Nobby Stiles, Alan Ball,** George Eastham, **John Connelly, Jimmy Greaves, Geoff Hurst.**

5 JULY 1966 (CHORZOW)
Poland 0 England 1 (Hunt 14)
Gordon Banks, George Cohen, Ray Wilson, Jack Charlton, Bobby Moore (capt), Nobby Stiles, Alan Ball, Martin Peters, Bobby Charlton, Jimmy Greaves, Roger Hunt.

Bibliography

NEWSPAPERS
Age, The
Associated Press
Birmingham Evening Mail & Despatch
Daily Express
Daily Mail
Daily Mirror
Daily Sketch
Daily Telegraph
Glasgow Herald
Guardian, The
Liverpool Daily Post
Liverpool Echo
London Evening Standard
Manchester Evening News & Chronicle
Miami News
Middlesbrough Evening Gazette
Montreal Gazette
News of the World
Observer, The
Ottawa Citizen
People, The
Reuters
Sheffield Morning Telegraph
Spokesman-Review
St Petersburg Times
Sunday Express

Sunday Mirror
Sunday Telegraph
Sunday Times
Sunderland Echo
Times, The
Virgin Islands Daily News
Yorkshire Post

BOOKS

Bowler, Dave; *Three Lions On The Shirt: Playing For England* (Orion, 1999)

Clack, Neil; *Animals! The Story of England v Argentina* (Pitch, 2011)

Dawson, Jeff; *Back Home: England And The 1970 World Cup* (Orion, 2001)

Dickinson, Matt; *Bobby Moore: The Man In Full* (Yellow Jersey, 2014)

Downing, David; *The Best Of Enemies: England v Germany* (Bloomsbury, 2000)

Freddi, Chris; *Complete Book Of The World Cup: 2006 edition* (Harper Sport, 2006)

Hutchinson, Roger, *'66: The Inside Story Of England's 1966 World Cup Triumph* (Mainstream, 1995)

McKinstry, Leo; *Sir Alf: A Major Reappraisal of the Life and Times of England's Greatest Football Manager* (Harper Sport, 2006)

Powell, Jeff; *Bobby Moore: The Life And Times Of A Sporting Hero* (Robson Books, 1993)

WORLD CUP DRAW

	LONDON GROUP 1	MIDLANDS GROUP 2	NORTH WEST GROUP 3	NORTH EAST GROUP 4
	URUGUAY	SWITZERLAND	BRAZIL	N.KOREA
	ENGLAND	W. GERMANY	BULGARIA	U.S.S.R.
	FRANCE	SPAIN	HUNGARY	CHILE
	MEXICO	ARGENTINA	PORTUGAL	ITALY

LONDON GROUP 1	MIDLANDS GROUP 2	NORTH WEST GROUP 3	NORTH EAST GROUP 4
JULY	JULY	JULY	JULY
11th ENGLAND v URUGUAY	12th W. GERMANY v SWITZERLAND	12th BULGARIA v BRAZIL	12th U.S.S.R. v N.KOREA
13th FRANCE v MEXICO	13th SPAIN v ARGENTINA	13th HUNGARY v PORTUGAL	13th ITALY v CHILE
15th URUGUAY v FRANCE	15th SWITZERLAND v SPAIN	15th BRAZIL v HUNGARY	15th N.KOREA v CHILE
16th MEXICO v ENGLAND	16th BRAZIL v W. GERMANY	16th PORTUGAL v BULGARIA	16th ITALY v U.S.S.R.
19th MEXICO v URUGUAY	19th ARGENTINA v W.GERMANY	19th PORTUGAL v BRAZIL	19th N.KOREA v ITALY
20th FRANCE v ENGLAND	20th SPAIN v W. GERMANY	20th HUNGARY v BULGARIA	20th CHILE v U.S.S.R.

Sir Stanley Rous (centre, front row) and FIFA colleagues at the draw in London in January, 1966, with the groups and fixtures displayed behind them.

Residents of Claudia Street near Goodison Park get in the World Cup spirit by decorating their street for the finals.

Queen Elizabeth II, flanked
by the Duke of Edinburgh and
Sir Stanley Rous, speaks at the
opening ceremony at Wembley.

Comic actor Norman Wisdom laughs with
Alf Ramsey during the England squad's visit
to Pinewood Studios the day after the opening
match against Uruguay.

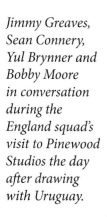

Jimmy Greaves,
Sean Connery,
Yul Brynner and
Bobby Moore
in conversation
during the
England squad's
visit to Pinewood
Studios the day
after drawing
with Uruguay.

The match officials try to restore order in the explosive Argentina-West Germany match as Rafael Albrecht (grounded, far left) is treated by the Argentine physio after a clash with Wolfgang Weber. When Albrecht got to his feet, he was sent off.

A young fan approaches Pelé for an autograph as the Brazil superstar proves his fitness in training in pouring rain in Bolton ahead of the vital match against Portugal.

Pelé, rendered almost lame by a serious knee injury, is treated on the touchline at Goodison Park during Brazil's calamitous defeat by Portugal.

England captain Bobby Moore commiserates with a disappointed Jimmy Greaves after the nation's record goalscorer learns that his shin injury will keep him out of the quarter-final against Argentina.

Referee Rudolf Kreitlein looks shell-shocked as he gets a police escort to the tunnel at the end of the controversial England-Argentina quarter-final.

Uruguay's Hector Silva (far left) is led away by police constables after his sending-off in the quarter-final against West Germany.

Dejected Portugal players after the semi-final defeat by England. Tearful tournament top scorer Eusébio is consoled by a photographer.

England players Jack Charlton, Ray Wilson, Bobby Moore, Jimmy Greaves and Bobby Charlton wait in vain for Muhammad Ali to show up at the gym where he is training for a fight with Brian London.

Jack and Bobby Charlton enjoy a drink with their mother, Cissie, after she travelled down to London from Northumberland for the final.

Linesman Tofik Bakhramov is unmoved by West German protests after ruling that Geoff Hurst's shot had crossed the line to put England 3-2 ahead in the final.

Photographers snap the iconic image of Bobby Moore being lifted shoulder-high by team-mates with the Jules Rimet Trophy on the Wembley pitch after the final.

Jubilant England supporters celebrate in the fountain at Trafalgar Square after the final.

Alf Ramsey and Prime Minister Harold Wilson in conversation at the post-final banquet, watched by Minister for Sport Denis Howell (centre).

The England squad delight a crowd of supporters below by showing off the Jules Rimet Trophy on the balcony of the Royal Garden Hotel.